REACHING
THE EAR
OF GOD

REACHING THE EAR OF GOD

PRAYING MORE . . . AND MORE LIKE JESUS

DR. WAYNE A. MACK

FOREWORD BY S. LANCE QUINN

P&R PUBLISHING

P.O. BOX 817 • PHILLIPSBURG • NEW JERSEY 08865-0817

D. Martyn-Lloyd Jones, *Studies in the Sermon on the Mount,* © 1959–60 D. Martyn-Lloyd Jones, Published by Wm. B. Eerdmans Publishing Co., Grand Rapids, MI. Used by permission.

Dan DeHaan, *The God You Can Know,* © 1982 Published by Moody Publishers. Used by permission.

Unless otherwise indicated, Scripture quotations are from the *NEW AMERICAN STANDARD BIBLE®.* © Copyright 1960, 1962, 1963, 1968, 1971, 1972, 1973, 1975, 1977 by The Lockman Foundation. Used by permission. (www.Lockman.org)

Scripture quotations marked NKJV are from The Holy Bible, New King James Version. Copyright © 1979, 1980, 1982, Thomas Nelson, Inc.

Italics within Scripture quotations indicate emphasis added.

Page design and typesetting by Lakeside Design Plus

Printed in the United States of America

Library of Congress Cataloging-in-Publication Data

Mack, Wayne A.
    Reaching the ear of God : praying more—and more like Jesus / Wayne A. Mack ; foreword by S. Lance Quinn.
        p. cm.
    Includes bibliographical references and index.
    ISBN 0-87552-613-6 (pbk.)
    1. Prayer—Christianity. I. Title.

BV210.3.M238 2004
248.3'2—dc22

2004053907

To our thirteen grandchildren
whom we love dearly and pray for regularly,
that each of them might personally know what it means
to pray and live more and more in accordance
with the teachings of our Lord Jesus Christ.

Courtney,

Nathan,

Stephanie,

David,

Ashley,

Michaela,

Audrey,

Jacob,

McKenna,

Cambria,

Catelyn,

Carolina,

and

Andrew

Contents

ACKNOWLEDGMENTS

Many people have been involved in helping me bring this book to fruition. To them I owe a great debt of gratitude. Without their help, in the midst of a very busy schedule, this book would have never come into existence. As you read the book, you may find some mistakes, in that I haven't been inspired as the biblical writers were. You may also find that the style is not as scintillating as you would like it to be. Please blame any negative thing about the book on me, and give these dear people who helped me the credit for any of the positives. They have been of immense help in birthing this book.

Who are these people? In a sense, all of the people of Grace Fellowship Church of the Lehigh Valley of Pennsylvania helped me to develop this book, in that the material presented in it was first presented to them in our training hour classes. They listened and responded to the material and hopefully grew in their Christian lives through it.

Several other people from the church were more specifically involved in getting this book ready for publication. Janet Dudek was initially responsible for typing and editing the contents. She spent many hours at this task. Her skill at helping me condense and phrase the material, her dedication, hard work, and support were invaluable. Her husband Jeff, an English teacher, looked over her shoulder (and figuratively speaking, mine as well) and gave valuable critique of grammar and style.

Gwen Knepp, from our church, also spent many hours typing some of the first manuscripts. My wife Carol did her usual thing—reading the manuscripts, making comments on better ways of stating the information, and then helping in developing the study questions scattered throughout the chapters and at the end of each chapter. And, oh yes, I also want to thank our daughter Beth who read the manuscript and gave some assistance to the study questions.

As you read this book, you will also become aware of two other people who gave me an immense amount of help in writing. These two people are now in heaven, but they are still speaking through their books. One of them is Thomas Watson and the other is Martyn Lloyd-Jones. Watson's book on the Lord's Prayer is superb—so biblical, practical, and interestingly written. Lloyd-Jones's input came from his *Studies in the Sermon on the Mount*. You will find quotes from these two men scattered throughout my book. So I would be remiss not to acknowledge the assistance I have received from them.

Thanks to all these people, but especially thanks to God for His goodness and for His giving me something to write about. I pray that this book will be used mightily to bring glory to our triune God and great blessing to His people for whom Christ died and rose again.

FOREWORD

Charles Spurgeon's famous statement that a Christian's life of prayer is like the slender nerve which moves the hand of omnipotence signals the huge level of importance God places upon our prayers. Could anything be more important and exciting to the Christian than seeing Almighty God being moved to answer your own specific prayers? Wayne Mack emphatically doesn't think so, and that is why he has written the marvelously helpful and instructive book on prayer which you now hold in your hand.

"Wait a minute!" you say. "You're trying to sell me on the idea of buying another book on prayer? No thanks. I've read my fair share of Christian books on prayer and I certainly don't need another one." I admit when this book first came across my desk, I might have been tempted to agree. I too have already read many Christian books on the subject of prayer (who hasn't?), and I too have seen Christian bookstore shelves lined with that many more books on prayer (again, who hasn't?!), so why yet another treatise on prayer? I suggest two main reasons should motivate you to purchase and read this one.

First, let me tell you a little about the author himself and why he is qualified to write on this vital topic. I have known Dr. Mack for many years now, and what has always stood out to me has been his own faithfulness and diligence in prayer. He is no armchair theologian or writer when it comes to his own devotion to prayer. He genuinely enjoys communing with his heavenly Father! I have seen this side of him, as some might say, in an "up close and personal" way. Indeed, I myself have been the beneficiary of his intense prayers for me. When I have had to make major ministry decisions, Wayne Mack was one of the first men I called to seek advice and counsel.

He carefully interceded for me, asking God to give me guidance and direction. Those experiences are etched in my mind as I read his book on prayer, seeing in a unique way how his prayer life and teaching intersect.

Second, I encourage you to move on from simply reading the foreword to actually reading and thereby profiting from this book's content. Let me explain what I mean. Christians often look "at" books, but never really read the book itself. They can sometimes be found "looking over" the covers or dust jackets (including being impressed by the endorsers), possibly even thumbing through certain chapters here and there, picking out sentences or maybe even paragraphs, but never really *reading* and *interacting* with the substance of the book's main thesis. Granted, this cursory acquaintance with a book may be all the time a person can devote when inside a bookstore, or when one is referencing several possible books for some future study. But when it comes to sitting down and reading a substantive book on a biblical topic as vital as prayer, you will want to devour *Reaching the Ear of God: Praying More . . . and More like Jesus.* As the subtitle suggests, it is this feature of the book that most stands out. As Dr. Mack shows us—on page after page—Jesus reveals His intimate relationship with God the Father, and how that kind of intimacy is also available to all true believers through prayer. He also shows us that it is available only through an intimacy with God's precepts and person, and only when done in the precise ways Jesus Himself prescribes. In an age when so much is done in a self-styled fashion, learning to pray in a Jesus-styled way is crucial. So, while you may have *seen* many books on prayer before, I think this might well be the book on prayer on which you should *focus* your attention.

Finally, as you study this resource on prayer, you'll notice some other considerable contributions. From the searching application questions (which show the author's dynamic counseling skills forged over forty years in ministry), to the extensive familiarity with the whole of Scripture (which shows the author's ministerial training, experience, and knowledge), to the interweaving of both the theological and practical elements of the Christian life (which shows the author's own rich reading of solid Christian literature), this book stands out above others on the subject. Wayne Mack is a reliable guide to a better prayer life, which is itself a way to greater intimacy with God. Who wouldn't want to have the kind of prayer life that can pave the way to greater intimacy? That is why Wayne Mack labored to write this book, and I for one thank God that he did. After you are finished reading it, I pray you will thank both of them.

S. Lance Quinn

Pastor-Teacher

The Bible Church of Little Rock

President of the National Association of Nouthetic
    Counselors (NANC)

Moderator of F.I.R.E. (Fellowship of Independent
    Reformed Evangelicals)

Little Rock, Arkansas

INTRODUCTION

Recently while reading a book on prayer by E. M. Bounds, I was struck by an illustration he used about the power of prayer. The book was called *The Possibilities of Prayer* and the chapter entitled "Wonders of God through Prayer." In that chapter Bounds uses an illustration about the power of prayer based on Revelation 8:3–5:

> Prayer is a tremendous force in the world. Consider this picture of prayer and its wonderful possibilities. God's cause is quiet and motionless on the earth. An angel, strong and impatient to be of service, waits around the throne of God in heaven. In order to move things on earth and give impetus to the movements of God's cause in the world, he gathers all the prayers of God's saints in all ages, and puts them before God just as Aaron used to perfume himself with the delicious incense when he entered the holy sanctuary, made awesome by the immediate presence of God. The angel impregnates the air with that holy offering of prayers, and thus takes its fiery body and casts it on the earth.
>
> Note the remarkable result. "There were voices, and thunderings, and lightnings, and an earthquake" (Rev. 8:5). What tremendous force is this that has convulsed the earth? The answer is that it is "*the prayers of the saints*" (v. 4), turned loose by the angel around the throne, who is in charge of those prayers. This mighty force is prayer, like the power of earth's mightiest dynamite.[1]

As I read these words by E. M. Bounds based on Scripture, I was gripped by the statement that prayer is a mighty force like the power of earth's mightiest dynamite. Then I was forced to ask the question: If this assessment by Bounds about the power of prayer

14

is true, why don't we see more of that dynamite being exploded in our churches and in our world today?

As I thought about this question, two possible answers came to mind. One, perhaps we're not seeing more of that dynamite because we don't pray enough. Perhaps we're not keeping the bowl of prayer full enough. And certainly, there's good reason to believe that is true. We don't have enough men like Bounds and the apostle Paul or Epaphras who prayed without ceasing and labored fervently in prayer (James 4:2; 1 Thess. 5:17).

And two, perhaps we aren't seeing much dynamite because we are not praying in the way we should be praying. John 4:23–24 indicates that acceptable worship must be in truth, and 1 John 5:14–15 indicates that effective prayer is prayer that is in accordance with the will of God. Perhaps we're not seeing more of that dynamite because we don't pray in accordance with the will of God, because we are, in the words of James 4:3, asking amiss.

In writing this book, I have two main purposes in mind: first, that all of us would be motivated to pray more than we have to this point. Most of us need motivation in that area. I have yet to meet any individuals who would say that they pray as much as they think they should. My second purpose is to help us to understand prayer Jesus' style. I want us to learn from history's greatest prayer expert. Jesus really knows everything there is to know about prayer. John 11:42 tells us that God the Father always heard Him. So in writing this book, I will be explaining and applying the passage in which He gave His clearest instructions on the subject—the passage in which He said three times, "When you pray" don't do this, and "when you pray" do this (Matt. 6:5–13). I have chosen to explain and apply this passage because if we pray the way He tells us to pray we can be sure that we will be praying for the things that are according to God's will.

Yes, Revelation 8:3–5 illustrates the fact that the right kind of prayer is powerful. It is like earth's mightiest dynamite. It was so in past times, and it still will be today as we pray the right kinds of prayers. So let's sit at the feet of Jesus and allow Him to teach us how to pray effectively. Come with a humble, teachable, hungry heart and listen carefully to what Jesus has to say about prayer His style.

THE NATURALNESS OF PRAYER

What would you include on your list of the major issues in the Christian life? I'm sure that many, perhaps most, Christian leaders would rate the subject we're dealing with in this book close to the top of their list. In this book, we're going to be studying the subject of effective prayer. We're going to be answering many questions about what it means to pray in a God-pleasing way. We're going to be learning lessons from history's greatest expert on the subject of prayer, the Lord Jesus Christ. We're going to be sitting at His feet and letting Him teach us how to really pray effectively. Could there be anything more important or exciting than that? How could it be otherwise when we have such a great teacher as the Lord Jesus Christ Himself and when we're studying one of the most important subjects that anyone could consider? Are you ready to learn? Are you ready to be a good student? I hope so because, as many others have said, this is one of the most important issues in the Christian life.

Prerequisites to the Study of Effective Prayer

A Desire to Learn

As we begin this study, there are a few preliminary issues about which we need to think. First, if we want to benefit from

17

this teaching, we must have a desire to learn. I once spoke with a woman who described to me a problem her son was having at school. It seems he was doing very well in every subject except one. This was not due to a lack of ability, but rather to a lack of interest. He did not learn because he did not care to learn.

A desire to learn is essential for any successful study. God does not force us to learn from Him. In Psalm 25:8–9 David said, "Good and upright is the LORD; therefore He instructs sinners in the way. He leads the humble in justice, and *He teaches the humble His way."* Jesus said much the same in Matthew 11:28–29, "Come to Me, all who are weary and heavy-laden, and I will give you rest. *Take My yoke upon you, and learn from Me, for I am gentle and humble in heart;* and you shall find rest for your souls." If we truly desire to learn from God, we must come humbly for instruction. James 4:6 says, "God is opposed to the proud, but *gives grace to the humble."* The proud do not learn from God. Proud people think that they know everything, and so God has no use for them. On the other hand, He will pour out His grace and favor on the humble.

In Matthew 5:6, Jesus taught us that God gives righteousness only to those who desire it: "Blessed are those who hunger and thirst for righteousness, for they shall be satisfied." Likewise, God instructs only those who desire to learn: "I praise Thee, O Father, Lord of heaven and earth, that Thou didst hide these things from the wise and intelligent and didst reveal them to babes" (Matt. 11:25). If we are not learning from God, it may be that we are not teachable. A humble desire to learn must accompany this study of prayer.

APPLICATION

Why is a desire to learn such an important part of learning to pray effectively? Record what the following verses indicate about this issue:

Psalm 25:8–9

Matthew 11:28–30

James 4:6

Matthew 11:25

1 Peter 2:3

Purity of Heart

Second, if we want to profit from this teaching, we must have purity of heart. In academics, there is no vital connection between knowledge and holiness. The most ungodly person in the world can earn a Ph.D. In the fourth century A.D. there lived a brilliant scholar named Augustine. He knew more than did all his professors, but his life was very immoral. He understood nothing of real Christianity, and others much less brilliant knew far more about spiritual things than he. It was not until Augustine was converted and turned his back on worldly wisdom that he became one of the greatest defenders of the Christian faith. He is considered largely responsible for the overthrow of two powerful heresies in the early church: Manicheanism and Donatism. Augustine is extolled even to this day for his brilliance in spiritual matters. None of this came about, however, until he became a Christian and pursued holiness.

Scripture clearly teaches a connection between holiness and growth in spiritual knowledge. In James 1:21 James said, "Therefore putting aside all filthiness and all that remains of wickedness, *in humility receive the word implanted,* which is able to save your souls."

God teaches only those who are willing to put aside sinful ways and who hunger for holiness. Peter said this in 1 Peter 2:1–2, "Therefore, putting aside all malice and all guile and hypocrisy and envy and all slander, like newborn babes, long for the pure milk of the word, that by it you may grow in respect to salvation." The ultimate goal of salvation is much more than gaining heaven; it is becoming more like our Lord Jesus Christ. That should be the consuming desire of every believer, but our hearts must be humble and holy for that work to be done in us.

If we do not hunger for God's Word—Bible study, godly preaching—one of two things is true. Either we are not believers at all, or our lives are clogged up with sin. I remember, as a child, watching my mother prepare dinner. Being impatient, I would see something I wanted right then, but my mother would always tell me that if I ate before dinner, I would spoil my appetite. This is what God says to us: if we want to eat the garbage of the world, we are going to spoil our appetite for spiritual things. Instead, we must clean the sin out of our lives to make room for the teaching and blessing of the Word of God. In order to profit from any godly teaching, we must come with a pure heart.

APPLICATION

Explain what the following verses indicate about the connection between humility and holiness and learning how to pray effectively.

James 1:21

1 Peter 2:1–2

Psalm 66:18

A Desire to Apply the Teaching

Finally, if we want to profit from the teaching of the Word, we must desire to apply what we have learned. God is not interested in simply filling our heads with facts. God wants us to take what we learn and act on it. James 1:25 says, "But one who looks intently at the perfect law, the law of liberty, and abides by it, not having become a forgetful hearer but *an effectual doer,* this man shall be blessed in what he does." We will be blessed when we become not just hearers of the Word, but doers of it.

If we are going to benefit from this teaching on prayer, we must be willing to apply it in our lives. I do not consider myself an expert on prayer; I feel as the disciples did in Luke 11. They saw Jesus praying and realized that, in comparison to their own prayers, they did not know how to pray at all. They came to Jesus and said, "Lord, teach us to pray." They noticed a great difference between the prayers of Jesus and their own prayers. Like Mary, we all need to sit at the feet of Jesus and learn more from Him.

APPLICATION

Explain what the following verses indicate about the connection between learning how to pray effectively and applying Scripture to our lives.

James 1:25

Philippians 4:6–8

John 7:17

The People of Effective Prayer

In Matthew 6:5–13 Jesus taught His disciples to pray with what is known as the Lord's Prayer. Let's look first at what Jesus taught about the people of effective prayer. In other words, to whom was this particular passage on prayer given? Some would say that Jesus was teaching everyone. If we look at the context of the passage, however, we will discover otherwise. The immediate context of the Lord's Prayer is found in verses 5 and 6: "And when you pray, you are not to be as the hypocrites. . . . But you, when you pray, go into your inner room, and when you have shut your door, *pray to your Father* who is in secret."

Jesus was not talking to everyone because He was not speaking to hypocrites. Jesus was teaching people who have a right to call God their Father. Those who do not know God as their Father are "children of wrath" (Eph. 2:3) and their father is the devil (John 8:44). John 1:12 says, *"But as many as received Him, to them He gave the right to become children of God,* even to those who *believe in His name."* When we have received Jesus Christ by believing in His name, God grants us the right to be called His sons. Jesus was teaching God's children how to pray.

He continued, "And when you are praying, do not use meaningless repetition, *as the Gentiles do"* (Matt. 6:7). At that time, the word

"Gentile" meant "unbeliever." Gentiles were outside the family of God and apart from God's covenant. Jesus was not teaching unbelievers to pray because the only prayer that God will hear from unbelievers is a prayer for mercy and forgiveness—in other words, a prayer for salvation. If a person has been praying and God does not seem to be answering, it may be that he or she is an unbeliever. God does not promise to hear the prayers of hypocrites or unbelievers.

Note also the larger context of this passage. This teaching is part of a sermon that Jesus preached, recorded in Matthew 5–7, called the Sermon on the Mount. It begins, "And when He saw the multitudes, He went up on the mountain; and after He sat down, *His disciples came to Him.* And opening His mouth He began to teach them" (5:1–2). Jesus was teaching those who were already His disciples and who had committed themselves to following Him. Later, in verses 13–14, Jesus said, "You are the salt of the earth; but if the salt has become tasteless, how will it be made salty again? . . . You are the light of the world. A city set on a hill cannot be hidden." Only believers are the salt of the earth and the light of the world. Jesus' teaching in the Lord's Prayer is addressed specifically to believers.

APPLICATION

1. Summarize what Jesus taught in Matthew 6:5–8 about the people of effective prayer.

2. List the various reasons why the prayer found in Matthew 6:9–13 can be prayed only by believers. Answer this question from this passage. Why does Jesus' teaching here not apply to non-Christians?

When, Not If, You Pray

Notice the significance of the word "when" in Matthew 6:5–7, "And *when you pray,* you are not to be as the hypocrites; for they love . . . to be seen by men. Truly I say to you, they have their reward in full. But you, *when you pray,* go into your inner room, and when you have shut your door, pray to your Father who is in secret. . . .

And *when you are praying,* do not use meaningless repetition, as the Gentiles do."

Jesus assumed that His disciples would pray. He does not say "if you pray," but "when you pray." Matthew Henry said, "You may as soon find a living man who does not breathe as a living Christian who does not pray." If a person does not pray, it is an evidence that he or she is not a believer. J. C. Ryle said:

> I have looked carefully over the lives of God's saints in the Bible. I cannot find one of whose history much is told us from Genesis to Revelation who is not a man of prayer. I find it mentioned as a characteristic of the godly, that they call on the Father and that they call on the name of the Lord Jesus. I find it recorded as a characteristic of the wicked that they do not call upon the Lord. I have read the lives of many eminent Christians that have been on earth since Bible days. Some of them, I see, were rich, some poor; some were learned, some unlearned, some of them were Episcopalians, some Presbyterians, some Baptists, some Independents, some were Calvinists and some Arminians, some have loved to use liturgy and some to use none. But one thing I see they all had in common; they have all been men of prayer. I have studied the reports of missionary societies in our own times. I see with what joy the heathen men and women are receiving the gospel in various parts of the globe. There are conversions in Africa, New Zealand, in India and South America. The people converted are naturally unlike one another in every respect, but one striking thing I observed at all missionary stations, the converted people always pray.
>
> I do not deny that a man may pray without heart and without sincerity. I do not for a moment pretend to say that the mere fact that a person is praying proves that he is a child of God. As in every other part of religion, so also in this, there is plenty of deception and hypocrisy. But this I do say, that not praying is a clear proof that a man is not yet a true Christian. He cannot really feel his sins, he cannot love God, he cannot feel himself a debtor to Christ, he cannot long after holiness, he cannot desire heaven. He has yet to be born again, he has yet to be made a new creature, he may boast confidently of election, grace, hope and knowledge and deceive ignorant people, but you may rest assured it is all vain talk if he does not pray.[1]

Jesus said "when you pray," because he knew that it is natural for a child of God to pray.

APPLICATION

Explain in your own words the significance of the words "when you pray" in Matthew 6:5–7.

Why It Is Natural for a Christian to Pray

It is natural for Christian to pray because *the Spirit of prayer dwells in them.* First Corinthians 6:19 says, "Or do you not know that *your body is a temple of the Holy Spirit* who is in you, whom you have from God, and that you are not your own?" When we become Christians, the Spirit of truth, faith, holiness, grace, and supplication comes to live in us. "And I will pour out on the house of David and on the inhabitants of Jerusalem, the *Spirit of grace and of supplication,* so that they will look on Me whom they have pierced" (Zech. 12:10). Paul said it this way in Romans 8:15, "For you have not received a spirit of slavery leading to fear again, but you have *received a spirit of adoption as sons by which we cry out, 'Abba! Father!' "*

The Spirit of God causes believers to pray. Romans 8:26 says, "And in the same way, the Spirit also helps our weakness; for we do not know how to pray as we should, but *the Spirit Himself intercedes for us with groanings too deep for words."* One of the ministries of the Spirit is to help us in our praying; therefore, where there is no prayer, there is no Spirit and thus no salvation. Romans 8:9 says, "However, you are not in the flesh but in the Spirit, if indeed the Spirit of God dwells in you. *But if anyone does not have the Spirit of Christ, he does not belong to Him."*

APPLICATION

1. Summarize why the fact that a Christian is indwelt by the Holy Spirit makes it natural to assume that a Christian will be a praying person.

2. Write out the verses of Scripture that support this concept.

It is natural to assume that believers will pray because *we are followers of Jesus Christ.* Jesus said in Luke 9:23, "If anyone wishes to come after Me, let him deny himself, and take up his cross daily, *and follow Me.*" First John 2:6 says, "The one who says he abides in Him *ought himself to walk in the same manner as He walked.*" John went on to say that, if anyone claims to abide in Christ and does not imitate Him, he is a liar. In other words, the Bible teaches that if anyone is not interested in following Jesus, he or she is not a Christian. Jesus said this Himself in John 10:27, "My sheep hear My voice, and I know them, and *they follow Me.*"

As followers of Christ, we should consider His example, and Jesus was a man of prayer. In Hebrews 5:7 we find this description, "In the days of His flesh, *He offered up both prayers and supplications* with loud crying and tears to the One able to save Him from death." There are more than thirty references in the Gospels to Jesus praying. In John 17:20 Jesus said, "I do not ask in behalf of these alone, *but for those also who believe in Me* through their word." In fact, He is still praying even now. *"He intercedes for the saints* according to the will of God" (Rom. 8:27), and "He is able to save forever those who draw near to God through Him, *since He always lives to make intercession for them*" (Heb. 7:25). One of the primary things Jesus is doing in heaven now is praying for us; as followers of Christ, we also should pray.

It is also natural to assume that we will pray because, as believers, we love Jesus Christ. This is one of the ways that the Bible describes Christians. In Ephesians 6:24 Paul closes his epistle, "Grace be with all those *who love our Lord Jesus Christ* with a love incorruptible." First Peter 1:8 says, "And though you have not seen Him, *you love Him.*" Who is it that loves Jesus? Jesus explained, *"If you love Me, you will keep My commandments"* (John 14:15); *"He who has My commandments and keeps them, he it is who loves Me"* (John 14:21); and *"If anyone loves Me, he will keep My word"* (John 14:23). Very simply, those who keep the Lord's commandments love Him. Consider, then, His commandments regarding prayer, "Ask and it shall be given to you" (Matt. 7:7); "at all times [men] ought to pray and not to lose heart" (Luke 18:1b); "Until now you have asked for nothing in My name; ask, and you will receive" (John 16:24). If we love Jesus, we will keep His command to pray.

APPLICATION

1. Summarize why being a follower of Jesus Christ makes it natural to assume that a Christian will be a praying person.
2. Write out the verses of Scripture that support this concept.

It is natural to assume that we will pray because *prayerlessness is a sin.* We often think of it as simply a problem of laziness or forgetfulness, but the Bible calls it sin. Isaiah 64:6 talks about the Israelite's sin: "For all of us have become like one who is unclean, and all our righteous deeds are like a filthy garment; and all of us wither like a leaf, and our iniquities, like the wind, take us away." In the next verse Isaiah explains what sin this is: "And *there is no one who calls on Thy name,* who arouses himself to take hold of Thee" (64:7). One of their sins was a failure to pray.

The Bible defines sin in many ways and one of these is found in James 4:17, "Therefore, to one who *knows the right thing to do, and does not do it, to him it is sin.*" Sin is not only doing what we should not do; sin is not doing what we should do. Since God says that we ought to "pray without ceasing" (1 Thess. 5:17), failing to pray is sin.

In 1 Samuel 12 the prophet Samuel told the Israelites that the Lord was angry with them because of their sins. Under conviction, they came to Samuel and said, *"Pray for your servants* to the LORD your God, so that we may not die" (12:19). Samuel answered them, "Do not fear. You have committed all this evil, yet do not turn aside from following the Lord, but serve the Lord with all your heart. . . . For the LORD will not abandon His people on account of His great name. . . . Moreover, as for me, far be it from me that I *should sin against the LORD by ceasing to pray for you"* (12:20–23). Samuel knew that he would be sinning against the Lord if he did not pray.

In Psalm 10:4 the Bible describes wicked people as those who do not pray. "The wicked, in the haughtiness of his countenance, *does not seek Him.* All his thoughts are, 'There is no God.' " Again, in

Psalm 14:4, Scripture says, "Do all the workers of wickedness not know, who eat up my people as they eat bread and *do not call upon the Lord?"* Wicked men do not seek God in prayer. As believers, we should hate all sin as our Lord hates all sin, and therefore, it is natural to assume that believers will pray because prayerlessness is a sin.

APPLICATION

1. Explain why prayerlessness is a sin.
2. Write out the verses of Scripture that support this concept.

Believers should also pray because **they claim God as their Father.** Psalm 100:3 says, "Know that the Lord Himself is God; it is He who has made us, and not we ourselves; we are His people and the sheep of His pasture." There is only one God, and we are not He. He is our Creator, and we, as believers, are His people through the blood of Christ. He brought us into His family and has put into our hearts His Spirit who allows us to pray to Him. He has taken care of us and provided everything that we need for life. *"All things came into being by Him,* and apart from Him nothing came into being that has come into being" (John 1:3).

We consider it a tragedy when earthly children refuse to talk to the parents who have brought them into this world and nurtured them. No one's parents are perfect—and some are even wicked—but it is a horrible thing when children, who owe so much to their parents, will have nothing to do with them. It is truly heartbreaking. Such ingratitude is unnatural even in the physical realm, but how much more so in the spiritual realm!

We have a heavenly Father who listens to us, and it is our privilege to talk to Him. Our Lord Jesus Christ was God manifest in the flesh, but while He walked this earth He laid aside the use of His divine attributes—His wisdom and power—and became man in every respect except sin. And Jesus, again and again, described God as His Father. He was totally dependent on the Father: "Truly, truly, I say to you, the Son can do nothing of Himself, unless it is something He sees the Father doing; for whatever the Father does, these things the Son also does in like manner" (John 5:19).

In John 8:28 the Lord Jesus said, "When you lift up the Son of Man, then you will know that I am He, and I do nothing on My own initiative, but I speak these things as the Father taught Me." Throughout the Gospels we find references to Jesus going out and spending whole nights in prayer to the Father. Jesus, as a man, needed and received in prayer instruction from His Father. He spent an entire night in prayer before choosing His twelve disciples. Jesus talked everything over with His Father because He and the Father were one.

We are familiar, of course, with His fervent prayers in the Garden of Gethsemane, just before going to the cross. Jesus cried out, "Father, if Thou art willing, remove this cup from Me; yet not My will, but Thine be done" (Luke 22:42). Jesus acknowledged God as His Father, and so it was natural for Him to be constantly talking to His Father. It is natural for us who call God "Father" to do the same.

APPLICATION

1. Summarize why God's being the heavenly Father of Christians makes it natural to assume that a Christian will be a praying person.

2. Write out the verses of Scripture that support this concept.

Finally, it should be natural for believers to pray because *prayer is connected to receiving blessings from God.* It is a means which God has appointed for us to obtain things from Him. In Matthew 7:7 Jesus instructed us, "Ask, and it shall be given to you." James 4:2 says, "You do not have because you do not ask." If we are not receiving from God, one of three things is true: one, we are not believers; two, we are asking with wrong motives—for our own selfish desires, says James 4:3; or three, we are simply not asking. To ask God for all our needs is to acknowledge our dependency on Him. "Until now you have asked for nothing in

My name; ask, and you will receive, that your joy may be made full" (John 16:24).

J. C. Ryle has commented:

Some without doubt have a larger cup of sorrow to drink than others, but few are to be found who live long without sorrows or cares of one sort or another. Our bodies, our property, our families, our children, our relations, our servants, our friends, our neighbors, our worldly callings—each and all of these are fountains of care. Sicknesses, deaths, losses, disappointments, partings, separations, ingratitude, slander—all of these are common things. We cannot get through life without them. Someday or other we find this out. The greater our affections, the deeper our afflictions, and the more we love, the more we have to weep. What is the best recipe for cheerfulness in such a world as this? How shall we get through this valley of tears with least pain? I know no better recipe than the habit of taking everything to God in prayer.

This was the practice of all the saints whose history we have recorded in Scripture. This is what Jacob did when he feared his brother Esau. This is what Moses did when the people were ready to stone him in the wilderness. This is what Joshua did when Israel was defeated before Ai. This is what David did when he was in danger at Keilah. This is what Hezekiah did when he received the letter from Sennacherib. This is what the church did when Peter was put in prison. This is what Paul did when he was cast into the dungeon at Philippi. The only way to be really happy in such a world as this is to be ever casting all of our cares on God. It is the trying to carry their own burdens that so often makes believers sad. If they will only tell their troubles to God, He will enable them to bear them as easily as Samson knocked down the gates of Gaza. If they are resolved to keep them to themselves they will find one day that the very grasshopper is a burden.

There is a friend ever waiting to help us if we will only unbosom to Him our sorrow. A friend who pitied the poor and sick and sorrowful when He was upon the earth. A friend who knows the heart of a man for He lived 33 years as a man amongst us. A friend who can weep with weepers for He was a man of sorrows and acquainted with grief. A friend who is able to help us for there never was earthly pain He could not cure. The friend is Jesus

Christ. The way to be happy is to be always opening our hearts to Him. Oh, that we were all like the poor Christian black person who only answered when threatened and punished, "I must tell the Lord." Jesus can make all happy who trust Him and call on Him whatever be their outward condition. He can give them peace of heart in a prison, contentment in the midst of poverty, comfort in the midst of bereavements, joy on the brink of the grave.

There is a mighty fullness in Him for all His believing members, a fullness that is ready to be poured out on everyone who will ask in prayer. Oh, that men would understand that happiness does not depend on outward circumstances, but on the state of the heart. Prayer can lighten crosses for us however heavy. It can bring down to our side one who will help us bear them. Prayer can open a door for us when our way seems hedged up. It can bring down one who will say, "This is the way, walk in it." Prayer can let in a ray of hope when all our earthly prospects seem darkened. It can bring down one who will say, "I will never leave you nor forsake you." Prayer can obtain relief for us when those we love most are taken away and the world feels empty. It can bring down one who can fill the gap in our hearts with Himself, and say to the waves within, "Peace, be still." Oh, that men were not so like Hagar in the wilderness, blind to the well of living waters close beside them.[2]

Considering all these things, it is natural to assume that we would pray. God has given us many promises and has said that one of the appointed means by which we obtain things from Him is by prayer. We do not know exactly the connection between God's sovereignty and our praying, but the Bible teaches it. In Acts 9, Saul was converted and God asked a man by the name of Ananias to go to him. Ananias, of course, knew who Saul was and why he had come to Damascus: to kill Christians and throw them in prison. Ananias was incredulous that God would ask him to go to such a man. But God reassured him of His purpose and confirmed Saul's conversion by telling Ananias, "He is praying" (Acts 9:11). As soon as Saul became a Christian, he began to pray. There is no reason to fear a person who prays the way Jesus taught us to pray because that person is a believer and loves God. May God challenge and stimulate us to devote ourselves to prayer. In the following chapters, we will continue by studying the principles and the pattern of prayer.

If you are reading this, and you are not a believer, you are a child of wrath and your father is the devil. Though this is not pleasant to hear, Jesus, who is the Truth, said it. I want to encourage you with this: there is a God in heaven who sent His only Son to keep the Law for you and to die on the cross to pay the penalty for your having broken the Law. If you will repent of your sins and trust in the Lord Jesus Christ, He will forgive you and save you. You will then receive His Spirit in your heart—the Spirit of adoption—and you will have a desire to fellowship with your Father. May God move you to pray to Him for mercy, for forgiveness, and for salvation, for Jesus' sake. If you do this, God, in His great mercy, will make you a member of His family and put His Holy Spirit in you. Then you also will be able to pray as Jesus taught us to pray.

APPLICATION

1. Summarize in your own words the encouragements to pray that are found in the lengthy quote from J. C. Ryle.

2. Summarize in your own words the most important truths presented in this chapter.

3. Write out and work on memorizing one or two verses found in this chapter.

4. In what ways were you encouraged, challenged, or convicted by the material in this chapter? In keeping with the material presented in this chapter, how should your prayer life be changed?

GETTING
THE BIG PICTURE

How important is prayer in the Christian life? What should be our attitude toward its place in our lives? Martyn Lloyd-Jones answers these questions in this way:

What is the place of prayer in your life? What prominence does it have in our lives? It is a question that I address to all. It is as necessary that it should reach the man who is well versed in the Scripture, and who has a knowledge of its doctrine and its theology, as that it should reach anyone else. What part does prayer play in our lives and how essential is it to us? Do we realize that without it we faint?

Our ultimate position as Christians is tested by the character of our prayer life. It is more important than knowledge and understanding. Do not imagine that I am detracting from the importance of knowledge. I spend most of my life trying to show the importance of having a knowledge of truth and an understanding of it. That is vitally important. There is only one thing that is more important, and that is prayer. The ultimate test of my understanding of the Scriptural teaching is the amount of time I spend in prayer. As theology is ultimately the knowledge of God, the more theology I know, the more it should drive me to seek to know God. Not to know about Him, but to know Him. The whole object of salvation is to bring me to a knowledge of

God. I may talk learnedly about regeneration, but what is eternal light? It is that they might know Thee, the only true God in Jesus Christ whom God has sent. If all my knowledge does not lead me to prayer there is something wrong somewhere. It is meant to do that. The value of the knowledge is that it gives me such an understanding of the value of prayer, that I devote time to prayer and delight in prayer. If it does not produce these results in my life, there is something wrong and spurious about it, or else I am handling it in a wrong manner.[1]

What a challenging and convicting statement! I ask, then, the following. If, as Martyn Lloyd-Jones states, our prayer lives are the ultimate test of our understanding of Scripture, if they are the ultimate test of our knowledge of God, if they are the ultimate test of our position as Christians, what do our prayer lives indicate about us? Sobering question, isn't it?

In similar fashion, John Piper emphasizes the crucial role that prayer should play in our lives:

It is true for individuals and churches: no prayer, no power. In Mark 9, we read about a time when the disciples were unsuccessful in casting a demon out of a young boy. After Jesus came and cast it out, the disciples asked Him why they had not been able to do it. Jesus answered, "This kind cannot be driven out by anything but *prayer*" (9:29). There are spiritual forces in this world that are difficult to overcome.

When Jesus told His disciples that their prayer was insufficient, He probably did not mean that they had neglected to pray over the demonized boy. That would seem to have been their first approach. More likely, He meant that they were not living in prayer; they had been caught in a prayerless period of life or frame of mind. Notice that when Jesus cast out the demon, the Bible does not indicate that He prayed at that moment.

Jesus, however, lived in prayer. He spent whole nights in prayer and He was ready when evil came. He would rise very early in order to pray before all the duties and responsibilities of His day, and He would spend whole nights in prayer as well. The disciples, on the other hand, had apparently become negligent in their praying and thus were powerless in the face of strong evil forces. Jesus' reply teaches us that without persistent prayer we have no offense in the battle with evil. Individually and as churches, we are meant to invade and plunder the strongholds of Satan. But, "No prayer, no power."

The same is true of spiritual defense. Consider Christ's words to the disciples when they fell asleep in the garden of Gethsemane instead of keeping up their guard against evil. "Watch and pray," Jesus had said. If we are not vigilant against evil, we will be ensnared by temptation. Our spiritual offense and defense is an earnest, persistent, believing prayer life. No prayer, no power.[2]

The Christian's Highest Activity

Prayer is tremendously important to believers for many reasons. Martyn Lloyd-Jones said, "Prayer is the highest activity of a Christian." What reasons do we have to believe that this is true?

The Difficulty of Prayer

Prayer may be the most difficult thing that Christians do. The Bible talks about people wrestling in prayer, striving in prayer, and laboring in prayer. In Romans 15:30 Paul said, "*Strive* together with me in your prayers." When Paul wrote to the Colossians, he noted that Epaphras is "always *laboring earnestly* for you in his prayers" (4:12).

Prayer is work. Unbelievers do not understand the difficulty of prayer, but those of us who are Christians know it well. Everything else in the Christian life is easier than prayer. It is far easier to read our Bibles than to pray. It is far easier to witness, to go to church, and to give to the poor than it is to pray. Why? The reason for this is that the closer we get to what is most important—what brings us most spiritual power, the more opposition we are going to get from the devil, the world, and our own flesh.

Those of us who have played football know well that the closer the offense gets to the goal line, the stronger the defending team's opposition becomes. It is much easier to move the ball down the first eighty yards of the field than it is to move it inside the "red zone" (the last twenty yards). This is true for the simple reason that scoring points is the only thing that really counts in football. All the other statistics of the game may be interesting, but ultimately, the only numbers that matter are the ones that make up the final score. In the Christian life, it is much the same. The stakes are highest when we do that which is most important. There is an old and wise saying: "Satan trembles when he sees a believer on his knees." Prayer is important because it is the most difficult thing we do.

APPLICATION

1. Considering what Martyn Lloyd-Jones says about our prayer life being the ultimate test of our understanding of Scripture, our knowledge of God, and our position as Christians, what does your prayer life indicate about you?

2. Why is prayer the most important thing we can do as Christians?

3. Would you agree that prayer is the most difficult thing we do?

4. Why is prayer so difficult?

The Example of Godly Men

Second, we know that prayer is the most important thing for a Christian to do from the example of godly men in history. It can be safely said that there never has been and never will be a truly godly man who does not pray. Godliness and prayerfulness are Siamese twins; never is one without the other.

Abraham is held up in Scripture as an example of a man who believed God (Heb. 11 and Rom. 4). He is called the father of the faithful. One of the first things that Abraham did wherever he went was to construct an altar to God for prayer and worship. Elijah, one of the greatest prophets in the Bible, was mightily used of God because he was a man of prayer. When James calls attention to Elijah's great faith, he uses these words, "Elijah was a *man with a nature like ours*, and *he prayed earnestly* that it might not rain; and it did not rain on the earth for three years and six months" (5:17).

Paul was also a great man of God and a great man of prayer. He said again and again in his letters to the churches that he was always praying for them. He began many of his epistles with prayer, and he ended almost every one by telling his readers what he was praying for them.

Jonathan Edwards was mightily used of God during the time of the Great Awakening when thousands were converted. Most of us know something of the way God used him in his preaching and of his intelligence and wisdom. Yet many people do not know that Edwards was a man who prayed constantly. He trusted in God, not his own understanding.

Consider these thoughts from mightily used servants of God on the necessity of prayer:

> What the church needs today is not more or better machinery, not new organizations, or more and novel methods. She needs men whom the Holy Spirit can use. Men of prayer. Men mighty in prayer. The Holy Spirit does not flow through methods, but through men. It does not come through machinery, but on men. He does not anoint plans, but men—men of prayer.[3]

> The principal cause of my leanness and unfruitfulness is due to an unaccountable backwardness to pray. I can write or read or converse or hear with a ready heart, but prayer is more spiritual and inward than any of these. And the more spiritual any duty is, the more my carnal heart is apt to stray from it. Prayer and patience and faith are never disappointed. I have long since learned that if I ever was to be a minister, faith and prayer must make me one. When I can find my heart dissolved in prayer, every-thing else is comparatively easy.[4]

> It may be considered a spiritual axiom that in every truly suc-cessful ministry, prayer is an evident and controlling force. It is evident and controlling in the life of the preacher, evident and controlling in the deep spirituality of his work. A ministry may be a very thought-provoking ministry without prayer. The

preacher may secure fame and popularity without prayer. The whole machinery of the preacher's life and work may be run without the oil of prayer, or with scarcely enough to grease one cog. But no ministry can be a spiritual one securing holiness in the preacher and in his people without prayer being made an evident and controlling force.[5]

A Means of Receiving Things from God

Third, prayer is extremely important because, according to the Bible, it is the means by which we obtain things from God and accomplish things for Him. In Matthew 7:7–8 Jesus said, "Ask, and it shall be given to you; seek, and you shall find; knock, and it shall be opened to you. For everyone who asks receives, and he who seeks finds, and to him who knocks it shall be opened." In Luke 11:13 He said, "If you then, being evil, know how to give good gifts to your children, how much more shall your heavenly Father give the Holy Spirit to those who ask Him?"

Acts 2:41–47 describes the day of Pentecost, when many repented of their sins and were baptized. Three thousand came to Christ that day. But we often overlook the work of a small band of believers prior to that event, recorded in Acts 1:14: "These all with one mind *were continually devoting themselves to prayer.*" There was a direct connection between the continuous prayer of God's people and the coming of the Spirit on the day of Pentecost. After Pentecost, Acts 2:42 says they continued in prayer.

The rest of the book of Acts demonstrates a powerful connection between the prayers of God's people and the working of God's Spirit. In Acts 9:40 Dorcas was raised from the dead as Peter prayed. In Acts 10 both Cornelius and Peter were in prayer. God directed them to each other through their prayers, and then brought them together for the purpose of bringing salvation to the Gentiles. While the church was in prayer in Acts 12:5–7, an angel released Peter from prison. In Acts 13 the Spirit of God said that He wanted the church to send out their first foreign missionaries: Paul and Barnabas. God's Spirit directed this through the prayers of the believers at Antioch, and they sent Paul and Barnabas out after even more prayer.

Paul was effective for the gospel on his missionary journeys because he prayed and had a church that constantly supported him in prayer. In Acts 16:13–14 Lydia's heart was opened to salvation during a time of prayer. Later, when Paul and Silas were in prison, there was an earthquake that opened the prison doors. Their jailer was brought to salvation because of this, and it all happened while Paul and Silas were praying (Acts 16:25).

The connection between prayer and the work of God is repeated again and again in the Scriptures. Neither preaching nor teaching nor even giving is the most important thing that we can ever do for the kingdom of God. It is to *pray*. The Bible says, "The effective prayer of a righteous man can accomplish much" (James 5:16).

APPLICATION

1. How did Abraham demonstrate the importance of prayer?

2. What Scripture shows that Paul was a man of prayer?

3. What three evidences were given that emphasize the importance of prayer?

The Principles of Effective Prayer

We turn now to the principles of effective prayer, which are found in Matthew 6:5–8:

> And when you pray, you are not to be as the hypocrites; for they love to stand and pray in the synagogues and on the street corners, in order to be seen by men. Truly I say to you, they have their reward in full. But you, when you pray, go into your inner room, and when you have shut your door, pray to your Father who is in secret, and your Father who sees in secret will repay you. And when you are praying, do not use meaningless repetition, as the Gentiles do, for they suppose that they will be heard for their many words. Therefore, do not be like them; for your Father knows what you need, before you ask Him.

True Prayer Must Be God-Centered

We will study two principles of effective prayer from this passage. One, true prayer is God-centered. That may seem rather obvious, but look again at what Jesus condemns in the prayers of the hypocrites. First, consider what He did *not* condemn; He did not condemn them because they stood to pray. In 1 Kings 8:22 Solomon stood in prayer as he dedicated the temple. Standing, in fact, is a very appropriate display of respect, as when people in a courtroom rise for a judge. In Leviticus the younger Israelites were commanded to show respect to their elders by standing when an elder entered their presence. Standing can also be a helpful way of focusing our minds during prayer because it is not physically comfortable for long periods of time.

Nor did Jesus condemn the hypocrites because they prayed in the synagogues or on the streets; He was not condemning public prayer. Some people believe that praying aloud in a prayer meeting is an ostentatious display, but the Scripture does not support their view. In 1 Timothy 2:8 Paul said he wanted "men in *every place* to pray." In John 6:11 Jesus prayed before more than five thousand people. In John 11:41 He prayed before His disciples, and there are many references in Acts to the believers praying together and in public.

What Jesus was condemning was the man-centered focus of the hypocrites' prayers. He was implying that though these men prayed on the street corners and in the synagogues, these were the only places they prayed. At that time the Jews had certain hours designated as hours of prayer. Acts 3:1 says, "Now Peter and John were going up to the temple at the ninth hour, the hour of prayer." There is, of course, nothing wrong with establishing regular times of prayer; in fact, it can be quite beneficial. Our days tend to get so filled up with other things that we may easily neglect to pray unless we plan for it.

The problem that Jesus was addressing in Matthew 6, however, was that these hypocrites prayed only when they were sure to be seen by other people—in common places and at the appointed times. Lloyd-Jones tells of a man who would frequently drop to his knees in prayer at any time and place. This may have been a mark of his spirituality, but it would depend on why he did it. In other words, it would depend on whether he was just as quick to pray when no one was around as he was when in public. Jesus was not condemning public prayer; he was condemning public prayer for the wrong reason. The hypocrites' prayers were man-centered.

A believer's prayer should be God-centered. The key is found in verse 6, when Jesus said, "But you, when you pray, *go into your inner room, and when you have shut your door,* pray to your Father who is in secret." Jesus was teaching us here that in order to pray properly, we must make an effort to shut out all distractions—other people and other things—and focus on God. The place is not essential; it is very possible to be in a closet and still not be focused on God. On the other hand, it is possible to be in the midst of a crowd and be completely focused on God in prayer.

Consider the example of Paul, who prayed without ceasing while in prison for several years. Prisoners were shackled to prison guards and had no privacy from other people. Paul could not have gotten away from people, and yet he persevered in prayer, not to impress others with his piety, but to focus his mind on God. Daniel is another example, among others, of a man whose prayers were God-centered. The first principle of prayer, then, is that God must be the focus of our prayers.

APPLICATION

1. What is the first principle of effective prayer mentioned here?

2. How does Matthew 6:5–8 illustrate a man-centered focus of prayer that Jesus condemned?

3. How does Matthew 6:5–8 teach the principle of God-centered prayer?

4. What will this first principle look like in your prayer life?

True Prayer Must Be Earnest and Full-Hearted

The second principle of effective prayer that we find in this passage is that true prayer must be earnest and full-hearted. In verse

7 Jesus says, "And when you are praying, do not use meaningless repetition, as the Gentiles do, for they suppose that they will be heard for their many words." Again, Jesus is not simply forbidding repetition in prayer. In Matthew 26:39–44 Jesus prayed three times for the same thing, "My Father, if it is possible, let this cup pass from Me." Paul, in 2 Corinthians 12:8, also prayed about the same thing three times. In Psalm 119 the psalmist asked seven times to be taught God's statutes and nine times for God to revive him.

Neither was Jesus condemning long prayers. Luke 6:12 says Jesus prayed all night. In Acts 12 the church continued in prayer all night. First Thessalonians 5:17 says we are to "pray without ceasing." Luke 18:1 says that we "ought to pray and not to lose heart."

Instead, Jesus was condemning vain prayers: mechanical prayers that lack heart. Some of us mindlessly repeat memorized prayers, or sometimes our prayers are just filled with meaningless repetitions of things God already knows about. He does not need us to tell Him every detail of our lives in prayer. Prayer should be a time to worship and praise our Father, to ask for our needs, and to confess our sins. Jesus was teaching us that we are not simply to speak many words to God when we pray.

Ultimately, the particular amount of time we spend in prayer is not important. Some believers, convicted by the lives of past saints, will themselves into passing many hours on their knees. If that were all that mattered, the Pharisees would have been very blessed by God. No, Jesus was not condemning the length of their prayers, but rather the lack of depth. They were not praying from burdened hearts.

In the Old Testament we often read about the "burden of the Lord" coming upon men of God. His prophets were men of passionate prayer. Hebrews 5:7 says that when Christ was in this world, "He offered up both prayers and supplications with *loud crying and tears.*" Earnest prayer characterized his life because He knew it was spiritual warfare. Luke 22:44 says, "And being in agony He was *praying very fervently.*" In Galatians 4:19 Paul said, "My children, with whom I am *again in labor* until Christ is formed in you."

James 5:16 says, "The effective, *fervent prayer* of a righteous man avails much" (NKJV). Our prayers are to be wholehearted and earnest. Do we struggle and agonize in prayer? Is it serious business, or is it just a routine? Real prayer warriors do not set their alarm clocks and pray for a determined amount of time. It is said that when David Brainerd would go out into the woods in the middle of winter, he would pray with such fervency that he would return soaked in sweat.

APPLICATION

1. What is the second principle of effective prayer?

2. What is Jesus forbidding in Matthew 6:7?

3. What Scripture emphasizes that our prayers should be wholehearted and earnest?

Prerequisites for Effective Prayer

How is this kind of prayer achieved? In order to pray this way, we must have a *relationship* with our Father in heaven. We must be born of God and receive Christ as prophet, priest, and king. There must also be *restraint;* we need to shut our door on the distractions around us and in us. This requires self-control and discipline. We must exclude all else and focus on God alone.

Further, there must be *reflection.* We must consider who we are and what we are before God—sinners. It is a tremendous privilege to come into the presence of God. Jesus said, "Abide in Me, and I in you. As the branch cannot bear fruit of itself, unless it abides in the vine, so *neither can you, unless you abide in Me*" (John 15:4). We are nothing without the help of God; thinking about this will help us to be wholehearted in our prayers. We need to also reflect on who and what God is: our caring Father, our all-wise God, our gracious Provider. If we want to pray fervently, we must prepare our hearts for it with right thinking.

Finally, there must be *righteousness* in our lives. James 5:16 refers to the "prayer of a *righteous* man." In order to achieve effective prayer, we have to be righteous in Christ and living rightly before

God. Psalm 66:18 says, "If I regard iniquity in my heart, the Lord will not hear."

Scripture asserts that "the effective, fervent prayer of a righteous man avails much." Friends, we have an enormous task before us that we cannot accomplish on our own. We will make no impact on this sinful world if we are not people of prayer. The early apostles were devoted first to prayer and then to the ministry of the Word—in that order (Acts 6:4). May God help us to take prayer seriously and to see that the most important thing we can ever do for ourselves and for our world is to become people who pray in the way that Jesus taught us in Matthew 6. To pray in that way is to pray effectively and it is to pray as Jesus taught us.

 **APPLICATION**

1. What are the four prerequisites for effective prayer?

2. Summarize in your own words the most important truths presented in this chapter.

3. Write out and work on memorizing one or two verses found in this chapter.

4. In what ways were you challenged or convicted by the material in this chapter? In keeping with the material presented in this chapter, how should your prayer life be changed?

COMING TO YOUR FATHER

*G*od has done everything possible in His Word to make us aware of the importance of prayer. We have countless examples in Scripture, including those of Jesus and the early church leaders. In reference to the importance of prayer, Martyn Lloyd-Jones said, "Prayer is, beyond any question, the highest activity of the human soul. Man is at his greatest and highest when upon his knees he comes face to face with God."[1] If we believe that is true, we must consider whether our conviction is borne out by the way we live and prioritize our time for prayer.

A Sad Reality

The sad reality is that, while most of us acknowledge that prayer is very important, most of us would also acknowledge that our prayer lives are woefully inadequate. There is probably no area in life in which we fail more and feel more inept than in the area of prayer. Jesus' disciples felt this way as well. On one occasion after they had watched Him pray, they said, "Lord, teach us to pray" (Luke 11:1). Certainly these men had prayed before, but there was something about Jesus' prayers that left them feeling as though they knew nothing about it at all.

44

In response, Jesus taught them the prayer that we find in Matthew 6:9–13. If we want to pray effectively and properly, we ought to thoroughly digest what our Lord Jesus Christ taught in this great passage on prayer. In this chapter, we will consider three things: one, the purpose of the prayer as a pattern; two, the structure of the prayer as a whole; and three, the meaning of the first part of the preface.

A Pattern for Effective Prayer

The primary purpose for which Jesus gave this instruction was so that we might have a *pattern* for prayer. Some people think that Jesus gave us these words to pray verbatim. There are churches that repeat the Lord's Prayer in every service. Of course, there is nothing wrong with praying this prayer word for word, but that is not its primary purpose. In Luke 11 we find a variation of the Lord's Prayer that Jesus taught His disciples on another occasion when they came to Him and asked, "Lord, teach us to pray." Though similar in structure, this prayer is not exactly the same in wording as the one in Matthew 6.

The point is that Jesus did not give this as a prayer to be repeated word for word, or the two prayers would have been exactly the same. Also, if we look through the recorded prayers of God's people in the Old and New Testaments, we never find this particular prayer repeated. We know that Paul did not repeat the Lord's Prayer when he prayed for the Ephesians and the Colossians because his prayers are recorded in those epistles. Nowhere in the Bible can you find someone other than Jesus praying this exact prayer. Its primary purpose was as a pattern for prayer.

Anyone who has done some sewing knows how a pattern is used. He or she uses the pattern as a guideline for constructing the garment, but two different people using the same pattern can easily have different results depending on their own needs and preferences. This is what Jesus expected us to do with this prayer. We are to use it as a pattern, or an outline, when we pray, but each person's words will be different than another's.

When I preach, I use an outline. As I prepare, I study carefully and exegete the passage. Then I consider the form in which I want to deliver my message; and finally, I write it out as an outline. The outline is not the sermon word for word. It is only the main points and subpoints. If I were to simply read my notes, my sermon would be very short. Likewise, Jesus gave us a prayer outline. In order to use it effectively, we ought to study it carefully to understand what Jesus is saying and then use it as a guide when we come to God in prayer.

APPLICATION

1. What is the primary purpose of the teaching of Jesus on prayer in Matthew 6:9–13?

2. How do we know that our Lord Jesus Christ didn't mean for us to pray this prayer verbatim?

3. What does it mean to say that this prayer should be an outline or guide for us when we come to God in prayer?

The Structure of the Prayer

Consider now the basic structure of the prayer as a whole. The Lord's Prayer can be divided into a preface (v. 9b), the main body (vv. 9c–13a), and the conclusion (v. 13b). Under each of these parts there are subpoints. In the preface, the two subpoints are "our Father" and "who art in heaven." The main body has two subpoints as well: three petitions relating particularly to God and His concerns, and three petitions relating to man and his concerns. In the conclusion, there are four subpoints in which Jesus makes assertions about the sovereignty of God, the omnipotence of God, the excellency of God, and the immutability of God.

As we look at the passage as a whole, we learn some general truths about prayer. One, we learn something about the attitude in which we should pray. We are entering the presence of our Father, to whom belong "the kingdom, and the power, and the glory, forever" (Matt. 6:13b). This truth ought to affect our attitude and our spirit as we come to pray. We need to take time to reflect on the fact that we are coming before the Almighty God.

Two, we learn something about the proper structure and focus of our prayers. In 1 Corinthians 14:15 Paul said, "I shall pray with the spirit and I shall pray *with the mind also.*" True prayer is not a free-for-all of thoughts and emotions. As we come before our great God, we should be concerned with how He wants us to pray and what He wants us to pray for. It is important to notice in this prayer that the Lord Jesus taught that our starting point and main focus should be God's concerns.

APPLICATION

1. What kind of attitude should we have when we pray?

2. What do we learn from this teaching of Jesus about the proper structure and focus of our prayers?

Three, we learn about the scope of our prayers. Our prayers should include big things, or God's concerns: "Hallowed be Thy name," "Thy kingdom come," and "Thy will be done." But at the same time Jesus indicated that it was appropriate to pray for small things, our concerns: "Give us this day our daily bread." He also taught that our prayers should include both spiritual and physical matters. Daily provisions are physical matters, and temptations and forgiveness are spiritual matters. It is important, however, to take note of the fact that there are many more petitions about spiritual things than there are about material things. This again indicates what the focus of our prayers should be—mainly spiritual things.

Quite often, a church's prayer request list is filled with physical concerns: surgeries, sicknesses, job needs. As we have noted, there is nothing wrong with praying about these things as long as they are not the emphasis of our prayers. If they are, we are out of accord with the teaching of Jesus in Matthew 6. Study the prayers of the apostles and others in the Scripture; spiritual matters are always the emphasis.

APPLICATION

1. What should be the scope of our prayers?
2. Summarize Ephesians 1:15–19.
3. How do your prayers reflect this emphasis?
4. List ten things you could pray for your spouse, children, pastors, or friends that would be in keeping with what this passage teaches about the scope of effective prayer.

The Lord's Prayer contains all the essential principles of prayer—no more and no less. Jesus' teaching was complete, and there is nothing that we could or should add to it in terms of basic principles. If we were to study the longest prayer that has ever been offered by a saint, we would find that it conforms to these principles. So, too, if we were to analyze what is known as our Lord's High Priestly Prayer, found in John 17, we would find that it can be reduced to the principles of this model prayer.

Using the Lord's Prayer as a pattern then, perfect in scope, all we need to do is to take the principles and base our petitions on them, expanding each one according to our own circumstances and needs. As we do this, we will agree with Augustine, Martin Luther, and many other saints who have said that there is nothing more wonderful in the entire Bible than the Lord's Prayer. The way in which Jesus summarized everything and reduced it all to a few sentences surely proclaims that the speaker was none other than the very Son of God.

Four, we learn that this prayer is meant not only for the disciples, but it is meant for all Christians everywhere and at all times. In the Sermon on the Mount, which includes the Lord's Prayer, Jesus was not only speaking to the people around Him at the time, but He was speaking to us as well. We ought to examine our thoughts and words as we pray in light of the teaching in Matthew 6. If we truly want to pray effectively, we must make every effort to follow the pattern that Jesus laid out in attitude, in structure, in scope, and in inclusiveness.

APPLICATION

1. How do you know that this prayer was not meant just for the disciples?

2. How should this teaching be reflected in your prayer life? In your attitude? In the structure and scope of your praying? In the inclusiveness of your prayers?

The Right to Call God "Father"

Finally, we turn to the meaning of the preface of the prayer. In verse 9 Jesus said, "Pray, then, in this way: 'Our Father.' " He was teaching us here to recognize that we are coming to our father, which requires that we be His children.

Jesus was certainly the Son of God; at His baptism, in Matthew 3:17, the heavens were opened and the Father said, "This is My beloved Son." John 1:14 says, "And the Word became flesh, and dwelt among us, and we beheld His glory, glory as of the only begotten from the Father." Jesus was the Son of God in a unique sense and rightly addressed God as His Father in prayer, "I praise Thee, O Father, Lord of heaven and earth" (Matt. 11:25). In Matthew 26:39–44, when Jesus was in the Garden of Gethsemane shortly before His crucifixion, He prayed several times, "My Father, if it is possible, let this cup pass from Me." From the cross He prayed, "Father, forgive them; for they do not know what they are doing" (Luke 23:34), and later, "Father, into Thy hands I commit My spirit" (23:46). The Scripture records numerous times when Jesus addressed God as His Father.

Who else has a right to call God "Father"? Some would say that everyone does since we were all created by God, but Creator and Father are not the same. In John 8:44 Jesus told some of the Pharisees, "You are of your father the devil." Paul said, in Ephesians 2:3, that before we became Christians we were by nature, not children of God, but "children of wrath." Clearly, not everyone has the right to call God "Father."

In John 1:12 we read, "But as many as received Him, to them He gave the right to become children of God, even to those who believe in His name." John 8:42 indicates that those who have a right to call God their Father are those who love Jesus. Jesus said, "If God were your Father, you would love Me." If we love Jesus as He is revealed in Scripture, then we have the right to call God our Father.

APPLICATION

1. How do you know that you can call God your Father?

2. On what Scripture do you base your answer?

Honoring Our Father

Those who have a right to call God their Father must also honor Him. In Exodus 20:12 we are commanded to honor our fathers. In Malachi 1:6 God said, "A son honors his father . . . , if I am a father, where is My honor?" Hebrews 12:9 asserts that honor for God is expressed by respect: "Furthermore, we had human fathers to discipline us, and we respected them; shall we not much rather be subject to the Father?" In Mark 7:9–12 Jesus said that honor is expressed to fathers and mothers by caring for their interests. If God is our Father, we must honor Him by caring about things He cares about. Ephesians 6:1 teaches children to obey their parents. If we, then, are the children of God, we will obey Him.

APPLICATION

1. How does your life show that you honor and respect God?

2. Write out John 5:23.

3. Write out John 14:15.

Resembling Our Father

The Bible also teaches that the sons of God will resemble their heavenly Father. Jesus, of course, perfectly resembled the Father, as He was the "exact representation of His nature" (Heb. 1:3). In fact, Jesus said, "He who has seen Me has seen the Father" (John 14:9). We can never resemble God the Father as Jesus did, but we are commanded to make every effort in that regard. Paul said in Ephesians 5:1, "Therefore be imitators of God, as beloved children." To some extent, the world ought to be able to look at us and see what God is like.

In fact, whether we like it or not, people often form their opinions about God by looking at the lives of believers. I have counseled people who have said that their father and mother were very "religious," yet they were cruel, harsh parents. These people came to the conclusion that if their parents were anything like God, then they wanted nothing to do with Him. As children of God, we ought to take care that we rightly resemble our Father. In Matthew 5:48 Jesus said, "Therefore you are to be perfect, as your heavenly Father is perfect." That will, to some extent, be true of us if we are really children of God.

APPLICATION

1. Why is it important that we resemble our heavenly Father?

2. What Scripture shows that Jesus was like God the Father?

3. Write out Ephesians 5:1.

4. What ideas about God will people form from looking at your life? Why?

5. What is the area in which you should change to be a better reflection of Christ?

Loving God's Family

Those who have the right to call God their Father will also love the other sons of God. First John 3:14 says, "We know that we have passed out of death into life, because we love the brethren. He who does not love abides in death." Calling God our Father means that we are not only going to love the Father, but we are going to love all those whom He loves as well.

I remember taking a long trip away from my family through Europe and the Middle East. I visited missionaries, preached at Bible colleges, and saw many biblical sites in the Holy Land. Though I enjoyed the fellowship with dear friends and the opportunities for ministry, I missed my family every day. At the end of the trip, we were scheduled to spend some time in England, but instead, I changed my ticket because I wanted to get home. I longed to be with my family and that has been true all of my life. We ought to long to be with God's family as well.

If we love God and He is our Father, we will love to be with His family. If we do not, there is reason to question if we are truly in God's family. Coming to God and praying "Our Father" includes all of these things: we must truly be His children, we must honor Him, we must strive to resemble him, and we must love His family.

Lloyd-Jones comments on the importance of beginning our prayers by addressing God as "Our Father":

Strange as it may seem to you, you start praying by saying nothing. You recollect what you are about to do.

I know the difficulty in this; we are but human and we are pressed by the urgency of our position, the cares, the anxieties, the troubles, the anguish of mind, the bleeding of heart, whatever it is. We are so full of this that like children we start speaking at once. If you want to make contact with God and if you want to feel His everlasting arms around you, put your hand upon your mouth for a moment. Stop for a moment and remind yourself of what you are about to do. We can put it in two words: "Our Father." I suggest that if you can say that from your heart, whatever your condition—"My Father"—in a sense, your prayer is already answered. It is just this realization of our relationship to God that we so sadly lack.

Perhaps we can put it in another way like this: there are people that believe it is a good thing to pray because it always does us good. They use various psychological reasons, and that of course is not prayer as the Bible understands it. Prayer means speaking to God—forgetting ourselves and realizing His presence. Then again, there are others, and sometimes I think they would claim for themselves an unusual degree of spirituality, who rather think that the hallmark of true prayer, of ease and facility in prayer, is that one's prayer is to be very brief and pointed. One should just simply make a particular request. That is something which is not true of the teaching of the Bible concerning prayer. Take any of the great prayers that are recorded in the Old Testament or the New, and none of them is what we might call this business-like prayer which simply makes a petition known to God and then ends. Every prayer recorded in the Bible starts with invocation. It does not matter how desperate the circumstance; it does not matter what the particular quandary might be in which those who pray find themselves. Invariably, they start with this worship, this adoration, this invocation.

We have a great and wonderful example of this in the ninth chapter of Daniel. There the prophet, in terrible perplexity, prays to God. But he does not start immediately with his petition. He starts by praising God. A perplexed Jeremiah does the same thing; confronted by the demand that he should buy a plot of land in a seemingly doomed country, Jeremiah could not understand it. It seemed all wrong to him. But he does not rush into the presence of God for this one matter; he starts by worshipping God. And so you will find in all the recorded prayers. Indeed, you even get it in the great High Priestly Prayer of our Lord Himself which is recorded in John 17. You remember also how Paul put it in writing to the Philippians. He says, "In nothing be anxious but in everything by prayer and supplication, with thanksgiving, let your requests be made known to God." That is the order; we must always start with invocation before we even begin to think about petition. And here it is once and forever put to us so perfectly in this model prayer. Jesus said when you pray, you reflect on the fact that you are coming to the Father. And what does that imply? That true prayer has a God-centered focus. It implies that we must come to God recognizing that we owe everything to Him, that He is our Father, and "He is the Father of lights, and every good and perfect gift comes from the Father."[2]

APPLICATION

1. In the past week, what are three ways in which you have shown that you love the family of God?

2. What are three things you will do next week to show this love?

3. Write out 1 Thessalonians 4:9.

A Main Mission of Jesus

At the very start of our Lord's teaching on how to pray, He teaches us that if we are going to pray effectively, we must be children of God and come to Him as a Father. Someone has said that one of the main missions that Jesus had in coming was to bring us into a relationship with God as our Father. Have you ever noticed when reading the Gospels how frequently Jesus refers to God as "our Father," or "My Father," or just as "Father"? In fact, He uses the word "Father" in reference to God more than any other name for God. Think about that; Jesus could have emphasized any other concept of God, but He specifically highlights the concept of God as Father.

He must have chosen to emphasize this concept of God for a specific reason. It's as if the members of the Trinity met prior to Christ's human birth and decided to lay a special emphasis on that one aspect of God's relationship to man. Jesus came into the world, kept the Law for us, died a substitutionary death on the cross, paid the penalty for our sin, rose again, and ascended into heaven. In a sense, He did all these things so that we might come into a familial relationship with God, so that we might come to know God as our Father.

There is no more glorious and wonderful truth in the Bible than that. Jesus came into the world to reveal or explain the Father to us (John 1:18; 14:9). He came into the world as the express image of God (Heb. 1:3). He came into the world to die "for sins once for all, the just for the unjust, in order that He might bring us to

God" (1 Peter 3:18). He came into this world so that we through Him might have access to the Father (Eph. 2:18). He came into this world so that we might receive the Spirit of adoption and thus be enabled to call God our Father (Rom. 8:15). He came into this world so that we might be adopted as sons through Jesus Christ to Himself (Eph. 1:5). No wonder that the apostle John cried out as he understood the wonder of having God as our Father, "See how great a love the Father has bestowed upon us, that we should be called children of God" (1 John 3:1).

Knowing God as Father is an indescribable benefit, and being able to approach God as Father is a glorious privilege. Knowing and approaching God in this way are also necessary prerequisites for praying effectively. To pray this way is to pray effectively, and it is to pray as Jesus taught us.

APPLICATION

1. Summarize in your own words the most important truths presented in this chapter.

2. Write out and work on memorizing one or two verses found in this chapter.

3. In what ways were you challenged or convicted by the material in this chapter? In keeping with the material presented in this chapter, how should your prayer life be changed?

COMING TO YOUR
HEAVENLY FATHER

*I*n chapter 3, we noted that praying effectively involves coming to God as Father. We also explored what it means to pray "Our Father." This concept is so important to our Christian lives in general, and to our prayer lives in particular, that we need to further study what it means to call God our Father, and more specifically, our *heavenly Father*.

Some time ago, an issue of *Moody Monthly* magazine contained an article in which Daniel DeHaan commented on this concept of God as Father:

> Jesus came to tell us that God is the Father. Christ's favorite way of addressing God and speaking about Him was "our Father," "your Father," "My Father," or just "Father." This is the most prominent truth Jesus taught us about God. The word "Father" is applied to God one hundred and eighty-nine times in the Gospels alone. Of those, one hundred and twenty-four are found in John's Gospel. Realizing that Jesus had the option of revealing any of several key concepts of God, we recognize His revelation of God as Father to be quite impressive.
>
> While God is an example of a good Father, Jesus the God-Man provides a good example of a good Son. It is as though heaven's councils met prior to Christ's human birth and decided to lay emphasis on that one aspect of God's relationship to man. If we view God as a Father, we will naturally respond by being

good children, good members of the family. That response puts all of the responses in balance.

As a father, I want my children to learn as quickly as they can. If they come home with a bad report card I am disappointed, but I am not as disappointed as I would be if they did not love each other. If I were simply their teacher, my primary concern would be their grades. But because I am their father, I would rather see C's for grades and have them love each other dearly, than see A's with little or no love. If I were only a master of my household, then I would desire only their obedience to the letter. As a father however, it is an even greater concern to me that they enjoy home and find it secure in every way. To see children happy and getting along with one another is a greater thrill to a father than seeing good performance.

As a family, we are to love and care for one another. I can go to school with you and never love you. I can sit in church with you and never really love you. Many are doing just that today. I can even go to war at your side and never love or care for you. But I cannot be in the same family with you and never love you. Only in the father-family concept does the church function as it should. We believers have failed to see God first of all as a Father. That is why the church does not function like a good family. "This is pure and undefiled religion in the sight of our God and Father, to visit orphans and widows in their distress." If God were not a Father He could have never said that.

In many places today, the church is performance-related. That would be fine if God had only one attribute, but He does not. Therefore, we should beware of the danger of intimidating others on the basis of performance. What characterizes your life? Is your church characterized by being an army, a classroom, or a family? If you are a family, that does not mean instruction and obedience are negated. Any effective father would include those things in bringing up his children. A man can be a teacher without being a father, but a true father will be a teacher. A man can be a lord without being a father, but a true father will be a good director of the home. A man can be a good provider without being a good father, but a true father will be a provider.[1]

APPLICATION

1. In Daniel DeHaan's article, why does he stress that the church should function according to the Father/family concept?

2. How does your church function as a family? Be specific.

God as Heavenly Father

In beginning His teaching on effective prayer with an emphasis on God as our Father, Jesus is surely teaching us that if we want to pray properly, we must know God as Father and come to Him as His children.

Note that in this phrase about approaching God as our Father (Matt. 6:9), Jesus didn't just say we should pray "Our Father." He said we should approach God recognizing Him as "our Father *who art in heaven.*" We must come to God recognizing that He is a Father who is in a class all by Himself.

By turning to other passages of Scripture where God is described as "Father," we can learn more about this unique concept of God as heavenly Father. Ephesians 1:3 tells us that our heavenly Father is the "God and Father of our Lord Jesus Christ, who has blessed us with every spiritual blessing in the heavenly places in Christ." God is called "Father" 189 times in the Gospels. In most of those places, it is Jesus who is calling God "the Father." God is not just any father; He is the God and Father of our Lord Jesus Christ. Jesus is the good Son, and God is a good Father. Jesus, as "the only begotten Son of God," reflects the Father. Hebrews 1:3 tells us that Jesus is the express image of God the Father. In John 14:9 Jesus says, "He who has seen Me has seen the Father." This means that when we think about God as our Father, we should think about someone who is like Jesus.

More than that, Ephesians 1:3 indicates that this One who is the God and Father of our Lord Jesus Christ—and through Christ, our Father as well—is One who blesses us. As a Father, this is what

He wants to do. In fact, the text says that He already "has blessed us with every spiritual blessing in the heavenly places in Christ." So as we come to God in prayer, we should come to Him with the attitude that we are coming to Him as our Father, our Father who is like Jesus, and our Father who blesses us.

APPLICATION

1. Why does Jesus begin the teaching on effective prayer by emphasizing that God is our Father?

2. How does the Bible show us that God is the Father who is in a class all by Himself?

3. Write out Ephesians 1:3.

4. How does remembering that God is the Father of our Lord Jesus Christ encourage us as we come to God in prayer?

5. List eight ways that God the Father has blessed you

The Father Of Glory

In Ephesians 1:17 Paul addresses God again, this time as the "Father of glory." God is the author of glory, and we should think of Him as One who is full of glory. In fact, He is so glorious that were we to see Him in His unveiled glory, we couldn't live. In Exodus 33 Moses asked to see God's glory. God answered him, "You cannot see My face, for *no man can see Me and live!* . . . Behold, there is a place by Me, and you shall stand there on the rock; and it will come about, while My glory is passing by, that I will put you in the cleft of the rock and cover you with My hand until I have passed by" (Ex. 33:20–22).

On that occasion, Moses learned something about how glorious God is, and through that and other biblical accounts, we can learn something about His glory as well. Our Father is incredibly glorious. As we come to our Father God in prayer, we need to remember that we are coming to One who is the Father of our Lord Jesus Christ, One who wants to bless us, and One who is glorious.

The Father of Mercies

In 2 Corinthians 1:3–4 we learn something else about our heavenly Father. Paul said, "Blessed be the God and Father of our Lord Jesus Christ, the *Father of mercies* and *God of all comfort.*" Note that the word "mercy" is in the plural. He has an abundance of mercy and He has many kinds of mercy. In fact, many kinds of mercy are His children, which means that He is the One who produces mercy. And just how merciful is our Father? Paul said in Ephesians 2:4 that God is "rich in mercy." We could never overestimate how merciful our Father is.

Not only is our heavenly Father full of glory and mercy, but Paul would have us to know that He is also the God of all comfort. He delights in comforting His children: "He "*comforts us in all our affliction.* . . . For just as the sufferings of Christ are ours in abundance, so also *our comfort is abundant through Christ*" (2 Cor. 1:4–5). In fact, He is able to comfort us so much that we, in turn, can comfort others with the comfort He has bestowed on us. When we come before God in prayer, we need to recognize that we are coming to One who is a merciful Father and who excels in bringing comfort to us when we are sorely afflicted.

APPLICATION

1. Write out Ephesians 2:4.

2. How has God comforted you in a time of affliction? Be specific.

3. How have you been able to use that comfort from God to comfort someone else? Be specific.

4. How does the knowledge that our Father is a God of mercy and comfort encourage you as you pray?

The Father of Love

In Matthew 5:44–45 we find another characteristic of our heavenly Father that should impact our prayer life. Jesus said, "But I say to you, *love your enemies,* and pray for those who persecute you, in order that you may be *sons of your Father who is in heaven*." Our Father loves His enemies. Even we were His enemies at one time, persecuting Him, ignoring Him, demeaning Him, and taking His name in vain. Yet He loved us and gave His Son for us.

In Matthew 5:45 Jesus continued, "For He causes His sun to rise on the evil and the good, and sends rain on the righteous and the unrighteous." We should imitate our Father in this as well, being devoted to helping all people, evil or good. Jesus explained, "For if you love those who love you, what reward have you? Do not even the tax-gatherers do the same? . . . Therefore you are to be perfect, as your heavenly Father is perfect" (5:46–48). With His perfect love, God loved us while we were still His enemies and did not love Him. We are called to be perfect in that kind of love, following the example of our Father.

Surely, Jesus is not saying in this passage that loving our enemies is the way we become sons of the Father, but rather He is saying that if we are children of God, we are to reflect our Father. In Ephesians 5:1 we are instructed to be "imitators of God, as beloved children." There are some ways in which we can't imitate God. For example, we can't imitate God in terms of His omniscience, His omnipotence, or His omnipresence. In a limited way, however, we can imitate God by loving our enemies and praying for those who persecute us. Because we have become His children and because we are to imitate our Father, we should be devoted and dedicated to helping people even if they are evil. The point is that God did not love us because we loved Him; God loved us even when we did not love Him. We are to follow the example of our Father by imitating Him in our love for others. As we come to God in prayer, we should remember that He is a Father who loved us while we were yet His enemies, and who continues to do so even when we act as if we are still His enemies. What a Father we have!

APPLICATION

1. With whom do you find it most difficult to be loving?

2. How could you show love to that person this week?

3. Write out Romans 12:20–21.

4. Write out 1 John 3:17.

The Father Who Knows and Rewards

Matthew 6:1 is another passage that should not be overlooked as we seek to get to know our heavenly Father. In this passage Jesus said, "Beware of practicing your righteous deeds before men to be noticed by them; otherwise you have no reward with your Father who is in heaven." This verse teaches us several things about our heavenly Father. For one, it teaches that He does reward us, even though we deserve nothing from God but hell. Yet in spite of this, God is so gracious and so merciful that He takes notice of the things that we do and says that He is going to reward us. That's how gracious and forgiving and magnanimous our heavenly Father is.

From Matthew 6:1 we also learn that our Father knows everything that we do. We have a heavenly Father who knows all about us. He knows every thought we have, every word we speak, every action we do, and every motive of our heart. Our Father who is in heaven knows these things and will still reward us. In Matthew 6:6 Jesus expanded on this thought about God's knowledge of us: "But you, when you pray, go into your inner room, and when you have shut your door, pray to your Father who is in secret, and your Father who sees in secret will repay you." Though we may be in our closet all alone where no one else sees us or even knows where we are, God is there with us. In that closet He sees us and pays close attention to what we do and say.

We should remember that the good things that we do that are not seen or recognized by others are always seen and recognized by our Father. We need to remember that our Father pays attention to the smallest and most insignificant things we do and some day will reward us openly. Again I say, what a Father we have! Jesus wants us to know that this is the kind of Father whom we are approaching when we come to Him in prayer.

APPLICATION

1. What practical significance does the fact that we can't hide anything from God have for us in prayer and in life in general?

2. Write out Hebrews 4:13.

The Father Who Keeps and Protects

In Matthew 18:14, in reference to God as our Father, Jesus said, "Thus it is *not the will of your Father who is in heaven that one of these little ones perish.*" Earthly fathers are limited in the protection they can give to their children. To some extent, they can protect them while at home, but even there, not perfectly. Children still fall out of trees and beds and do all sorts of other harmful things that cannot be prevented. When away from home, children are in even greater danger because fathers are not omnipresent. But our heavenly Father is, and what a tremendous encouragement it is to know that He promises to watch over us and care for us. In John 10:28–29 Jesus said, "And I give eternal life to them, and *they shall never perish; and no one shall snatch them out of My hand.*" Jesus said that none of God's children would ever perish. Why won't they perish? Because they are in the hands of their heavenly Father, who is greater than every enemy or difficulty they could ever face (John 10:29). Again I say, what a Father we have!

APPLICATION

1. What practical significance does the fact that our Father keeps and protects us have for us in prayer and in life in general?

2. Write out Hebrews 13:5–6.

The Holy and Righteous Father

In John 17 Jesus used two very important adjectives to describe the kind of Father our God is. In verse 11 Jesus addressed God as

"Holy Father," and in verse 25 He addressed Him as "Righteous Father." So then, as we come to God our Father in prayer, we must come remembering that He is holy and righteous and that this is His very nature. We need to come with the awareness that His eyes are too pure to approve evil and that He cannot look on wickedness with favor (Hab. 1:13). We must come with the awareness that our heavenly Father takes sins seriously, and because He takes sin seriously, He doesn't just say, "Oh, you've sinned. Well, never mind, it doesn't matter." No, our holy and righteous Father says that sin is so serious that we need to seek His forgiveness (1 John 1:9). We can count on the fact that if we confess and forsake our sin and trust in the atonement of Jesus Christ for it (Prov. 28:13), He will forgive us (Ps. 130:8; Eph. 1:7; Rom. 3:25).

Scripture contains many illustrations of the fact that God takes the sins of His children seriously. For example, Mark 11:25–26 indicates that our Father takes the sin of bitterness and resentment, which result in an unwillingness to forgive, very seriously. So seriously that if, while praying, we remember that we are bitter toward another person, we are commanded to deal with that resentment before we continue our prayer. God says, "I want My children to get along and to love one another. Before I hear your prayer and forgive you, you need to go and get it straightened out with anyone against whom you have resentment and bitterness." Matthew 6:14–15 reminds us of this same truth. Jesus said that if we will not forgive the trespasses of others against us, our relationship with our heavenly Father is going to be affected. Our Father is a holy and righteous Father who hates sin of every kind and description. To pray effectively, we must recognize that and confess and forsake our sin as we come to Him in prayer.

APPLICATION

1. What practical significance does the fact that God is holy and righteous have for us in prayer and in life in general?

2. Write out Habakkuk 1:13.

3. How does Mark 11:25–26 illustrate that God takes sin seriously?

The Father Who Is Altogether Trustworthy

Luke 12:29–32 reminds us of another important truth about our heavenly Father. In verse 29 Jesus said, "Do not keep worrying." Nice thought, right? Why shouldn't we worry? Fortunately, Jesus gave us some good reasons for not worrying. "For all these things the nations of the world eagerly seek; but your Father knows that you need these things" (v. 30). In other words, "Don't worry: you aren't an orphan. You are not without a Father. On the contrary, you have the best Father possible, One who knows all about your situation, your needs, your difficulties, your struggles, and He is in control." According to Jesus, we have nothing in this world—terrorism or war or hunger—to worry about. Awful things might happen, but the promise of God is that He already knows and is in control. We can trust our Father to take care of us and to do what is best for us. We need only to focus on obeying Him and seeking to do the things that please Him, and He will take care of us (Luke 12:31).

APPLICATION

1. What is something you are tempted to worry about?
2. How will knowing that God is our heavenly Father help us not to worry?
3. Write out Luke 12:29.

The Father Who Disciplines

We learn more about our heavenly Father in Hebrews 12:5–6: "And you have forgotten the exhortation *which is addressed to you as sons:* 'My son, *do not regard lightly the discipline of the Lord,* nor faint when you are reproved by Him. For those whom the Lord loves He disciplines." When we experience our Father's discipline, we must take it seriously, but not allow it to cause us to despair. Though painful at the time, God's discipline is an expression of His love for us. If He did not love us, then He would not discipline us.

Jesus said in Luke 6:40, "A pupil . . . after he has been fully trained, *will be like his teacher.* "The purpose of discipline is to make us like the Lord Jesus Christ, and so we are to endure. "It is for discipline that you endure; God deals with you as with sons" (Heb. 12:7). All loving fathers discipline their children, and so if God is truly our Father, He will discipline us. In fact, if He did not, we would be "illegitimate children and not sons" (Heb. 12:8).

When there have been children in my home that were not mine, I did not discipline them, but I did discipline my own children. I disciplined them because they were my children and I was their father. God gave me that responsibility, and if I had failed to discipline them, it would have been evidence that I did not love them. The writer to the Hebrews said, "Furthermore, we had earthly fathers to discipline us, and we respected them; shall we not much rather be subject to the Father of spirits, and live? *For they disciplined us for a short time as seemed best to them, but He disciplines us for our good"* (12:9–10a).

As our heavenly Father, God disciplines us in terms of what is best for us and when it is best for us. Earthly parents have only thirteen or so years in which to establish authority over their children. If they do not use the opportunity they are given, their ability to influence their children rapidly diminishes. Many parents today miss that opportunity and this is one reason why there are so many teenagers with problems. We have only a short time in which to discipline our children.

God, however, disciplines us not just for a short time, but for our whole lives because we are always His children. As far as God is concerned, there is always room for growth, and so He disciplines us for our good, *"that we may share His holiness.* All discipline for the moment seems not to be joyful, but sorrowful; *yet to those who have been trained by it, afterwards it yields the peaceable fruit of righteousness"* (12:10b–11). Our heavenly Father is active in discipline because He desires righteousness in us.

APPLICATION

1. Why does God discipline His children?

2. How does this discipline reflect His fatherly love for us?

3. Write out Hebrews 12:5.

The Father Who Is like Jesus

Finally, we can learn something from John 14:6–10 on the subject of our heavenly Father. Jesus said to His disciples, "I am the way, and the truth, and the life; no one comes to the Father, but through Me." Philip did not understand His words, so Christ explained, "He who has seen Me has seen the Father. . . . Do you not believe that I am in the Father, and the Father is in Me?" Jesus was teaching them that He was like the Father and that He had come to reveal the Father.

As we come in prayer saying, "Our Father, who art in heaven," we need to reflect on the fact that God the Father is like Jesus. We know what Jesus was like from what has been recorded in the Gospels: He blessed little children, He was merciful, He was gracious, He was gentle, and He stood for what was right. He was also full of truth. Since Jesus is the "exact representation" of God (Heb. 1:3), then our heavenly Father is also full of truth. We need to remember all these things when we come to God in prayer.

The Father Who Excels

As we study the nature of our heavenly Father, it is helpful to consider the examples of our earthly fathers. There are some who say we form our image of God from our earthly fathers. Sometimes that is true, though in reality it should be the reverse. We should learn what an earthly father is to be like from considering what our heavenly Father is like. Earthly fathers do not naturally imitate their heavenly Father as Christ did.

In Matthew 7:11 Jesus said, *"If you then, being evil, know how to give good gifts* to your children, how much more shall your Father who is in heaven give what is good to those who ask Him!" Jesus taught us two things about earthly fathers in this verse: one, that some of them do give good things to their children; and two, that they are all sinful. Earthly fathers do not just give good things; many times they give bad things to their children. They do that because *"all have sinned* and fall short of the glory of God" (Rom. 3:23). We noted earlier (in Heb. 12:7–10) that fathers do discipline their children, but they discipline according to what seems best to them (12:10).

Usually, when I disciplined my children, I did it because I thought it was best for them. But no father is as wise as God the Father, and the discipline that an earthly father imposes on his children will never be perfect, however much he strives for it to conform to biblical principles. The godliest human father will not always do what is best for his children because his wisdom and knowledge are not perfect as God's are.

Additionally, earthly fathers can discipline their children only "for a short time," in other words, while they are young. Many times, they do not even do it for that short time. There are many parents today who are abdicating their responsibility to discipline their children. Children do whatever they want without fear of correction or training of any kind. It is amazing how many Christian families do not have a time of devotions together. Parents do not spend time with their children in the Word of God or require them to memorize Scripture verses. They do not ask their children to pray or memorize the catechism or sing hymns. Many do not even bring their children to Sunday school to be taught the Word of God. Earthly fathers fail in many ways in this matter of discipline.

Lot is an example of an earthly father who failed. In Genesis 19, after being delivered from Sodom and Gomorrah, he allowed his two daughters to get him drunk. They seduced their father and he committed incest with them. Lot was a terrible example of a father. The Bible also tells us about Isaac, who was deceived by his son Jacob in Genesis 27. Jacob pretended to be his brother Esau and deceived his father Isaac into giving him Esau's birthright. Our heavenly Father will never be deceived by His children.

In Genesis 31 we read about Laban, the father of Rachel and Leah. Genesis 31:2 says, "And Jacob saw the attitude of Laban, and behold, it was not friendly toward him as formerly." Laban had a bad attitude toward his son-in-law, and both Jacob and his wives noticed it. Together, they deceived Laban and stole from him. When Laban found out, he was angry and came after them, intending to kill Jacob. He was a terrible example of an earthly father.

In Genesis 37 Jacob was the sinful father because he loved his son Joseph more than his other children. He treated Joseph in such a partial way that Joseph's brothers became envious of him and were willing to kill him. Later, in verses 31–34, we find another instance where Jacob was a bad example of an earthly father. The sons of Jacob came back from selling Joseph into Egypt and deceived their father. Earthly fathers can be fooled, yes, but our heavenly Father knows everything and can never be fooled.

Earthly fathers are also mortal and, in Genesis 49:33, we read that Jacob died. All earthly fathers will someday die, and their children can no longer come to them for advice or help. There is going to come a day when I can no longer be a help and guide to my children because I am going to be gone. Our daughter calls us just about every day from California. Someday, she will not be able to call me and ask me what I think about something. Not so with our heavenly Father. He is eternal: "Even from everlasting to everlasting, Thou art God" (Ps. 90:2).

Achan was an earthly father who disobeyed God by lying, cheating, and deceiving. Joshua 7 tells about his sin and God's punishment on him and his whole family. They were all killed for what Achan did. The disobedience of earthly fathers not only affects them personally, but it affects their children as well. In 1 Samuel 2 we read about Eli. The Bible says Eli did not rebuke his two sons when they were sinning. Because he was not willing to honor God more than he honored his sons, God told Eli, "On the same day both of them shall die" (2:34). Eli's sons were destroyed and Eli was removed from the priesthood because he did not fulfill his responsibilities as a godly father.

In 1 Kings 1 we learn about David's failure as a father. "Now Adonijah the son of Haggith exalted himself, saying, 'I will be king.' So he prepared for himself chariots and horsemen with fifty men to run before him. And his father had never crossed him at any time by asking, 'Why have you done so?' " (1:5–6). David never took a stand against his son Adonijah or demanded his obedience, and so Adonijah did as he pleased. In 1 Samuel 20, King Saul threw a javelin at his own son Jonathan and shouted at him. Tragically, earthly fathers do all these sinful things.

Consider now how our heavenly Father contrasts with earthly fathers. Sometimes earthly fathers are neglectful of or unavailable to their children. Not so with our heavenly Father, "for He Himself has said, 'I will never desert you, nor will I ever forsake you' " (Heb. 13:5). Sometimes, earthly fathers are physically or verbally abusive to their children, but our Father never abuses us. "The LORD is compassionate and gracious, slow to anger and abounding in lovingkindness" (Ps. 103:8). Sometimes earthly fathers are constantly finding fault with their children and demeaning them. Not so our heavenly Father; "The LORD is near to the brokenhearted, and saves those who are crushed in spirit" (Ps. 34:18).

Sometimes earthly fathers refuse to listen to their children. Not so with our heavenly Father; "The eyes of the LORD are toward the righteous, and His ears are open to their cry" (Ps. 34:15). Sometimes earthly fathers are poor examples to their children, but God the Father is a perfect example to us. "But like the Holy One who called you, be holy yourselves also in all your behavior; because it is written, 'You shall be holy, for I am holy' " (1 Peter 1:15).

Sometimes earthly fathers are legalistic and performance-oriented in their relationship with their children. By their rigid expectations, they communicate "I'll love you if" or "I'll love you when" or "I'll love you because." God said, "I will love them freely" (Hos. 14:4), "I have loved you with an everlasting love" (Jer. 31:3); indeed "We love, because He first loved us" (1 John 4:19).

Sometimes earthly fathers are overly permissive. They fail to establish biblical standards or they fail to enforce those standards with firm discipline. They forget that "foolishness is bound up in the heart of a child" (Prov. 22:15), and "a child who gets his own way brings shame to his mother" (Prov. 29:15). But God the Father always disciplines His children. Job acknowledged this, "If I sin, then Thou wouldst take note of me, and wouldst not acquit me of my guilt" (10:14). God has established His standards for us in Scripture, and because He loves us, He disciplines us when we disobey them. "For whom the LORD loves He reproves" (Prov. 3:12).

Our heavenly Father commanded earthly fathers to do the same, "He who spares his rod hates his son, but he who loves him disciplines him diligently" (Prov. 13:24). Proverbs 20:30 says, "Stripes that wound scour away evil, and strokes reach the innermost parts." God teaches us that discipline must hurt in order to be effective. This does not, however, in any way condone child abuse or child beating. Sometimes earthly fathers discipline their children excessively or harshly. They are overly restrictive and have unreasonable demands and expectations. Not so our heavenly Father, for He gives us the power of the Holy Spirit to do everything He asks us to do. "His divine power has granted to us everything pertaining to life and godliness" (2 Peter 1:3).

Sometimes earthly fathers allow their children to manipulate and intimidate them; they are scared of their own children. Their home is a child-centered home, not a God-centered home. God the Father, of course, will never be manipulated or controlled by His children. He knows what is right and will never lower His standards, regardless of how we sputter and fume and disagree. At the end of his trials and arguing, Job finally acknowledged, "I know that Thou canst do all things, and that no purpose of Thine can be thwarted" (Job 42:2).

Sometimes earthly fathers are not in agreement with their wives. They do not stand together in discipline and in their standards for their children. Not so with our heavenly Father. He operates in concert with the other members of the Trinity. God the Father never disagrees with God the Son, and the Father and the Son never disagree with God the Holy Spirit. "For He whom God has sent speaks the words of God; for He gives the Spirit without measure. The Father loves the Son, and has given all things into His hand" (John 3:34–35).

Martyn Lloyd-Jones's exposition of the phrase "Our Father who art in heaven" is worth quoting at length:

> There are many people in this world, alas, to whom the idea of fatherhood is not one of love. Imagine a little boy who is the son of a father who is a drunkard and a wife beater and was nothing but a cruel beast. That little boy knows nothing in life but constant and undeserving thrashings and kicking. He sees his father spend

all his money on himself and his lust while he himself has to starve. That is his idea of fatherhood. If you tell him that God is his Father and leave it at that, it is not very helpful and it is not very kind. The poor boy in necessity has the wrong idea of fatherhood. That is his notion of a father: a man who behaves like that. So our human sinful notions of our fatherhood need constant correction.

Our Lord says, "Our Father who art in heaven." Paul says, "The God and Father of our Lord Jesus Christ." Anyone like Christ, says Paul, must have a wonderful Father. And thank God, God is such a Father, the Father of our Lord Jesus Christ. It is vital when we pray to God and call Him our Father that we should remind ourselves that He is our "Father who is in heaven." We should remind ourselves of His majesty and greatness and of His almighty power. When in your weakness and your heart of humiliation you drop on your knees before God, in your anguish of mind and heart, you remember that He knows all things about you. The Scripture says all things are naked and open under the eyes of Him with whom we have to do.

Remember also that at some times you rush into the presence of God and want something for yourself or are praying for forgiveness for a sin you have committed. God has seen and knows all about it. It is not surprising that when he wrote Psalm 51, David said in the anguish of his heart, "You desire truth in the inward parts." If you want to be blessed of God you have to be absolutely honest. You have to realize He knows everything and that there is nothing hidden from Him. Remember also that He has all power to punish and all power to bless. He is able to save; He is able to destroy.

Indeed, as the wise man who wrote the book of Ecclesiastes put it, it is vital when we pray to God that we should remember that He is in heaven and we are upon the earth. That is the way to pray. It says to take these two things together and never separate these truths. Remember that you are approaching the almighty, eternal, ever-blessed God. And remember also that that God in Christ has become your Father, who not only knows all about you in the sense that He is omniscient, He knows all about you in a sense that a father knows all about his child. He knows what is good for His child.

Put these two things together. God in His almightiness is looking at you with a holy love and knows your every need; He hears your every sigh and loves you with an everlasting love. He desires nothing so much as your blessing, your happiness, your joy and your prosperity. And remember this: that He is able to do exceedingly abundantly above all that we ask or think. As your Father who is in heaven, He is much more anxious to bless than you are to be blessed. There is also no limit to His almighty power; He can bless you with all the blessings of heaven. He has put them all in Christ and put you into Christ so your life can be enriched with all the glory and riches of the grace in God Himself.[2]

Jesus taught so much with these few words, "Our Father, who art in heaven." When we come to God in prayer, we need to first remember and reflect on what it really means to call God our *heavenly Father*. That is all part of being effective in prayer and of learning to pray Jesus' way.

APPLICATION

1. List some of the ways in which earthly fathers fail in contrast to what is true of our heavenly Father.

2. Summarize in your own words the most important truths presented in this chapter.

3. Write out and work on memorizing one or two verses found in this chapter.

4. In what ways were you encouraged or challenged or convicted by the material in this chapter? In keeping with the material presented in this chapter, how should your prayer life be changed?

PUTTING GOD'S
CONCERNS FIRST

Wouldn't it be wonderful if we had a rock-solid promise that our prayers would always be answered—not maybe, not perhaps, not sometimes—but *always* answered? I've got good news for you: there is such a promise, and you can count on it because God doesn't lie! It's found in 1 John 5:14–15. "And *this is the confidence* which we have before Him, that, if we ask anything *according to His will, He hears us.* And if we know that He hears us in whatever we ask, *we know that we have the requests* which we have asked from Him."

Two Amazing Truths about Prayer

The inspired statement from the apostle John in 1 John 5:14–15 reveals two amazing truths about prayer. One, it teaches us that we can pray with confidence, knowing that God hears us and will grant our requests. Two, it teaches us that this confidence is ours if we ask according to His will. Therefore, it is tremendously important for us to know the will of God if we want to pray effectively. God has not promised to hear us if our prayer doesn't reflect His will, but we can pray with absolute confidence that God will hear our prayers and grant our requests if we pray according to His will.

Knowing God's Will from the Commands, Promises, and Prayers in His Word

In fact, the Bible says that we need to know God's will. "So then do not be foolish, *but understand what the will of the Lord is*" (Eph. 5:17). How then do we know what His will is? God has revealed His will to us through His Word. In Hebrews 10:7 the Lord Jesus said, "Behold, I have come (in the roll of the book it is written of Me) to do Thy will, O God." Jesus came to do God's will which is found in the "roll of the book," or the Word of God. Thus, if we desire to pray with confidence that God will hear and answer us, we must know His Word.

More specifically, we must know God's commands in His Word. Any amount of study quickly shows that God's Word is full of commands for us. In 1 Thessalonians 4:3 the Bible says, "For this is the will of God, *your sanctification.*" First Thessalonians 5:18 says, *"In everything give thanks;* for this is God's will for you in Christ Jesus." Whenever we find a command in God's Word, we can pray confidently for help in fulfilling it because we know that all of God's commands are His will for us.

God's will is also revealed through His many promises. For example, in John 6:37–40 Jesus spoke concerning the will of God: "All that the Father gives Me shall come to Me, and the one who comes to Me I will certainly not cast out. For I have come down from heaven, *not to do My own will, but the will of Him who sent Me.* And this is the will of Him who sent Me, that of all that He has given Me I lose nothing, but raise it up on the last day. *For this is the will of My Father,* that everyone who beholds the Son and believes in Him, may have eternal life; and I Myself will raise him up on the last day." God promised here that those whom He has chosen for salvation will be brought to repentance and faith in Jesus Christ. Therefore, we can pray with confidence that the Lord will bring His own to Himself because God has said that it's His will for this to happen.

In Galatians 1:3–4 we find another wonderful promise that we can bring to God in prayer: "The Lord Jesus Christ . . . gave Himself for our sins, that He might *deliver us out of this present evil age, according to the will of our God and Father.*" It is God's will that we should be set apart from this world as holy people. When we pray for deliverance from sinful influence and temptation, we are praying in the will of God and can have confidence that He hears us and will grant our request.

In addition to God's commands and promises, we can also know the will of God by the prayers that are found in the Bible, since they are part of the inspired Word of God. God's will is revealed in the prayers of Jesus, the apostles, and the Old Testament saints. Jesus' prayer in Matthew 6 is one such prayer. When we pray for the things for which Jesus taught us to pray, we can be confident that we are praying according to God's will and that He will hear and grant our request.

APPLICATION

1. What promise does God give that the right kind of prayers will always be effective?

2. What two truths does this promise of God present?

3. What are three ways by which we can know what the will of God is?

Where Prayers Should Begin

Knowing this, we return to our study of the Lord's Prayer to consider the next few words Jesus used in Matthew 6:9, "Hallowed be Thy name." To properly understand this teaching, we first need to learn what the word "name" means in the Bible. Jesus Christ is referred to in Scripture as "Lord," which means He is sovereign. Romans 10:9 says, "If you confess with your mouth *Jesus as Lord* . . . you shall be saved." The name "Lord" stands for who and what Jesus is.

In John 10:25 Jesus said, "I told you, and you do not believe; the works that I do *in My Father's name,* these bear witness of Me." Jesus came as God's representative and whatever He did was with God's authority. Jesus said in John 12:28, "Father, *glorify Thy name.*"

In other words, He was glorifying who and what God is. And in John 14:23–26 Jesus said: "If anyone loves Me, he will keep My word . . . and the word which you hear is not Mine, but the Father's who sent Me. These things I have spoken to you, while abiding with you. But the Helper, *the Holy Spirit, whom the Father will send in My name,* He will teach you all things, and bring to your remembrance all that I said to you." It is the work of the Holy Spirit to represent Jesus by revealing who and what Jesus is.

In Acts 4:12 we read, "For there is *no other name under heaven* that has been given among men, by which we must be saved." We are saved only through the name of Jesus. John 1:12 says, "But as many as received Him, to them He gave the right to become children of God, *even to those who believe in His name.*" In other words, salvation comes by believing that Jesus is who His names reveal Him to be. In Acts 5:41 we read of the early Christians, "So they went on their way from the presence of the Council, rejoicing that they had been considered worthy to suffer shame *for His name.*" These believers suffered persecution because they revealed to people who Jesus was.

All in all, there are some two hundred names for God in the Scripture. Like most people, I have three names and none of them reveal much about me. They identify me, but they were never intended to describe me. The name "Wayne," for example, means "burden bearer" or "wagon master." My parents did not give me that name because they really expected me to be a wagon master; they just liked the name. Obviously, they had no choice about giving me the name "Mack."

God, however, has two hundred names and every one of them reveals who and what He is. As we pray "Hallowed be Thy name," we are praying that everything God is, everything God has done, and everything there is about God will be hallowed. In Psalm 20:1 David said, "May the LORD answer you in the day of trouble! May the *name of the God of Jacob* set you securely on high!" What does the name "God of Jacob" reveal about God? The God of Jacob was a God of *grace.* Jacob blew it time and again; he was a deceiver and a usurper and yet God was gracious to him. David was praying that the God who is gracious—who gives us what we do not deserve—

would make him secure. Every blessing that we receive from God comes to us because of His grace.

David continued in verse 7, "Some boast in chariots, and some in horses; but we will boast in the *name of the LORD, our God.*" Speaking in modern terms, we are going to trust not in our nuclear bombs or our Green Berets, but we are going to trust in God for deliverance. Though God sometimes uses horses and chariots, ultimately the victory is not because of them. If we are victorious, it is because God has ordained that we should be. Therefore, we trust in the name of our God and in everything that His name reveals about Him.

Jesus in John 17:6 said, "I manifested *Thy name* to the men whom Thou gavest Me." Jesus meant that He had revealed the character of God to them. In John 1:18 He said, "The only begotten Son, who is in the bosom of the Father, *He has explained Him.*" In John 14:9 Jesus said, "He who has seen Me has seen the Father." Hebrews 1:3 tells us that Jesus is the "exact representation of [the Father's] nature." Jesus revealed God the Father's name to us because He is one with the Father.

APPLICATION

1. What do the names of God tell us about God?

2. What relevance does the fact that God's names reveal who and what He is have for our prayer lives? Be specific.

What Does It Mean to Pray "Hallowed Be Thy Name"?

What, then, are we praying for when we pray "Hallowed be Thy name"? The Greek word used here is *hagiazō*, which literally means "to make holy." To hallow means to set apart, to highly respect, and to venerate. When we pray these words, we are praying that God would be made holy.

To understand what it means to pray that God would be made holy, let's look at some Old Testament passages. In Exodus 20:11 we find the same Greek word (in the Septuagint—the Greek translation of the original Hebrew Scriptures) meaning to make holy. "For in six days the LORD made the heavens and the earth . . . and rested on the seventh day; therefore the LORD blessed the sabbath day and *made it holy.*" God meant by this that He had set the Sabbath, or seventh, day apart from every other day in the week; it was to be a hallowed day. The Sabbath is set apart as a day of rest from career activities and is to be devoted to worship.

In the same way, when we pray "Hallowed be Thy name," we pray that God's name would be set apart from every other name. We desire for God to be regarded in a different way from everyone else just as the Sabbath day was to be regarded differently from the other days of the week. We are praying that we might have respect and reverence for God that transcends our regard for anyone or anything else.

In Leviticus 10:1–3 we read about two men who were functioning as priests:

> Now Nadab and Abihu, the sons of Aaron, took their respective firepans, and after putting fire in them, placed incense on it and offered strange fire before the LORD, which He had not commanded them. And fire came out from the presence of the LORD and consumed them, and they died before the LORD. Then Moses said to Aaron, "It is what the LORD spoke, saying, 'By those who come near Me *I will be treated as holy,* and *before all the people I will be honored.*'"

Nadab and Abihu were not treating God as holy. They were not honoring Him because they offered "strange fire," meaning some kind of worship that God had not prescribed for Himself. God says in His Word that He is to be worshiped in a particular way and we ought to be concerned that our worship conforms to what He desires. Nadab and Abihu have not been the only ones to worship God incorrectly, and if God dealt with all men as He did with them, there would be many deaths today. But He put this in His Word to show us that worship is serious business. He may not kill us when we worship Him inappropriately, but He is still greatly displeased and we will someday answer for it. If we want to hallow God's name, we must worship Him properly.

Nadab and Abihu were Aaron's sons. Notice the end of verse 3, "So Aaron, therefore, kept silent." Aaron did not protest God's judgment with cries of "Unfair!" No, he recognized God's right to do whatever He chose and kept silent before Him. He knew that God is holy and only does what is right. If God took his sons, then it was right for Him to do so. If we want to hallow God's name, we must, like Aaron, acknowledge God's right to act as He pleases, even if it touches something or someone very dear to us.

In 2 Samuel 7:26 David said, "[May] *Thy name . . . be magnified forever,* by saying, 'The LORD of hosts is God over Israel'; and may the house of Thy servant David be established before Thee." David was praying here, in effect, that God's name would be hallowed. When God's name is magnified, it is enlarged so that others can see how great and marvelous God is. A magnifying glass enlarges objects so that they can be better seen. David wanted to show people how wonderful his God was. Not that he could make *God* any bigger than He already is, but so that people could have their *views of God* enlarged.

APPLICATION

1. What does it mean to pray "Hallowed be Thy name"? What are we really praying for? Be specific.

2. Write out Psalm 8:1.

3. Write out Psalm 145:21.

4. How does your life magnify or hallow the name of your God?

5. How do you see God's name being hallowed in the lives of other people?

6. How is God's name not being hallowed in the church and in the world?

More Specifics on the Meaning of "Hallowed Be Thy Name"

For sixteen years of my life, I never thought about hallowing God's name. I heard about God in church, but I had no desire to know Him. God was not important to me at all, but at age sixteen the Lord brought me to Himself. He turned me around so that my desire in life became to be a magnifying glass through which people can see the greatness and glory of God. That is what it means to pray "Hallowed be Thy name."

In 1 Kings 8:43 Solomon prayed for God's name to be hallowed. He said, "Hear Thou in heaven Thy dwelling place, and do according to all for which the foreigner calls to Thee, in order that all the peoples of the earth may know *Thy name,* to fear Thee, as do Thy people Israel, and that they may know that this house which I have built is called by *Thy name.*" Solomon used the word "name" twice in this verse. He prayed for God's name to be hallowed by all the peoples of the earth knowing who and what God is. He wanted everyone to know God's glory and majesty when they came to the place where they worshiped Him. He also wanted everyone to know that God's people would be meeting together in God's name.

Part of what we are praying for when we pray "Hallowed be Thy name" is that people may know through the church—God's dwelling place in the New Testament—that God is among His people when they meet together. We want the world to know that church is a special place where God meets with His people. There ought to be something so different about us when we leave church that people acknowledge that God is among us and is changing us into His image.

David prayed in 1 Chronicles 17:24, "And *let Thy name be established and magnified* forever, saying, 'The LORD of hosts is the God of Israel, even a God to Israel; and the house of David Thy servant is established before Thee.'" Again, this prayer was really for God's name to be hallowed in that David prayed for his family to be established before God so that people would know that David's family served God and belonged to God.

In summary of this point, consider the words of Martyn Lloyd-Jones as he commented on the phrase "Hallowed be Thy name":

What does that mean? . . . The word "hallowed" means to sanctify or revere, to make and keep holy. Why does He say, "Hallowed be Thy name"? What does this term "Thy name" stand for? We are familiar with the fact that it was the way in which the Jews commonly referred to God Himself. Whatever we may say about the Jews in the Old Testament times, and however great their failures, there was one respect, at any rate, in which they were most commendable. I refer to their sense of the greatness and the majesty and the holiness of God. You remember that they had such a sense of this that it became their custom not to use the name Jehovah. They felt that the very name, the very letters as it were, were so holy and sacred, and they were so small and unworthy, that they dare not mention the name Jehovah. They referred to God as "The Name" in order to avoid the actual term "Jehovah." So "Thy name" here means God Himself and we see that the purpose of the petition is to express this desire that God Himself may be revered, may be sanctified. That the very name of God and all it denotes and represents may be honored among men, may be holy throughout the entire world. But perhaps in the light of the Old Testament teaching, it is good for us to enlarge on this just a little. "Thy Name," in other words, means all that is true of God, all that has been revealed concerning God. *That means God in all His attributes, God in all that He is, in and of Himself, and God in all that He has done and all that He is doing.*[1]

APPLICATION

1. In specific ways, what does praying "Hallowed be Thy name" mean in reference to the church? To your family?

2. Summarize what Lloyd-Jones is teaching about the phrase "hallowed be Thy name."

Ways to Hallow and Unhallow God's Name

Exodus 20:7, the third of the Ten Commandments, is an excellent commentary on what it means to pray "Hallowed be Thy name." It says, "You shall not take the name of the LORD your God in vain, for the LORD will not leave him unpunished who takes His name in vain." When we pray for God's name to be hallowed, we are asking God to help us not take His name in vain. Thomas Watson, in his book on the Ten Commandments, listed several ways in which we take the name of God in vain:

1. We take God's name in vain by speaking slightly or irreverently of Him. In other words, we use God's name in a way that we might use anyone else's name. When we mention a king's name, we use some title of honor. So also we should speak of God with the sacred reverence that is due the Lord God Almighty, Maker of heaven and earth. When we speak carelessly of Him, God interprets it as contempt for Him and His name.

2. We take God's name in vain when we profess God's name as believers but fail to live answerably to it. Watson uses the phrase from Titus 1:16, "They profess to know God, but *by their deeds they deny Him.*" When we claim to love God, trust God, and want to serve God, but our lives do not match our words, we are taking His name in vain.

3. We take God's name in vain by using it in idle talk, such as "Oh God," "Oh Christ," or "God save my soul." We hear these phrases all the time; but by using them, we take the name of God lightly and in vain.

4. We take God's name in vain by worshiping Him with our lips but not with our heart. Proverbs 23:26 says, "Give me your heart, my son." The heart is the chief thing in worship and the altar that sanctifies the offering. In Isaiah 29:13 God said, "This people draw near with their words and honor Me with their lip service, *but they remove their hearts far from Me.*" When we simply go through the motions of worship—say the right prayers, sing the right hymns—but it does not come from our hearts, we are taking God's name in vain.

5. We take God's name in vain when we pray to Him but do not believe that He hears us. We can go through the motions of prayer and still not believe that God will answer. When we pray "Hallowed be Thy name," we are asking God to help us to really believe His promise to always hear our prayers.

6. We take God's name in vain when we, in any way, profane or abuse His Word. Psalm 138:2 says, "For Thou hast *magnified Thy word according to all Thy name.*" In other words, when we fail to treat the Word of God respectfully and love what it has to say, we are taking God's name in vain because His Word is a revelation of Him.

7. We take God's name in vain when we swear by His name carelessly or wickedly. Jesus taught us not to swear by heaven or by earth (Matt. 5:34–35). When we say, "As God is my witness," and do it lightly or in telling a lie, we are using the name of God in a vain way.

8. We take God's name in vain when we mention God's name in connection with wicked actions. In 2 Samuel 15:7 Absalom said, "Please let me go and pay my vow which I have vowed to the LORD, in Hebron." Then in verse 10 he said, "As soon as you hear the sound of the trumpet, then you shall say, 'Absalom is king in Hebron.' " Absalom invoked God's name as worthy of his honor and then turned around and sought honor for himself. He used the name of God to support his wickedness.

9. We take God's name in vain when we use our tongue to dishonor His name. We do this when we curse in anger, but also when we make rash or unlawful vows—promising to do something that we won't or shouldn't do—and use God's name to make that promise seem trustworthy to others. Many couples make marriage vows in the name of God, but fail to keep those commitments afterward. When becoming members of a church, people often make a covenant with God before the church body to do certain things. When they fail to keep those commitments, they are taking God's name in vain.

10. We take God's name in vain when we speak evil of God by murmuring at—complaining about—His providences. We murmur at His justice, "It's not fair!" When we get upset about our circumstances and cry out against them, we are really raging against God because He is in control of all things. When we pray "Hallowed be Thy name," we are praying, "Lord, please help me not to complain about anything You bring into my life. Help me never to entertain the thought that what You are doing is not fair." Murmuring springs from a bitter root; it comes from pride and discontent. Murmuring reproaches God and therefore takes His name in vain.

11. We take God's name in vain when we falsify our promises. For example, if we ask God to spare our life or the life of a loved one in a time of great distress and then forget about it later, we make our promise false.[2]

Watson also noted that the third commandment ends by saying, "For the Lord will not leave him unpunished who takes His name in vain." God takes this sin seriously. When we pray "Hallowed be Thy name," part of what we are praying for is His help in not taking His name in vain in all these different ways.

APPLICATION

1. What are some ways people take God's name in vain?
2. What are some of the ways in which you have taken His name in vain and thus failed to hallow His name?

There are many verses in Scripture that help us to understand what it means to take God's name in vain in other specific ways. In Isaiah 29:23–24 God said of people who please Him, *"They will sanctify My name;* indeed, they will sanctify the Holy One of Jacob, and *will stand in awe of the God of Israel.* And those who err in mind *will know the truth,* and those who criticize *will accept instruction."* God said that to sanctify, or hallow, His name, we must show great reverence for Him but we must also *know the truth.* In other words, we must hallow His Word by wanting to know it. When we pray "Hallowed be Thy name," we are asking God to help us to know the truth in His Word. And further, we must *accept instruction.* The proud say, "I don't need instruction." Proverbs 14:12 says, "There is a way which seems right to a man, but its end is the way of death." But Proverbs 15:10 says, "Stern discipline is for him who forsakes the way; *he who hates reproof will die."* And more than that, if we disregard instruction, then we are not hallowing God's name. Hallowing God's name requires that we open our hearts to hear God's Word through reading and teaching.

Psalm 69:7 gives us additional insight into what it means to hallow God's name: "Because *for Thy sake I have borne reproach;* dishonor has covered my face." In other words, if we really desire to hallow God's name, we will be willing to be dishonored and to experience ridicule for His sake. Though we may be demeaned and despised, we bear it gladly because we are more concerned about pleasing God than about pleasing others. When we pray "Hallowed be Thy name," we are praying, "Lord, help me to be more concerned about honoring You than about impressing people or being accepted by them."

APPLICATION

What are three ways we can show in our words and in our lives that we hallow God's name?

It is fitting to close this chapter with some additional thoughts from Lloyd-Jones:

> This petition means . . . we should all have a consuming passion that the whole world might come to know God. There is an interesting expression used in the Old Testament with regard to this which must sometimes have astonished us. The psalmist in Psalm 34 invites everyone to join him in magnifying the Lord. What a strange idea! "Oh," he says, "magnify the Lord with me and let us exalt His name together!" At first sight, that appears to be quite ridiculous. God is the eternal, the self-existent One, absolute and perfect in all His qualities. How can a feeble man ever magnify such a being? How can we ever make God great or greater, which is what we mean by magnify? How can we exalt the name that is highly exalted over all? It seems preposterous and quite ridiculous. And yet, of course, if we but realize the way in which the psalmist uses it, we shall see exactly what he means. He does not mean that we can add to the greatness of God for that is impossible. But he does mean that this greatness of God may appear to be greater among men. Thus, it comes to pass that, among ourselves and this world, we can magnify the name of God. We can do so by words and by our lives, by being reflectors of the greatness and glory of God and of His glorious attributes.
>
> That is the meaning of this petition. It means a burning desire that the whole world may bow before God in adoration, in reverence, in praise and worship, in honor and thanksgiving. Is that your supreme desire? Is that the thing that is always uppermost in your mind when you pray to God? I would remind you again that it should be so whatever your circumstance. It is when you look at it in that way that you see how utterly valueless much of your praying must be.[3]

"Hallowed be Thy name." Jesus was teaching that when we come to God, even though we may be in desperate conditions and circumstances, we must pause for a moment and realize that our greatest desire should be for our great God and Father to be honored, worshiped, and magnified among men. This has always been so in the prayers of every true saint of God that has lived. Their main concern was that our glorious God might be rightly represented for people.

That is what it means to pray according to the will of God. When we do, we can have the confidence that John talks about in 1 John 5:14–15. "If we ask anything according to His will, He hears us . . . [and] we know that we have the requests which we have asked from Him." Since it is God's will for His name to be hallowed, we must evaluate our prayers in the light of this great first petition. Is this the main thing that we are concerned about in our prayers? It should be. To pray in this way is to pray effectively and it is to pray Jesus' way.

APPLICATION

1. Summarize in your own words the most important truths presented in this chapter.

2. Write out and work on memorizing one or two verses found in this chapter.

3. In what ways were you encouraged or challenged or convicted by the material in this chapter? In keeping with the material presented in this chapter, how should your prayer life be changed?

KINGDOM PRAYING

In his book *Theology of Christian Counseling* Jay Adams writes:

> In this materialistic age, surely one may ask, "What is prayer?" and not in the least be facetious when doing so. The present generation has grown up prayerless. Even where giving of thanks at meals still prevails, all too often it is but the hollow vestigial remains of a worn-out tradition. Few children are taught how to bring their problems to God. At home and in school, they are reared according to an uneasy doctrine of self-sufficiency that leads to a radical self-centered pride and arrogance, or conversely to an unhealthy dependence upon parents and society.[1]

My wife and I recently heard a preacher on a supposedly Christian program say that many people do not think highly enough of themselves and do not realize how much they deserve. Schools are telling our children this kind of thing all the time. This teaching flies directly in the face of the teaching of the Bible, which says that we are to be completely dependent on God. The message of self-reliance and self-importance, however, leads us to think that we really do not need to pray. Adams continues:

> Without prayer, God is in a picture on the wall. Without prayer, there is no vital connection with God: no confession, adoration,

thanksgiving or petition. That is to say, no communication is established with God. . . .

But even for Christians who pray, and all Christians do or they are not Christians, the universal word is that prayer is the hardest discipline of all. So on both counts, it is quite proper to ask the question, "What is prayer?" The comment, "Everyone knows what prayer is," is both correct and false. Just about everyone has a vague idea about prayer. The picture of someone with his head bowed, talking to God, is perhaps the most common connotation of prayer, yet even that stereotyped image has been shattered recently by the common charismatic stance of face and hands raised toward heaven in prayer. Members of the Unity cult, for instance, repeat "truth sayings" in an attempt to further indoctrinate one another in the idea that one prays to himself since he is as much God as any other. So it is not really true that everyone knows what prayer is. Clearly, there are quite different concepts of prayer in content and form, some of which are plainly contradictory to others.[2]

I agree wholeheartedly with Jay Adams that most people really do not know what true prayer is. More importantly, though, I am convinced that our Lord Jesus Christ would also agree that most people do not know how to pray. That is why He included this thorough teaching on prayer in His Sermon on the Mount.

In Matthew 6:9b–13, our Lord Jesus Christ, who is God manifest in the flesh, taught us what we should pray for by giving us this pattern for prayer. In this chapter we will begin to study the teaching of Jesus in the second petition, "Thy kingdom come." Here and in the following chapter we will look at three things that stand out about this particular petition: its importance, its implications, and its ingredients, or the things for which it calls us to pray.

The Importance of Kingdom Praying

Emphasis in the Sermon on the Mount

The *importance* of the second petition is emphasized in a number of ways. Its place in the prayer is one of them. Immediately after we are taught to pray that God's name would be hallowed, we are taught to pray that His kingdom would come. As we noted earlier, there are many Bible scholars who believe that the most important petition of all in the Lord's Prayer is the first, "Hallowed be Thy name." The main concern of our prayers and lives should be that God's name would be sanctified and glorified. "Whether, then, you eat or drink or whatever you do, *do all to the glory of God*" (1 Cor. 10:31).

We also know that the second petition is tremendously important because of the emphasis that the kingdom of God had in the teaching of our Lord Jesus Christ. In Matthew 4:17 we read, "From that time Jesus began to preach and say, 'Repent, for the *kingdom of heaven* is at hand.' " This was the beginning of His public ministry, and His message was repentance and the coming of God's kingdom. Matthew 4:23 says, "And Jesus was going about in all Galilee, teaching in their synagogues, and proclaiming the *gospel of the kingdom.*"

In Matthew 5–7, the Sermon on the Mount, Jesus talked about the kingdom of heaven or the kingdom of God many times. The Beatitudes, which paint a verbal picture of a true believer, mention the kingdom of heaven twice. "Blessed are the poor in spirit, for theirs is *the kingdom of heaven*" (5:3). "Blessed are those who have been persecuted for the sake of righteousness, for theirs is *the kingdom of heaven*" (5:10). Later, in verses 19–20, Jesus says: "Whoever then annuls one of the least of these commandments, and so teaches others, shall be called least in the *kingdom of heaven;* but whoever keeps and teaches them, he shall be called great in the *kingdom of heaven.* For I say to you, that unless your righteousness surpasses that of the scribes and Pharisees, you shall not enter the *kingdom of heaven.*" Similarly, in His teaching on prayer in Matthew 6:9–13, Jesus referred to God's kingdom twice: verse 10, "Thy kingdom come," and verse 13, "For thine is the kingdom." Further on, in Matthew 6:33 Jesus taught, "But seek first *His kingdom* and His righteousness; and all these things shall be added to you." In Matthew 7:21, He said, "Not everyone who says to Me, 'Lord, Lord,' will enter the *kingdom of heaven;* but he who does the will of My Father who is in heaven."

Beyond the Sermon on the Mount

Beyond the Sermon on the Mount, there are many more times throughout Christ's ministry and teaching that He emphasized this matter of the kingdom of heaven. In Matthew 9:35 we read that Jesus continued to do what He began to do at the beginning of His ministry. He was still "teaching . . . and proclaiming the *gospel of the kingdom.*" In Matthew 10:7 He sent out His disciples, "And as you go, preach, saying, 'The *kingdom of heaven* is at hand.' " In Matthew 11:11–12, in reference to John the Baptist, He says, "Truly, I say to you, among those born of women there has not arisen anyone greater than John the Baptist; yet he who is least in the *kingdom of heaven* is greater than he. And from the days of John the Baptist until now the *kingdom of heaven* suffers violence, and violent men take it by force."

At the very end of His time on earth, Jesus' message was the same. When our Lord met with the disciples before ascending into heaven, He spoke of the kingdom. "To these He also presented Himself alive, after His suffering, by many convincing proofs, appearing to them over a period of forty days, and speaking of the things concerning the *kingdom of God*" (Acts 1:3). The kingdom of God was a central theme in Jesus' ministry from beginning to end.

APPLICATION

1. What are the three things that stand out in reference to the petition "Thy kingdom come"?

2. How is this petition emphasized in the Sermon on the Mount?

3. How did Jesus in other places emphasize the importance of the kingdom of God in His teaching?

The Kingdom in the Apostle Paul's Thinking and Preaching

While this petition regarding God's kingdom is of great importance because of its position in the Lord's Prayer and its emphasis in Christ's teaching, it is also important because of its emphasis in the thinking and teaching of the early Christians. It was the focus of Philip the Evangelist's message to the Samaritans in Acts 8:12, "They believed Philip preaching the good news about the *kingdom of God* and the name of Jesus Christ."

The good news of the kingdom of God was central in the preaching of the apostle Paul as well. In Acts 14:21–22 the first missionary journey of Paul and Barnabas is reported. "And after they had preached the gospel to that city [Derbe] and had made many disciples, they returned . . . strengthening the souls of the disciples, encouraging them to continue in the faith, and saying, 'Through many tribulations we must enter the *kingdom of God.*' " In Acts 19:8 we read that Paul "entered the synagogue and continued speaking out boldly for three months, reasoning and persuading them about the *kingdom of God.*"

In fact, Paul's preaching about the kingdom of God had such an impact that though many were saved, others were very upset by it. Acts 19:20 reports, "So the word of the Lord was growing mightily and prevailing," and verse 23, "And about that time there arose no small disturbance concerning the Way." When Paul was taken to Rome as a prisoner near the end of his ministry, his message about the kingdom of God was still a focus. Acts 28:23 tells us, "They came to him at his lodging in large numbers; and he was explaining to them by solemnly testifying about the *kingdom of God,* and trying to persuade them concerning Jesus." Verses 30–31 continue, "He . . . was welcoming all who came to him, preaching the *kingdom of God,* and teaching concerning the Lord Jesus Christ with all openness, unhindered." The message of the kingdom of God was tremendously important to the apostle Paul.

In the same way, the teaching of the other apostles emphasized the kingdom of God. In 2 Peter 1:11 Peter said, "For in this way the entrance into the *eternal kingdom of our Lord* and Savior Jesus Christ will be abundantly supplied to you." In Revelation 1:9 John the apostle said, "I, John, your brother and fellow partaker in the tribulation and *kingdom* and perseverance which are in Jesus." If this concept of the kingdom of God was so important to Jesus and the apostles who carried His message to the world, then it ought to be important to every one of us who names the name of Jesus Christ. As believers, we are part of this kingdom.

APPLICATION

1. How did Paul emphasize the importance of the kingdom of God?

2. What impact did this teaching have on the people who heard Paul preach?

3. In what ways is it evident in your teaching and praying that the kingdom of God is important to you?

The Implications of Kingdom Praying

Our God Is the King

Having considered the importance, we now consider the *implications* of this petition. When we pray "Thy kingdom come," we are acknowledging that God is King because a kingdom must have a king. Psalm 47:7–8 says, "For *God is the King* of all the earth; sing praises with a skillful psalm. *God reigns* over the nations, *God sits on His holy throne."* In Hebrews 1:8 we read, "But of the Son He says, *'Thy throne, O God,* is forever and ever, and the righteous scepter is the *scepter of His kingdom.'*" This verse demonstrates the divinity of Christ as well; both God the Father and the Lord Jesus Christ are declared to be King. Revelation 19:12 says, "And His eyes are a flame of fire, and upon *His head are many diadems"*—or crowns. He wears many crowns because He is, in fact, King.

In Revelation 4:1–4 John was allowed to see scenes in heaven:

> After these things I looked, and behold, a door standing open in heaven. . . . Immediately I was in the Spirit; and behold, a throne was standing in heaven, and One sitting on the throne. And He who was sitting was like a jasper stone and a sardius in appearance; and there was a rainbow around the throne, like an emerald in appearance. And around the throne were twenty-four

thrones; and upon the thrones I saw twenty-four elders sitting, clothed in white garments, and golden crowns on their heads.

Later John said, "The twenty-four elders will fall down before *Him who sits on the throne*" (4:10). "Thy kingdom come" is an acknowledgment of God as our King.

What kind of King is God our Father? The Almighty God is a *glorious* King. David wrote Psalm 24 for the children of Israel to sing to God as they entered the place of worship.

> Lift up your heads, O gates,
> And lift them up, O ancient doors,
> That the *King of glory* may come in!
> Who is this *King of glory?*
> The LORD of hosts,
> He is the *King of glory.* (24:9–10)

Would that we all came to worship with such excitement and praise for our God the King!

The King that we worship is a King of glory and majesty. Psalm 93:1–2 says:

> The LORD reigns, He is clothed with majesty;
> The LORD has clothed and girded Himself with strength;
> Indeed, the world is firmly established, it will not be moved.
> Thy throne is established from of old;
> Thou art from everlasting.

And Psalm 89:6–7:

> For who in the skies is comparable to the LORD?
> Who among the sons of the mighty is like the LORD,
> A God greatly feared in the council of the holy ones,
> And awesome above all those who are around Him?

The "holy ones" are angels, and this psalm teaches us that God is *greatly feared* even among the angels who have never sinned and dwell constantly in His presence. How much more then should we fear the Almighty God? The awesome glory and majesty of our God ought to strike fear and awe in our hearts as we come into His presence in prayer.

APPLICATION

1. What impact does the fact that God is King have on your life? How does this truth manifest itself in your life and praying?

2. Write out 1 Timothy 6:15–16.

The Bible also teaches that **God is the great King.** Psalm 95:3 affirms, "For the LORD is a *great God,* and a *great King* above all gods." In Jeremiah 23:24 God's greatness is described in this way: " 'Can a man hide himself in hiding places, so I do not see him?' declares the LORD. 'Do I not fill the heavens and the earth?' declares the LORD." Only our great King can be everywhere at once, unlike earthly kings. In 1 Kings 8:27, as Solomon prayed at the dedication of the temple, he asked, "But will God indeed dwell on the earth?" Scientists continue to grapple with the enormity of our universe, discovering galaxies even beyond what they imagined to be the farthest galaxies. God cannot be limited to the earth, or our galaxy, or even to the universe. Psalm 102:15–16 says, "So the *nations will fear the name of the LORD,* and all the *kings of the earth Thy glory.* For the LORD has built up Zion; *He has appeared in His glory."* He is indeed a great King. Praying "Thy kingdom come" implies that we know and honor Him as a glorious and great King.

He is also an *eternal* king. Psalm 10:16 says, "The LORD is King forever and ever." In Psalm 145:13 the Bible emphasizes God's eternal kingship: "Thy kingdom is an *everlasting* kingdom, and Thy dominion *endures throughout all generations."* History has recorded the rise and fall of many great kings of the earth—Nebuchadnezzar, pharaohs, kings of Europe, and others. They lasted for a brief time, but our Lord is an eternal King who has an eternal kingdom. Second Peter 1:11 talks about our "entrance into the *eternal kingdom.*" First Timothy 1:17 says, "Now to the *King eternal,* immortal, invisible, the only God, be honor and glory *forever and ever.* Amen."

APPLICATION

1. How does God demonstrate that He is a great King?
2. How do you know that God is an eternal King?

The fact that God is a great, glorious, and eternal king *should affect our attitude toward service.* First, it should make us eager to submit ourselves to Him because He is all-wise. It is our privilege to serve the King of kings. Second, it should affect our attitude toward life. God is the King of kings, and that should encourage us to trust Him and to fear Him. It should make us hopeful and courageous as we look to the future because His kingdom is everlasting and He will never be defeated. It also means that we should never be ashamed of Him or His cause. He is the King of kings! What is there to be ashamed of? It should also humble us; He is the King of kings and we are not. Finally, it should cause us to see the folly of rebelling against Him. Job 9:4 says, "Wise in heart and mighty in strength, who has defied Him without harm?" Ultimately, no one has ever resisted the King of kings and been successful. When we pray "Thy kingdom come," we are acknowledging God as King—glorious, great, and eternal.

APPLICATION

1. What effect does this truth about your heavenly Father have on your prayers and life? Be specific.
2. How does this great truth affect your attitude toward service? Toward the future?
3. Why is it the height of folly to rebel against God?

The Aspects of the Kingdom of God

There is a sense in which the kingdom of God has not yet fully come. To understand what this means, we need to consider the three aspects of God's kingdom, beginning with **His kingdom of power.** Jesus referred to this in Matthew 6:13 when He said, "Thine is the kingdom." God has always ruled His kingdom of power. Ephesians 1:20–22 teaches that our Lord Jesus Christ already rules in this kingdom. It says that after God raised Christ from the dead, He "seated Him at His right hand in the heavenly places. . . . And He put all things in subjection under His feet, and gave Him as head over all things to the church." In 1 Timothy 6:14–16 Paul said that we are to be holy "until the appearing of our Lord Jesus Christ, which He will bring about at the proper time—He who is the blessed and only Sovereign, the King of kings and Lord of lords; who alone possesses immortality and dwells in unapproachable light; whom no man has seen or can see. To Him be honor and eternal dominion!"

Our God is reigning right now. Psalm 103:19 says, "The LORD has established His throne in the heavens; and His sovereignty rules over all." In 1 Chronicles 29:11 the Bible says, "Thine, O LORD, is the greatness and the power and the glory and the victory and the majesty, indeed everything that is in the heavens and the earth; Thine is the dominion, O LORD, and Thou dost exalt Thyself as head over all." In Daniel 4:35 Nebuchadnezzar, having been humbled by God acknowledged, "But He does according to His will in the host of heaven and among the inhabitants of earth; and no one can ward off His hand or say to Him, 'What hast Thou done?' " Psalm 115:3 reminds us, "But our God is in the heavens; He does whatever He pleases." In some way that we will never fully understand, everything that happens in our world happens because it pleases God. He may one day explain it to us, but right now the truth is that He is King over *all* and His kingdom is a kingdom of power. What a tremendous comfort that is for believers, to know that in all things God reigns with power!

Second, we must understand **God's kingdom of grace.** We enter the kingdom of grace when God works in our hearts to bring us to salvation through Jesus Christ. Jesus referred to this kingdom when He said to Nicodemus, "Unless one is born again, he cannot see the *kingdom of God*" (John 3:3). By "kingdom of God," Jesus meant the kingdom of grace wherein people come to repentance and faith in Him as their Savior and Lord. In Mark 1:15 Jesus called people to enter this kingdom through repentance: "The *kingdom of God* is at hand; repent and believe in the gospel." In Matthew 5:10 He said, "Blessed are those who have been persecuted for the sake of righteousness, for theirs is the *kingdom of heaven*." In Matthew 10:7 Jesus told His disciples to preach, "The kingdom of heaven is at hand." He was calling the lost to enter into the kingdom of God through His saving grace. In Colossians 1:13 Paul wrote about what happens to us when we are saved: "For He delivered us from the domain of darkness, and *transferred us to the kingdom of His beloved Son*." Through faith in Christ Jesus, we are right now a part of this kingdom of grace.

The apostle Paul preached the gospel of the kingdom of grace. "For the *kingdom of God* is not eating and drinking, but righteousness and peace and joy in the Holy Spirit" (Rom. 14:17). In other words, if we are part of God's kingdom, our lives should be characterized by the things of God because we belong to Him. We acknowledge also that Jesus Christ is King and Lord of our lives. We say to Christ, "You rule my life. My life is about what You want, not what I want, because You are my King." The gospel, or good news, is that God has a kingdom that we can be part of through repentance and faith in Jesus Christ. That is the gospel of the kingdom of grace.

Why is grace called a kingdom? When we become Christians, grace not only saves us, but grace begins to rule our lives. Romans 5:19–21 says, "For as through the one man's disobedience the many were made sinners, even so through the obedience of the One the many will be made righteous . . . that, as sin reigned in death, even so *grace might reign* through righteousness to eternal life through Jesus Christ our Lord." The purpose of the Law was to show us how much we sin against God. Before we were saved, sin reigned in our lives and controlled us. When we enter the kingdom of grace, grace rules our lives through Jesus Christ. Thomas Watson said, "When grace comes, there is a kingly government set up in the soul. Grace rules the will and the affections and brings the whole man in subjection to Christ. It reigns in the soul, sways the scepter, subdues mutinous lusts, and keeps the soul in spiritual decorum." Jesus wants to reign in our lives, and it is our responsibility and privilege to submit to Him as our King. When we pray "Thy kingdom come," we pray that the kingdom of God's grace might come and might reign more fully.

APPLICATION

1. How does the fact that God is reigning right now comfort you?

2. How do we become part of the kingdom of grace?

3. If we are part of the kingdom of grace, what will characterize our lives?

4. In what ways does your life manifest that you are a part of the kingdom of grace?

5. Write out Colossians 1:13.

Third, we must understand *God's kingdom of glory.* When we pray "Thy kingdom come," we are not praying that God's kingdom of power would come because God already reigns. We are praying that His kingdom of grace would continue to come because there are people yet to be brought into it by salvation. We are also praying that His kingdom of glory would come, which has not yet come in a literal sense.

What is the kingdom of glory? In Matthew 8:11 Jesus referred to this kingdom: "And I say to you, that many shall come from east and west, and recline at the table with Abraham, and Isaac, and Jacob, in the *kingdom of heaven.*" One day, after our Lord Jesus returns, we are all going to sit together in fellowship with all the saints; that is the kingdom of glory. In Matthew 25:31–34 Jesus described His second coming: "But when the Son of Man comes in *His glory,* and all the angels with Him, then He will sit on His *glorious throne.* And all the nations will be gathered before Him; and He will separate them from one another . . . and He will put the sheep on His right, and the goats on the left. Then the King will say to those on His right, 'Come, you who are blessed of My Father, *inherit the kingdom* prepared for you from the foundation of the world.' " Which kingdom did Jesus mean? His sheep had already inherited the kingdom of grace; now, they would inherit the kingdom of glory.

In 1 Peter 5:10–11 Peter wrote about this coming kingdom of glory: "And after you have suffered for a little while, the God of all grace, who *called you to His eternal glory* in Christ, will Himself perfect, confirm, strengthen and establish you." He referred to it again in 2 Peter 1:11, "For in this way the entrance into the *eternal kingdom* of our Lord and Savior Jesus Christ will be abundantly supplied to you." Second Timothy 4:18 says, "The Lord will deliver me from every evil deed, and *will bring me safely to His heavenly kingdom; to Him be the glory forever and ever. Amen.*" Remember the old hymn that says "Only glory by and by"? We look forward to a time when it will be only glory for our Lord Jesus Christ and for those of us who belong to Him. When we pray "Thy kingdom come," we are praying that this kingdom of glory would come.

APPLICATION

1. What are the three aspects of the kingdom of God?

2. What is the kingdom of glory?

3. Write out 1 Timothy 1:17.

Summary of the Implications of Kingdom Praying

In summary, the implications of this petition are threefold. One, it implies that God the Father and Jesus Christ are King. Two, it implies that they have a kingdom that has not yet fully come in at least two ways: the kingdom of grace is not yet complete because some of the elect have not yet come in, and the kingdom of glory is yet to come. Three, it implies that we *believe that the kingdom of God will come* in its fullest sense. Unless we believe that, there is no point in praying this prayer. We will consider the third implication in the following chapter, along with the ingredients of this petition.

There are many people in our world who enter churches and do what they call prayer. Some go to cathedrals, light candles, and cross themselves. Some kneel down on prayer mats several times a day. That is not prayer. There are people in churches all over the world repeating the Lord's Prayer who do not really want God's name to be hallowed and His kingdom to come. They repeat the words, but they do not understand their meaning. When true believers pray "Thy kingdom come," they must believe every word that they say and everything that those words imply. They must believe that the kingdom of God will come in its fullest sense.

Jesus is teaching us how to pray. If we really want to pray, we must have a relationship with God so that we can honestly call Him *"Father."* We must recognize that He is a *heavenly Father,* with all which that means, and we must desire that His name be hallowed. We must also acknowledge that He is a glorious, great, and eternal King and His kingdom is one of power. We must know personally, through faith in Jesus Christ, that His kingdom is one of grace as well. And we must long for the day when Jesus returns and takes us with Him into His kingdom of glory. According to Jesus, this is how we are to pray if we want to pray effectively. This is what it means to pray in Jesus' way.

APPLICATION

1. Summarize in your own words the most important truths presented in this chapter.

2. Write out and work on memorizing one or two verses found in this chapter.

3. In what ways were you encouraged, challenged, or convicted by the material in this chapter? In keeping with the material presented in this chapter, how should your prayer life be changed?

PRAYING FOR THE KINGDOM TO COME

*D*uring the latter part of the nineteenth century, the most influential church for the work of God may well have been the Metropolitan Tabernacle in London, England, where Charles Spurgeon was pastor. I recently finished reading a biography of this great preacher, and it was a reminder to me of the incredible impact that this one church had on much of the English-speaking world of that time. Sixty-six different ministries were spawned from the church including an orphanage, an elder-care home, a pastor's college, and a book-selling society. Thousands of people were brought to Christ. Services were so packed with people who wanted to hear the Word of God that many were turned away for lack of room. On occasion, Spurgeon would ask the members of the church not to come to the evening service in order to make room for newcomers to hear the Word of God. This church had a fantastic ministry.

Spurgeon on the Importance of Prayer

Why was the ministry of the Metropolitan Tabernacle so powerful? If we were to ask Spurgeon, his answer would be, "My people pray." When Spurgeon was called at age nineteen to pastor New Park Street Chapel, he told the people that he would come on one condition; they must pray for him. He said, "One thing is due; namely, that in private and as well as public, you must all wrestle in prayer that I may be sustained in this great work."

Spurgeon did not make the gathering of a crowd his first interest. In view of the spiritual warfare in which the Christian is placed, he was concerned first of all that his people learn truly to pray. To Spurgeon, prayer was something far superior to mere surface activity. He talked with God in reverence, but with freedom and familiarity. In his prayers, there were none of the tired expressions many ministers used. He spoke as a child coming to a loving parent. A fellow minister declared, "Prayer was the instinct of his soul and the atmosphere of his life." It was his vital breath and native air. He sped on eagle wings into the heaven of God as he prayed.

So real was Spurgeon's praying that the formal effort showed in glaring contrast beside it. "I can readily tell," Spurgeon said, "when a brother is praying, or when he is only performing or playing at prayer. Oh, for a living groan! One sigh of the soul has more power in it than half an hour's recitation of pretty pious words. Oh, for a sob from the soul or a tear from the heart." Spurgeon truly expected to see God answer prayer both in the individual life and in the life of the church. He recognized unanswered prayer beyond human understanding, but he also experienced numerous instances in which God moved in response to his cry. He knew that God's power was manifested in the services in proportion as God's people truly prayed, and that, in such proportion also, souls were brought under conviction and drawn to Christ.

Spurgeon's own praying proved a great influence on his people. Deeply moved by the reality of his intercession, many of them became ashamed of their own pretty pious words. Some of them, undoubtedly, had a difficult struggle to overcome the formal practice of previous years, but they persisted and, little by little, they began to wrestle with God in prayer. Spurgeon said, "I can never forget how earnestly my people prayed. Sometimes they seem to plead as though they could really see the angel of the covenant present with them. More than once we were all so awestruck with the solemnity of the meeting that we sat silent for some moments while the Lord's power appeared to overshadow us. We had prayer meetings in New Park Street that moved our very souls. Each man seemed like a crusader besieging the new Jerusalem. Each one appeared determined to storm the celestial city by the might of intercession and soon the blessing came down upon us in such abundance that we had not room to receive it."

To consider the rest of Spurgeon's life, we must bear in mind the manner in which his people prayed. Numerous men and women were converted, several institutions developed, various buildings were erected, and their work had its effect to the ends of the earth. All the time, true prayer rose to God. When someone once asked Spurgeon the secret of his success, he replied, "My people pray for me." He meant not prayer in the usual formal and unexpectant manner, but wrestling with God in living faith that He would answer.[1]

Charles Spurgeon truly believed that "the effective prayer of a righteous man can accomplish much" (James 5:16), and so do I. If we are going to impact our community and our world, it will only be as we learn to pray. It is not enough for a church to have many meetings or pastors who prepare well. All that is important; but without prayer, it will all be ineffective. That is why we must study to learn how to pray. In the last chapter, we began to study what it means to pray "Thy kingdom come." We considered first the importance of this petition and then we looked at two implications. In this chapter we will study the third implication and the ingredients of this petition.

APPLICATION

1. What was the one condition that Charles Spurgeon required before he accepted the pastorate of New Park Street Chapel in London, England?

2. What does this indicate about Charles Spurgeon?

3. How would you answer the question, what is the most important aspect of an effective and fruitful church ministry?

4. In the last week, does the way you prayed for your pastors/elders and church leaders demonstrate that you believe that prayer is the most important part of an effective ministry?

Implications of Praying "Thy Kingdom Come"

One of the implications we considered already was that God is King. We noted in Scripture that He is a glorious, great, and eternal King. Second, we considered that this petition implies that there is a sense in which the kingdom of God has not yet fully come. We learned that there are three aspects to the kingdom of God. He has a kingdom of power that has already come because God has always reigned, and will always reign. He has a kingdom of grace, which we enter when we come to salvation in Jesus Christ. And He has a kingdom of glory, which will come when Christ returns to receive all the glory that is due His name. Thomas Watson has described the nature of the kingdoms of grace and glory and their relation to each other:

> When Christ teaches us to pray, "Thy kingdom come," He does not mean a political or earthly kingdom. The apostles did indeed desire Christ's temporal reign. "Wilt Thou at this time restore the kingdom again to Israel?" they asked Jesus in Acts 1:6. But Christ said His kingdom was not of this world. So that when Christ taught His disciples to pray, "Thy kingdom come," He did not mean it of an earthly kingdom, that He should reign here in outward pomp and splendor. Secondly, it is not meant of God's providential kingdom. His kingdom rules over all, that is, the kingdom of His providence. This kingdom we do not pray for when we say, "Thy kingdom come," for this kingdom is already come. God exercises the kingdom of His providence in the world. He puts down one and sets up another. Nothing stirs in the world but God has a hand in it. He sets every wheel at work. He humbles the proud and raises the poor out of the darkness to set them among princes. The kingdom of God's providence rules over all. Kings do nothing, but what His providence permits and orders. The kingdom of God's providence we do not pray should come for it is already come.

What kingdom then is meant when we say, "Thy kingdom come"? Positively, a two-fold kingdom is meant. One, the kingdom of grace, which God exercises in the conscience of His people. This is God's lesser kingdom. When we pray, "Thy kingdom come," we pray that the kingdom of grace may be set up in our hearts and increase. We pray also that the kingdom of glory may hasten and that we may, in God's good time, be translated into it. These two kingdoms—grace and glory—differ not specifically but gradually. They differ not in nature, but in degree only. The kingdom of grace is nothing but the beginning of the kingdom of glory. The kingdom of grace is glory in the seed, and the kingdom of glory is grace in the flower. The kingdom of grace is glory in the daybreak, and the kingdom of glory is grace in the full sunshine. The kingdom of grace is glory militant, and the kingdom of glory is grace triumphant.

There is such an inseparable connection between these two kingdoms, grace and glory, that there is no passing into the one but by the other. If you are going to get into the kingdom of glory, you are going to have to get into it by means of the kingdom of grace. At Athens, there were two temples, a temple of virtue and a temple of honor, and there was no going into the temple of honor but through the temple of virtue. So the kingdoms of grace and glory are so closely joined together that we cannot go into the kingdom of glory but through the kingdom of grace. Many people aspire after the kingdom of glory but never look after grace. But these two, which God has joined together, may not be put asunder. The kingdom of grace leads to the kingdom of glory. And so, when we pray, "Thy kingdom come," we are praying God's kingdom of grace and God's kingdom of glory would come more fully.[2]

APPLICATION

1. What does Thomas Watson state that Christ did not mean when He referred to the kingdom in Matthew 6:10? What is the kingdom that Watson says has already come?

2. When Watson refers to the kingdom of grace, what is he referring to?

3. When Watson writes of the kingdom of glory, what is he referring to?

4. What does Watson say is the connection between the kingdom of grace and the kingdom of glory?

5. What does Watson say Jesus is teaching us to pray for in this petition?

The Confessional Nature of "Thy Kingdom Come"

Once we know what these two kingdoms are, what then are the implications of praying for God's kingdom of grace and glory to come? When we pray "Thy kingdom come," we are confessing our belief that all these things will indeed take place: all that the Father has given to our Lord Jesus Christ will come to Him and be translated into His glorious kingdom. In other words, every person for whom Jesus Christ died will be brought to repentance and faith and will someday enjoy eternity with Him. According to Isaiah 53:11, our Lord Jesus "as a result of the anguish of His soul . . . *he will see it and be satisfied. By His knowledge the Righteous One, My Servant, will justify the many.*" In John 6:39 Jesus said, "And this is the will of Him who sent Me, *that of all that He has given Me I lose nothing, but raise it up on the last day.*" Our prayer implies that we believe these things will come to pass.

We are confessing also that we believe that Jesus is going to come again as the angels said in Acts 1:11: "This Jesus, who has been taken up from you into heaven, *will come in just the same way as you have watched Him go into heaven.*" We believe in Christ's bodily return though others may doubt and even scoff. Second Peter 3:3–4 warns, "Know this first of all, that in the last days mockers will come . . . saying, 'Where is the promise of His coming?' " One day, however, every person who ever lived is going to acknowledge that Jesus reigns because the Bible says "that *at the name of Jesus every knee should bow . . . and that every tongue should confess that Jesus Christ is Lord,* to the glory of God the Father" (Phil. 2:10–11). As Christians, we believe with all our hearts that He really will return.

When we pray "Thy kingdom come," we are confessing that we believe that only God is able to bring in His kingdom of grace and of glory. Zechariah 4:6 says, " 'Not by might nor by power, *but by My Spirit,'* says the LORD of hosts." We are confessing what Jonah said in Jonah 2:9, *"Salvation is from the LORD,"* and what Paul said in 1 Corinthians 3:7, "So then neither the one who plants nor the one who waters is anything, *but God who causes the growth."* We profess Romans 9:16, "So then it does not depend on the man who wills or the man who runs, *but on God who has mercy."* And we believe John 1:13, which says that we "were born not of blood, nor of the will of the flesh, nor of the will of man, *but of God."* We are confessing that we believe that God is the One who must bring in His kingdom.

Al Mohler, president of Southern Seminary, points to Martin Luther's belief that the kingdom of grace and the kingdom of glory have to be brought in by God:

> I want to point back in history almost five hundred years ago to March 10, 1522. It was a Monday, and Martin Luther was the preacher of the hour. On this particular Monday, Luther had a problem on his hands. The problem was his seminary students. As the Reformation had made its course, starting in Wittenberg and spreading throughout Germany, he had attracted to the university an innumerous group of men who were training for the ministry. They were fervently committed to the ideals of the Reformation and to the doctrines of the Reformation. They had zeal, but they had zeal without knowledge, and Luther had a problem with them. On the previous weekend, they had gone into the houses of German nobility who were still practicing the Catholic private mass. These students had forced their way into the homes and destroyed the altars. They were right in terms of theological judgment on the abhorrence of the bloody mass. They knew it was a travesty and a horrible thing, and yet Luther had a problem because the Reformation was going to hit some pretty rough reefs if the students went into the houses of the nobility and tore up the altars.
>
> But he knew that his pragmatic problem was of less significance than the theological problem it betrayed. He gathered his

students together and he said, "Students, you are right to see the abhorrence of the mass, but you are wrong to go into private homes and tear out the altars because the Reformation cannot come by force. It can only come by the Word of God. You can tear up the altars and even pull people away from the altars by their hair, but as soon as you leave them, put back the altar and to the altar again they will go. We should preach the Word, but the results must be left solely to God's good pleasure. Certainly, to hold the mass in such a manner is sinful, and yet no one should be dragged away from it by the hair. For it should be left to God; His Word should be allowed to work alone without interference.

"Why? Because it is not in my power to handle or fashion the hearts of men as the potter molds the clay and fashions them at his pleasure. Their hearts I cannot reach. I can get no further than their ears. And since I cannot pour faith into their hearts, I cannot, nor should I, force anyone to have faith. That is God's work alone who causes faith to live in the heart. Therefore, we should give free course to the Word of God and not add our works to it. If you preach the Word and trust the Word, the Word will sink into the heart and do its work. God would accomplish more with His Word than if you and I were to merge all our power into one heap."[3]

God is the only One who can bring in the kingdom; however, as God often brings in the kingdom of grace through our prayers, there is a sense in which He will bring in the kingdom of glory through our prayers as well. This, of course, was what Jesus intended when He taught us to pray "Thy kingdom come."

Still further, when we pray this petition, we are confessing that we are longing to see these two aspects of His kingdom more fully realized. We are praying, "Lord, I long for more people to be saved." Paul earnestly prayed this in Romans 9:1–3: "I am telling the truth in Christ, I am not lying, my conscience bearing me witness in the Holy Spirit, that I have great sorrow and unceasing grief in my heart. *For I could wish that I myself were accursed, separated from Christ for the sake of my brethren, my kinsmen according to the flesh.*" If we are rightly praying "Thy kingdom come," we, like Paul, have a yearning in our hearts to see people saved for God's glory and their good.

In Romans 10:1 Paul said, "Brethren, *my heart's desire and my prayer to God for them is for their salvation.*"

As we long for more people to know Christ, we also long to be taken into glory. Romans 8:23 says, "Having the first fruits of the Spirit, even we ourselves groan within ourselves, *waiting eagerly for our adoption as sons, the redemption of our body.*" As believers, we look forward to the kingdom of glory. In 1 Thessalonians 1:9–10 Paul says, "You turned to God from idols to serve a living and true God, and *to wait for His Son from heaven.*" In Titus 2:13 the apostle Paul tells us about *"the blessed hope and the appearing* of the glory of our great God and Savior, Christ Jesus." Hebrews 9:28 says, "So Christ also, having been offered once to bear the sins of many, *shall appear a second time for salvation without reference to sin, to those who eagerly await Him.*" When we pray "Thy kingdom come," we say to God, "Lord, I long for more people to know You, and I long for Your return from heaven."

APPLICATION

1. What confessions are we making when we pray this petition aright?

2. Do the contents of your prayers reflect the fact that you are longing to see God's kingdom of grace move forward in an abundant way?

3. Do the contents of your prayers reflect the fact that you are longing to see God's kingdom of glory ushered in?

4. Reflect on Paul's intense concern that the kingdom of grace be extended (Rom. 9:1–3 and 10:1). Ask yourself, do I have that same kind of longing? Is a longing for the kingdom of grace to expand reflected in my prayer life?

5. Reflect on Paul's words about what our attitude should be regarding the kingdom of glory coming. Ask yourself, do I have that same kind of longing and attitude that is described in these verses? Is that longing for the kingdom of glory reflected in my prayer life?

The Ingredients of This Petition

Now that we have studied the implications of this petition, let's turn to the *ingredients*. What is it that we are praying for? First, when we pray "Thy kingdom come," we pray for the increase of the kingdom of God in our lives. In other words, we want to "seek first His kingdom and His righteousness" as Jesus taught in Matthew 6:33. We want to be like the people Jesus described in Matthew 5:3, "Blessed are the poor in spirit, for theirs is the kingdom of heaven," and verse 10, "Blessed are those who have been persecuted for the sake of righteousness, for theirs is the kingdom of heaven." We are praying that God would make us so committed to the truth that we would never compromise, even if that means persecution, because we know that God has called us to persevere. "Through many tribulations we must enter the kingdom of God" (Acts 14:22).

When we pray "Thy kingdom come," we are praying for the grace to live the godly life that we have been called to in Christ Jesus. In Ephesians 4:1–2 Paul said, "I, therefore, the prisoner of the Lord, entreat you to *walk in a manner worthy of the calling with which you have been called*, with all humility and gentleness, with patience, showing forbearance to one another in love." He said also in Romans 14:17, "For the kingdom of God is not eating and drinking, *but righteousness and peace and joy in the Holy Spirit.*" We are praying for Christ to reign in our hearts more and more.

At the same time, we are praying that God would deliver us from the "deeds of the flesh" listed in Galatians 5:19–21 because "those who practice such things shall not inherit the kingdom of God." When we pray "Thy kingdom come," we are praying that God would keep us from all immorality and impurity—things that are not of His kingdom. We are praying also that God would open our hearts to receive His word of truth, as Paul said in 1 Thessalonians 2:13: "And for this reason we also constantly thank God that *when you received from us the word of God's message, you accepted it* not as the word of men, but *for what it really is, the word of God, which also performs its work in you who believe.*" As we come to God in prayer and worship, we should be praying for God to reign in our lives in power, not just in words that we say without thought or intention. "For the *kingdom of God does not consist in words, but in power"* (1 Cor. 4:20). We must not simply talk about Christ as King; He must truly reign in our hearts.

Thomas Watson comments on this petition:

When we pray, "Thy kingdom come," we are praying that God would help us to know Him better and to love Him more. We are praying that God would give us more strength to resist temptation, to forgive our enemies, and to suffer affliction. We are praying that God would help us to grieve for and fight against sin. We are praying that God would help us to learn to live by faith and that God would make us full of holy zeal. We are praying that God would make us diligent in our callings, that He would establish us in the belief of His truth and in the love of His truth, and that God would grant that our labors would be instrumental in setting up the kingdom in others.

When a Christian has further degrees in grace, there is more oil in his lamp, his knowledge is clear, and his love is more inflamed. Grace is capable of degrees, and may rise higher as the sun in the horizon. It is not with us as it was with Christ, who received the Spirit without measure. He could not be more holy than He was, but our grace is receptive of further degrees. We may have more holiness; we may add more cubits to our spiritual stature. The kingdom of grace increases when a Christian has got more strength than he had. "He that hath clean hands shall be stronger and stronger" (Job 17:9). He shall add to his strength. A Christian has strength to resist temptation, to forgive his enemies, and to suffer affliction. It is not easy to suffer; a man must deny himself before he can take up the cross. The way to heaven is like the way which Jonathan and his armor-bearer had in climbing up a steep place. There was a sharp rock, the Bible says, on the one side and a sharp rock on the other. It requires much strength to climb up this rocky way, that grace would carry us through. Prosperity will not carry us through sufferings. The ship needs stronger tackling to carry it through a storm than a calm. Now when we are so strong in grace that we can bear up under affliction without murmuring or fainting, the kingdom of grace is increased. What mighty strength of grace had he who told the emperor Valentinian, "You may take away my life, but you cannot take away my love for the truth." The kingdom of grace increases when a Christian has most conflict with spiritual corruptions, when he not only abstains from gross evils, but has a combat with inward, hidden, close corruptions—pride, envy, hypocrisy, vain thoughts, carnal confidence—and they defile and disturb. Let us cleanse ourselves from all filthiness of the flesh and of the spirit.

There are two sorts of corruptions, one of the flesh and the other of the spirit. When we grieve for and combat with spiritual sin, which is the root of all gross sins, then the kingdom of grace increases and spreads in the territories in the soul. The kingdom of grace flourishes when a Christian has learned to live by faith. "I live by the faith of the Son of God" (Gal. 2:20). There is the habit of faith and the drawing of this habit into exercise. For a Christian, to graft his hope of salvation only upon the stock of Christ's righteousness and make Christ all in justification; to live on the promises as a bee on the flower and suck out the sweetness of them; to trust God where we cannot trace Him; to believe His love through a frown; to persuade ourselves when He has the face of the enemy that He has the heart of a Father; when we have arrived at this, the kingdom of grace is flourishing in our souls.

It flourishes when a Christian is full of holy zeal. In Numbers 25:13 we are told that Phinehas was zealous for his God. Zeal is the flame of the affections; it turns the saint into a seraphim. A zealous Christian is impatient when God is dishonored. He will wrestle with difficulties; he will swim to Christ through a sea of blood. Zeal loves truth when it is despised and opposed. "They have made void Thy law, therefore I love Thy commandments," said the psalmist. Zeal resembles the Holy Ghost. "There appeared cloven tongues like as a fire and sat upon each of them" (Acts 2:3). Tongues of fire were an emblem of that fire of zeal which the Spirit poured on them. The kingdom of grace increases when a Christian is as diligent in his particular calling as he is devout in his general calling. He is the wise Christian that carries things equally; that so lives by faith that he lives in a calling. Therefore, it is worthy of notice that when the apostle had exhorted the Thessalonians to increase in grace, he presently adds, "And that you do your own business and work with your own hands."

It's a sign grace is increasing when Christians go cheerfully about their calling. Indeed, to be all the day in the mount with God and to have the mind fixed on glory is more sweet to a man's self and is heaven upon earth, but to be conversant in our calling is more profitable to others. Paul says, "To be with Christ is far better; nevertheless, to abide in the flesh is more needful for you." So to converse with God in prayer and sweet meditation all the week long is more for the comfort of a man's own person, but to be sometimes employed in the business of a calling is more profitable for the family to which he belongs. It is not good to be as the lilies, "which toil not, neither do they spin." It shows the increase of grace when a Christian keeps a due decorum. He joins piety and industry when zeal runs forth in religion and diligence is put forth in a calling.

The kingdom of grace increases when a Christian is established in the belief and the love of the truth. The heart, by nature, is a ship without a ballast, that wavers and fluctuates. Such as are wandering stars will be falling stars. But when a soul is built on the rock Christ, and no winds of temptation can blow it away, a kingdom of glory flourishes.

The kingdom of grace increases in a man's own heart when he labors to be instrumental to set up this kingdom in others. Though it is the greatest benefit to have grace wrought in ourselves, it is the greatest honor to be instrumental to work it in others. "My little children, of whom I travail in birth again until Christ be formed in you," is what Paul said in Galatians 4:19. Such as our masters of a family should endeavor to see the kingdom of grace set up in their service. Such as are godly parents should not let God alone by prayer till they see grace in their children. What a comfort to be both a natural and spiritual father of your children. Augustine says that his mother Monica traveled and travailed with greater care and pain for his new birth than for his natural birth. As water abounds in the river when it overflows and runs into the meadows, so grace increases in the soul when it has influence upon others and we seek their salvation.[4]

For all of these things we ask when praying "Thy kingdom come" in a proper way.

APPLICATION

1. What does this section indicate about the implications of praying this petition?

2. What does Watson indicate are the evidences that the kingdom of grace is increasing in our lives? How can we know that the kingdom of grace is increasing in our lives?

3. Compare your life with these evidences and evaluate how much the kingdom of grace is really growing in your life.

Further Ingredients of This Petition

There are various reasons to pray for the increase of the kingdom of God in our lives. For example, we have much work to do, and a little grace will not carry us through. In 2 Corinthians 9:8 the apostle Paul said, "And *God is able to make all grace abound to you,* that always having all sufficiency in everything, *you may have an abundance for every good deed."* A little grace is not enough; we need to grow in grace. If the kingdom of God does not increase, it will decay. As believers, we must either grow stronger or become weaker in our faith and knowledge of God. The Lord Jesus said to the church at Ephesus, "You have left your first love" (Rev. 2:4).

We also pray for the increase of the kingdom of God in our lives because a lack of growth may indicate a lack of life. A baby that does not grow is not likely to live, and as it is in the physical realm, so also in the spiritual. If we are not growing spiritually, then there is reason to believe that we have never been born again.

In addition, we pray for the increase of the kingdom of God in our lives so that our comforts would increase. The more grace that we have, the more we grow in the peace and power and joy of Romans 14:17. "Grace turns to joy as churned cream turns to butter." If we lack joy, the kingdom of God is in a deficient state in our lives. When we pray "Thy kingdom come," we are praying for the kingdom of God to increase in our lives in these many ways.

As we pray for God's kingdom to increase in our own lives, we are also asking that God would send forth laborers into His harvest field. Jesus said, "Therefore beseech the Lord of the harvest to send out workers into His harvest" (Matt. 9:38). God has determined to bring people into the kingdom of grace through the preaching of the Word. Paul asked, "And how shall they believe in Him whom they have not heard? And *how shall they hear without a preacher?*" (Rom. 10:14).

I received an e-mail in which a friend related to me the interesting way in which politicians campaigned in recent elections in England. The politicians got their message out primarily by preaching. These politicians believed in the power and effectiveness of preaching their political views. My friend compared this to the church today, noting that we have often turned aside from seeking to reach people by preaching the Word of God. We have drama and dancing and all sorts of other things that are supposed to draw people to Christ. My friend's point was that we need to remember that it is through the preaching of the Word that God saves. This was always the practice of Jesus and the apostles. "Thy kingdom come" is a prayer for God to send forth workers into His harvest field to preach the gospel.

We are also praying that God would give us opportunities for preaching. Paul asked the Colossians to pray for him "so that we may speak forth the mystery of Christ" (Col. 4:3). In Ephesians 6:19 he said, "And pray on my behalf, *that utterance may be given to me in the opening of my mouth,* to make known with boldness the mystery of the gospel." When we pray "Thy kingdom come," we are praying for God to help us see people around us who need to hear the gospel.

Along with opportunity, we are praying that God would give us unction and authority as we preach the Word. As Paul said, we can plant the seed and water it, but only God can make it grow. When Peter preached on the day of Pentecost, "they were *pierced to the heart*" (Acts 2:37). When we pray "Thy kingdom come," we should be praying for what happened in Acts 14:1 to the apostle Paul: "And it came about that in Iconium they entered the synagogue of the Jews together, and *spoke in such a manner that a great multitude believed,* both of Jews and of Greeks." We ought to pray that God would give such authority to our preaching of His Word that unbelievers would hear and be saved.

When we pray "Thy kingdom come," we are also praying that God would remove all obstacles to the advance of the gospel and the coming of His kingdom. In 1 Corinthians 16:9 Paul noted, "A wide door for effective service has opened to me, and *there are many adversaries.* "What are these obstacles and adversaries? One of them is the devil himself. In Mark 4 Jesus told a parable about a sower spreading seed on different soils. He explained regarding one type of soil, "And these are the ones who are beside the road where the word is sown; *and when they hear, immediately Satan comes and takes away the word which has been sown in them*" (Mark 4:15). When we pray this petition, we are praying that God would not allow the devil to take His Word from the hearts of people who have heard it.

In 2 Thessalonians 3:1–2 Paul asked, "Pray for us . . . that we may be *delivered from perverse and evil men.* "As we pray "Thy kingdom come," we are praying for God to remove the obstacle of people who try to undermine the preaching of the gospel. There are many accounts in the New Testament of perverse and evil men who tried to hinder the apostle Paul.

Another obstacle is the inconsistencies of Christians. Paul warned about this in Titus 2. He urged believers to live in such a way "that they may adorn the doctrine of God our Savior in every respect" (Titus 2:10) so as not to hinder the gospel. The prophet Nathan told David that because of his sin of adultery, "You have given occasion to the enemies of the LORD to blaspheme" (2 Sam. 12:14). From a human point of view, the sin and inconsistencies of Christians hinder God's kingdom of grace. In this petition, we are praying that God would make us more consistent in godliness.

When we pray "Thy kingdom come," we are also praying that God would remove the obstacle of false prophets and teachers. In 2 Peter 2:1 Peter warned, "But false prophets also arose among the people, *just as there will also be false teachers among you.* "Today there are false prophets everywhere: on our television sets, in our bookstores, in our schools, and in many churches as well. All of these are an obstacle to the coming of the kingdoms of grace and glory.

Finally, we are praying that God would remove the obstacle of our own fears and cowardice. Paul said in Romans 1:16, "For *I am not ashamed of the gospel,* for it is the power of God for salvation to everyone who believes, to the Jew first and also to the Greek." Unfortunately, many of us are afraid to speak up for Christ when we should be proclaiming Him boldly. Second Timothy 1:7 says, *"For God has not given us a spirit of timidity,* but of power and love and discipline." Paul was encouraging Timothy because Paul knew that Timothy was faced with struggles that might have caused him to become fearful. When we pray "Thy kingdom come," we are praying for the Lord to deliver us from the spirit of fear and to give us the spirit of power, love, and a sound mind.

APPLICATION

1. Reflect on what this section teaches about the meaning of praying "Thy Kingdom come," and list the various things that are included in praying this petition.

2. Compare your prayer life to the items mentioned in this section and evaluate how your prayer life measures up to this teaching. Do you pray for these things daily, sometimes (every now and then), seldom (not very often), or never?

3. Can you really say you are praying for the things and in the way that Jesus wants you to pray?

4. In terms of our Lord's teaching in this petition, how should your prayer life improve? What changes should you make?

Jesus was including all these things when He taught us to pray "Thy kingdom come." This petition is important because it is God's will for us to pray for all these things and all their implications. We need to remember what the ingredients of this petition are so that we can pray according to God's will. The Bible says that if we pray according to His will, we can know that we have what we have asked of Him.

His words were few, but His teaching was great. When these three words, "Thy kingdom come," are properly understood in the full light of Scripture, our hearts are opened to tremendous truths. Ultimately, of course, we are praying that Jesus Christ would return. As believers, we long to see Him face to face. Our heart's desire is the same as the apostle John's in Revelation 22:20: "He who testifies to these things says, 'Yes, I am coming quickly.' Amen. *Come, Lord Jesus.*" To pray effectively means that we will pray as Jesus taught us. This is the kind of prayer that pleases God, and this is the kind of prayer that God loves to answer. How could it be otherwise when it was Jesus Christ, the Son of God, who taught us to pray in this way?

 **APPLICATION**

1. Reflect back over this whole chapter and summarize in your own words the most important truths presented.

2. Write out and work on memorizing one or two verses found in this chapter.

3. In what ways were you challenged or convicted by the material in this chapter? In keeping with the material presented in this chapter, how should your prayer life be changed?

ASPECTS OF GOD'S WILL

As we learn how to pray as Jesus taught us, we should remember that our Lord has given us a pattern, or outline, for prayer in the passage that we are studying in Matthew 6. In other words, this prayer was not given for the purpose of being recited word for word. Though there is nothing wrong with that, all too often this prayer is used only in that way. Jesus' primary purpose for this teaching is indicated in Matthew 6:9, "Pray, then, *in this way:* 'Our Father who art in heaven, hallowed be Thy name . . .'" When we pray for the things that Jesus taught in this prayer, we can be assured that we are praying according to the will of God and that He will hear us and give us what we ask of Him.

With that in mind, we come to the third petition of this prayer, "Thy will be done, on earth as it is in heaven" (Matt. 6:10b). In this chapter we're going to study just one word in this petition, the word "will." In later chapters we will consider the words "be done," "Thy," "on earth," and "as it is in heaven."

Three Aspects of God's Will

What did Jesus mean when He taught us to pray that God's *will* be done? A careful study of God's Word reveals that there are three aspects of the will of God. Unless we understand this, we may be confused when reading the word "will" in Scripture. In some contexts, God's "will" refers to His sovereign, or "decretive," will. In other places, "will" refers to God's moral, or preceptive, will. A third meaning of "will" in the Scripture is the individual, or personal, will of God for each person. Jesus was teaching us to pray for all three of these aspects of the will of God when He taught us to pray "Thy *will* be done."

APPLICATION

1. What was the primary purpose of Jesus in giving this teaching on prayer?
2. What are the three aspects of the will of God?
3. Write out Matthew 6:9–10.

God's Sovereign Will

First, let's consider what Jesus meant in reference to praying for God's *sovereign* will. The sovereign will of God is that which always comes to pass. We know the sovereign will of God in two ways. One, we know it by what He has said that He is going to do in His Word. When God says He will do something, it is always done. Two, we know the sovereign will of God by providence and by history. In other words, we understand that something was the will of God because it came to pass, since nothing can happen aside from the will of God. In fact, there are many elements of the sovereign will of God that we cannot know in detail until they actually come to pass.

This is what Paul was referring to in Ephesians 1:11 when he said that God *"works all things after the counsel of His will."* Everything that happens is according to God's sovereign will, or it would not take place. This is also the aspect of God's will that is referred to in Proverbs 19:21, "Many are the plans in a man's heart, but *the counsel of the Lord, it will stand."* We can make all kinds of plans, but the only things that will come to pass are the things that correspond to God's sovereign will. Proverbs 16:9 says the same, "The mind of man plans his way, but *the Lord directs his steps."*

In Ephesians 3:11 the apostle Paul said, "This was in accordance with *the eternal purpose which He carried out in Christ Jesus our Lord.*" Paul was talking about the coming of Christ. It was part of God's sovereign will that Christ would come to the earth at a particular time, be born the way that He was born, die the way that He died, and be raised the way that He was raised. Nothing could have prevented Jesus from coming and living and dying as God intended because it was part of God's sovereign will that those things would come to pass.

Nebuchadnezzar referred to the sovereign will of God when he said in Daniel 4:35, "But He does according to His will in the host of heaven and among the inhabitants of earth; and no one can ward off His hand." What God has purposed to do, no one can stop Him from accomplishing. Psalm 115:3 sums it up this way, "But our God is in the heavens; He does whatever He pleases." If it doesn't please God, it doesn't happen.

Deuteronomy 29:29 is one of the most important statements in the Bible concerning the will of God: *"The secret things belong to the LORD our God,* but the things revealed belong to us and to our sons forever, that we may observe all the words of this law." The first part of this verse is referring specifically to the sovereign will of God. The "secret things" are the things that only God knows about—what He wants to do and what He's going to accomplish—and that He has not been pleased to reveal to us. We learn, primarily, what His sovereign will is through providence, or what actually takes place in history.

When Jesus taught us to pray, "Thy *will* be done, on earth as it is in heaven," He was teaching us, at least in part, to pray that God's sovereign will would be done.

APPLICATION

1. Define what is meant by God's sovereign will.

2. In what two ways do we come to know His sovereign will?

3. What is the teaching of Deuteronomy 29:29 about God's sovereign will?

His Moral Will

A second aspect of the will of God is what we could call the preceptive, or *moral,* will of God. A precept is a command, and the moral will of God is revealed in His commands. While God's sovereign will is revealed broadly in the Word and specifically in history, His moral will is what He directly commands in the Scripture that we are to do and believe. When we pray "Thy *will* be done," we are also praying that God's moral will would be done in our lives and in our world.

Matthew 7:21 refers to this aspect of the will of God when it says, "Not everyone who says to Me, 'Lord, Lord,' will enter the kingdom of heaven; but he who *does the will of My Father* who is in heaven." Jesus was talking here about the moral will of God. If we do what God commands, then we have reason to believe that we really are children of God. Jesus referred to God's moral will again in Matthew 12:50. "For whoever *does the will of My Father* who is in heaven, he is My brother and sister and mother." In John 7:17 Jesus said, "If any man is *willing to do His will,* he shall know of the teaching, whether it is of God, or whether I speak from Myself." The "will" in these verses refers to the moral will of God. If we are willing to obey God's commands and live under the lordship of Christ—God's moral will for us—we will recognize and understand His teachings.

Likewise, Ephesians 6:6 refers to the moral will of God when it says, "not by way of eyeservice, as men-pleasers, but as slaves of Christ, *doing the will of God from the heart.* " Paul was teaching us how to work in that verse. God's will for us is to do our work faithfully because it pleases Him when we live under His lordship. When we work this way, we are acknowledging that God is our Master. First Thessalonians 4:3 says, "For *this is the will of God,* your sanctification; that is, that you abstain from sexual immorality." Part of God's moral will for us is that we are to be holy in all areas of our lives. First Thessalonians 5:18 teaches that the moral will of God for us includes always being thankful: "In everything give thanks; for *this is God's will* for you in Christ Jesus." When we pray "Thy *will* be done," we are praying that God would help us to please Him in our work, in our holiness, and in our thanksgiving.

Hebrews 13:21 also refers to God's moral will when the writer prays that Jesus would "equip you in every good thing *to do His will,* working in us that which is pleasing in His sight, through Jesus Christ, to whom be the glory forever and ever. Amen." It is the will of God for us to live the way He wants us to live. Psalm 40:8 says, *"I delight to do Thy will,* O my God; Thy Law is within my heart." What will is meant here? Primarily the moral will of God because David was talking about doing things according to God's Law. Though David wrote these words, we know that this is also what Jesus did and how Jesus taught us to live (Heb. 10:1–18).

Looking again at Deuteronomy 29:29, we see that the second part of this verse refers to the moral, or preceptive, will of God. "The secret things belong to the LORD our God, *but the things revealed belong to us and to our sons forever, that we may observe all the words of this law."* The "things revealed" are what we have been given in the words of the Scripture—the commands of God. These are God's moral will for us, and we are instructed to learn them and to teach them to our children. When we pray "Thy *will* be done," we are referring to the moral will of God.

APPLICATION

1. Define what is meant by God's moral or preceptive will.

2. How is God's moral will revealed?

3. What does Deuteronomy 29:29 indicate about His moral will?

4. What specific biblical examples of God's moral will were mentioned in this section?

His Will for the What, When, Where, and Who Issues of Life

There is a third aspect to the will of God that we should also pray about. This will addresses the "what," "when," "where," and "who" of our life. In other words, "Lord, *who* should I share the gospel with at work today?" or "Lord, *what* do you want me to do with my time today?" or "Lord, *when* should I confront this person?" Certainly, in His moral will, God has given us general directions regarding how we are to live our lives. It is in the specifics, however, that we wish we had more directions, in that the general principles do not speak to our individual situations. For example, we may be faced with several choices for spending our time on a particular day, all of them conforming to the moral will of God. Since we are commanded to "redeem the time" by making the most of every opportunity for His glory, how then do we decide what God's individual will for us is at any particular point in time? These things fall into the *individual,* or personal, will of God.

Jesus had to make decisions in terms of whom He was going to minister to, and when and where. We have to make these decisions as well. We know that we should help people, but we also know that we cannot minister to all of them. Further, how do we balance our ministry with other obligations—family, church, and work? How do we decide what amount of time or money or other resources to give to each? As believers, we know that we are to marry someone who loves the Lord as we do. But if there are several God-fearing people in our lives that we could marry, how do we know which one is God's will for us? In this case, just knowing that we are to marry another believer is not enough to decide our individual situation.

Sometimes the Bible reveals God's will in terms of a very specific issue. For example, in Acts 21:8–14 Paul was confronted with the will of God:

> We departed and came to Caesarea; and entering the house of Philip the evangelist, who was one of the seven, we stayed with him. Now this man had four virgin daughters who were prophetesses. And as we were staying there for some days, a certain prophet named Agabus came down from Judea. And coming to us, he took Paul's belt and bound his own feet and hands, and said, "This is what the Holy Spirit says: 'In this way the Jews at Jerusalem will bind the man who owns this belt and deliver him into the hands of the Gentiles.' " And when we had heard this, we as well as the local residents began begging him not to go up

to Jerusalem. Then Paul answered, "What are you doing, weeping and breaking my heart? For I am ready not only to be bound, but even to die at Jerusalem for the name of the Lord Jesus." And since he would not be persuaded, we fell silent, remarking, "The will of the Lord be done!"

Clearly, it was not the will of God that everyone should go to Jerusalem, but it was God's individual will for the apostle Paul to go there and for these things to happen to him.

Acts 22:1–10 gives us another example of God's individual will. Paul was on trial in Jerusalem, giving his testimony to the people. After telling them how he was saved, Paul continued, "And I said, 'What shall I do, Lord?' And the Lord said to me, 'Arise and go on into Damascus; and there you will be told of *all that has been appointed for you to do.*'" God had something special for Paul to do in Damascus and it was for Paul alone. The things that God called Paul to specifically do for Him at that time were not for any other believer. God had an individual will for Paul in terms of his ministry.

When Jesus taught us to pray "Thy *will* be done," part of what He was teaching us to pray for was God's individual will for us. We ought to look for God's specific direction in every matter of our lives. In Romans 12:1–2 Paul said, "I urge you therefore, brethren, by the mercies of God, to present your bodies a living and holy sacrifice, acceptable to God, which is your spiritual service of worship. And do not be conformed to this world, but be transformed by the renewing of your mind, that you may prove *what the will of God is,* that which is good and acceptable and perfect." This passage refers to many things that are God's moral will for all of us: to present our bodies as living sacrifices, to not be conformed to this world, and to renew our minds. But I believe that this passage also includes the individual will of God, that we might each prove in our individual lives what is "good and acceptable and perfect" for us to do. Since there are some things that God wants certain believers to do that He has not willed for other believers to do, each of us ought to desire the knowledge of what the will of God is for us in the specifics.

In 1 Corinthians 1:1 Paul says that he is an apostle by the will of God. It was God's will for Paul and a few other men at that time in history, but it is not God's will for all of us to be apostles. Paul said again in 2 Corinthians 1:1, "Paul, *an apostle of Christ Jesus by the will of God.*" Paul did not become an apostle because he volunteered for it, or because the church took a vote, but because it was God's individual will for him. In verses 9 and 10 Paul said, "Indeed, we had the sentence of death within ourselves in order that we should not trust in ourselves, but in God who raises the dead; who delivered us from so great a peril of death, and will deliver us, He on whom we have set our hope. And He will yet deliver us." It was also God's individual will for Paul that he would face death many times—by stoning, by shipwreck, by beatings—in order that he would trust in God alone. God wants us all to learn that lesson, but He accomplishes it differently in each of our lives. We were not called to the same life as the apostle Paul was.

Paul prayed about God's individual will, at least in part, in Colossians 1:9: "For this reason also, since the day we heard of it, we have not ceased to pray for you and to ask that you may be *filled with the knowledge of His will in all spiritual wisdom and understanding.*" The knowledge of God's will certainly includes the moral aspect of His will, but it also includes application to our individual situations through "spiritual wisdom and understanding." First Peter 2:13–15 addresses both the moral and individual will of God: "Submit yourselves for the Lord's sake to every human institution, whether to a king as the one in authority, or to governors as sent by him for the punishment of evildoers and the praise of those who do right. *For such is the will of God* that by doing right you may silence the ignorance of foolish men." Our submission to authority fulfills God's moral will for us, but our submission to our particular authorities—elders, teachers, bosses—is God's individual will for us.

In John 4:34–35 Jesus referred to God's moral and individual wills when He said, "My food is *to do the will of Him who sent Me,* and to accomplish His work." There is a sense in which Jesus' words apply to our lives; our food, or sustenance, should be to do what is pleasing to God. That is God's moral will. But Jesus' words also referred to God's individual will for Him, because Jesus was called by God to do things that we are not. Jesus was called to go to the cross and die for the sins of the world. God commissioned and empowered His Son to do things that were for His Son alone. His life is an example to us in terms of God's moral will, but not in terms of God's individual will.

In John 5:30 Jesus referred to God's individual will for Him when He said, "I can do nothing on My own initiative. As I hear, I judge; and My judgment is just, because I do not seek My own will, *but the will of Him who sent Me.*" Just before His trial and crucifixion, Jesus prayed in the Garden of Gethsemane, "My Father, if it is possible, let this cup pass from Me; yet not as I will, *but as Thou wilt*" (Matt. 26:39). Jesus was clearly talking about God's individual will in this prayer because it was not God's will for anyone but Him to die on the cross and bear the sins of the world. (See chapter 9 for more on how to know God's individual will.)

APPLICATION

1. What is meant by the individual will of God?

2. What are some of the specific areas in which you want to know what is the godly thing to do?

3. How do you go about making decisions on the individual issues of life?

Praying for All Three Aspects of God's Will

All three of these aspects of God's will should be in our minds as we come to God in prayer, saying, "Thy *will* be done." When Jesus gave us these words, He was teaching us that our prayers should include a petition for God's sovereign will for all creation, God's moral will for all His people, and God's individual will for each of us. In the next chapter we will consider the meaning of the words "be done" and the implications that they have for our prayer "Thy will be done, on earth as it is in heaven." To pray this way is to pray as our Lord taught us, and it is to pray effectively. How could it be otherwise? May our prayers continue to be enriched and informed by Jesus' great teaching on the subject of true and effective prayer.

APPLICATION

1. Summarize in your own words the most important truths presented in this chapter.

2. Write out and work on memorizing one or two verses found in this chapter.

3. In what ways were you challenged or convicted by the material in this chapter? In keeping with the material presented in this chapter, how should your prayer life be changed?

PRAYING FOR GOD'S
WILL TO BE DONE

*M*atthew 6:9–13, though commonly called the Lord's Prayer, is really the disciples' prayer because Jesus is teaching us, His disciples, how to pray. This is the longest passage devoted specifically to the subject of *how* to pray. To properly understand this or any other passage in Scripture, we need to carefully study each word. This is called exegesis. We have been doing this with the Lord's Prayer, and this is what we should also be doing in our own Bible study. We believe in the plenary, verbal inspiration of Scripture. "Plenary" means absolute and complete. In other words, we believe that the entirety of Scripture is inspired. "Verbal" means that we believe that God did not inspire merely the thoughts and ideas of the writers, but rather every word that they wrote down. Because of this, every word in the Scripture is important and should be examined carefully.

In the last chapter we began to study the meaning of God's "will" in connection with the third petition of the Lord's Prayer, "Thy will be done, on earth as it is in heaven." We learned that the Bible reveals that there are three aspects to God's will. First, there is the *sovereign* will of God. God's sovereign will always has and always will come to pass. We know it in detail for the past by what has already occurred, and we know it in general for the future by what God has outlined in His Word about what is to come. Second, there is the *moral,* or preceptive, will of God. God's moral will is revealed to us in the Bible and is summarized in the Ten Commandments. Jesus summarized God's will even further when He said, "You shall love the Lord your God with all your heart, and with all your soul, and with all your mind. . . . You shall love your neighbor as yourself" (Matt. 22:37–39). Third, there is the *individual* will of God. This will addresses the matter of God's desires for us personally on a daily basis—what, where, when, and how to do things. When we pray "Thy *will* be done," our prayer encompasses all three of these aspects of God's will.

The Meaning of "Be Done"

We turn now to the important words "be done." What does it mean to pray that God's will *be done?* Jesus was teaching us to acknowledge our submission to and satisfaction with the will of God. When we pray "Thy will *be done,"* we are saying, "Lord, I acknowledge your sovereignty in this world and I submit myself to it."

What does that look like in the particulars? Saying "Thy will *be done"* means that we are going to give thanks to God in everything (1 Thess. 5:18). Ephesians 5:20 says, *"Always giving thanks for all things* in the name of our Lord Jesus Christ to God." We are saying to God, "Lord, I thank you for everything you bring into my life because I know you are God and you are wise and loving in all things." Philippians 2:14 says, "Do all things without grumbling or disputing." When we pray "Thy will *be done,"* we are saying, "Lord, I'm not going to complain or argue with you about anything that happens because I am satisfied with your sovereign will."

In Psalm 37:7–8 David said, "Rest in the LORD and wait patiently for Him; *do not fret* because of him who prospers in his way, because of the man who carries out wicked schemes. *Cease from anger,* and forsake wrath; do not fret, it leads only to evildoing." When we become worried or angry about something, it is most certainly due to the fact that we are not living out "Thy will *be done."* If we are worried, it's because we are not satisfied with God's will, and if we are angry, it's because we are not submitting to God's will.

We may say that our anger is with a person, not God, but if God wanted that person to act differently, he would. Ultimately, our anger is against God. "The king's heart is like channels of water in the hand of the LORD; He turns it wherever He wishes" (Prov. 21:1). When we pray for God's sovereign will to "be done," we must repent of our anxiety and anger and pray for a heart that is satisfied in the Lord.

Philippians 4:4 says, *"Rejoice* in the Lord always; again I will say, rejoice!" Why would we not rejoice? If we are not rejoicing, it's because we are not satisfied with God's sovereign will. We need to repent, submit ourselves to God, and pray, "Thy will *be done.*" Psalm 27:14 says, *"Wait for the LORD;* be strong, and *let your heart take courage;* yes, wait for the LORD." If we want God's sovereign will to *be done,* then we must wait for His timing in all things. We cannot force things or push people around. If we lose courage, it's because we are unhappy with the challenges that we are facing. We are saying, *"My* will be done." God is teaching us through this petition that we must acknowledge His will and be satisfied with it.

APPLICATION

1. What are the practical implications of praying that God's will be done? What does praying this prayer actually mean in your prayer life?

2. In what circumstances, at what times in your past or present life have you had difficulty praying this petition with sincerity and honesty?

Examples of People Who Rejoiced in God's Sovereign Will

There are many examples in the Bible of God's people living in submission to and satisfaction with God's sovereign will. After God took all of Job's children away and allowed all his possessions to be lost, "Job arose and tore his robe and shaved his head, and he fell to the ground and *worshiped.* And he said, 'Naked I came from my mother's womb, and naked I shall return there. The Lord gave and the Lord has taken away. Blessed be the name of the Lord.'

Through all this Job did not sin nor did he blame God" (Job 1:20–22). Job's first reaction to the calamity that came upon him was "Thy will *be done.*" Though he wasn't happy, he determined his heart to be satisfied.

Another example of someone who lived out this teaching is the priest Eli. In 1 Samuel 3:10–18 the Bible records God's judgment on the house of Eli. The Lord gave His judgment on Eli to young Samuel, who was serving with Eli in the temple:

> And the Lord said to Samuel, "Behold, I am about to do a thing in Israel at which both ears of everyone who hears it will tingle. In that day I will carry out against Eli all that I have spoken concerning his house, from beginning to end. For I have told him that I am about to judge his house forever for the iniquity which he knew, because his sons brought a curse on themselves and he did not rebuke them. And therefore I have sworn to the house of Eli that the iniquity of Eli's house shall not be atoned for by sacrifice or offering forever."

Later, Eli insisted on hearing God's words. "So Samuel told him everything and hid nothing from him. And [Eli] said, *'It is the Lord; let Him do what seems good to Him.'* " Eli's response was remarkable, considering the circumstances, but it was also the right one. Eli was willing to submit to the sovereign will of God and be satisfied.

In Psalm 34:1 David affirmed, *"I will bless the Lord at all times; His praise shall continually be in my mouth."* David vowed to praise God whether his circumstances seemed good or bad to him, and he kept that vow. In 2 Samuel 12 the prophet Nathan came to David with a message from God. He told David that God would forgive his sin of adultery, but that he would not escape the consequences—his son would die. When David heard the words of the Lord, he did not protest or become angry. Instead, he accepted God's sovereign will as just and right for him. In Psalm 51, David's great prayer of confession and penitence, he said, "Against Thee, Thee only, I have sinned, and done what is evil in Thy sight, so that Thou art justified when Thou dost speak, and blameless when Thou dost judge" (v. 4).

In 2 Corinthians 11 Paul listed some of the difficulties that he had faced in his ministry: beatings, dangers from robbers and shipwrecks, lack of food and clothing, criticism and insults, and persecutions of every kind. Through it all, Paul was able to say, "I am content." He wrote, "And He has said to me, 'My grace is sufficient for you, for power is perfected in weakness.' Most gladly, therefore, *I will rather boast about my weaknesses, that the power of Christ may dwell in me*" (2 Cor. 12:9). The prayer of Paul's heart was "Thy will *be done.*"

When we pray "Thy will *be done,*" part of what we are praying for is that God would help us to be satisfied with whatever He brings into our lives because we have submitted ourselves to His sovereign will. We are content with whatever He gives us—whether physical problems or good health, financial abundance or constant need, rebellious children or a happy family—and we can say with conviction, "Thy will *be done.*"

 **APPLICATION**

1. What examples were given in this section of people who lived in subjection to God's sovereign will?

2. Describe what was going on in their lives that may have made it difficult for them to pray this prayer.

Several Cautions

At this point, there are several cautions, or qualifications, that we must be sure to understand clearly. First, praying "Thy will *be done*" does not mean that it's wrong to pray for a change in our circumstances. If we are sick, it is not wrong to ask God for healing. If we need a job, it is not wrong to ask God for an opportunity to work. The apostle Paul asked God three times to remove the thorn in his flesh (2 Cor. 12:8). It *is* wrong, however, to get upset with God if He doesn't answer our prayer as we expect or desire. When God refused to remove Paul's thorn, Paul was content and submitted to God's will. We must do the same.

Second, we need to understand that this truth does not free us from the responsibility to continue in prayer and obedience. If we are struggling with a financial or family problem, we need to pray about it and we need to do everything God has commanded us to do to remedy the problem. If our children are rebellious, then we do not simply shrug our shoulders and say, "Whatever. That's what God wants." No, saying "Thy will *be done*" means that after we have done all that we are supposed to do—living in obedience, instructing and correcting, pleading with God in prayer—we are content to rest in the Lord and wait patiently for Him. If it's God's will for us to go bankrupt, or for our children to turn their backs on God, and we have been obedient in all things, then we must be content with whatever outcome God brings about.

Third, praying "Thy will *be done*" does not mean that we accept all things without emotion. If a loved one dies, it is not wrong to sorrow over their death, but we do not grieve as those who have no hope (1 Thess. 4:13). It also does not mean that if we cannot understand why something is happening, it is necessarily wrong to ask God what His purpose is. There are many places in the Psalms where the writer asked God, "Why?" Even Jesus, while on the cross, said, "My God, My God, why hast Thou forsaken Me?" (Matt. 27:46). It is not wrong to ask "why" with an open hand, but it is wrong to ask with a clenched fist. If our heart is saying, "Not fair!" we are wrong. Praying "Thy will *be done*" does not exclude a prayer for help in understanding our circumstances. If God is pleased to tell us, then we can thank Him for it, but we must be satisfied with His sovereign will even if He does not.

APPLICATION

What are three things that praying for God's will to be done doesn't mean?

More about What It Means to Pray "Thy Will Be Done"

Having considered these important qualifications, let's continue looking at what praying "Thy will *be done*" means in a positive way. When we pray for God's will to *be done,* we are asking God to enable us to do what He says we should do. Paul prayed for this in

Colossians 1:9–10 when he wrote, "We have not ceased to pray for you and to ask that you may be filled with the knowledge of His will in all spiritual wisdom and understanding, so that you may walk in a manner worthy of the Lord, to please Him in all respects, bearing fruit in every good work and increasing in the knowledge of God." Paul wanted God's people to be filled with the knowledge of God's will so that they would *be able* to do it. He prayed this again in Philippians 1:9–10: "And this I pray, that your love may abound still more and more in real knowledge and all discernment, *so that you may approve* the things that are excellent, *in order to be* sincere and blameless until the day of Christ."

When we pray "Thy will *be done,*" we are also asking God to help us to know what His will is—His sovereign, moral, and individual will—in order that we would be able to do what is best. Paul used the word "excellent" in regard to what we are to pray about. By reading God's Word, it is not difficult to figure out the evil things we should *not* do. But if we want to do more than just what is good and not evil—to do that which is excellent—we need to pray for God to give us the necessary wisdom and understanding.

This is what the psalmist prayed for in Psalm 119:18–20 when he said, "Open my eyes, that I may behold wonderful things from Thy law. I am a stranger in the earth; do not hide Thy commandments from me. My soul is crushed with longing after Thine ordinances at all times." He asked first that God would help him to know His will. Then he continued in verses 26–27, "I have told of my ways, and Thou hast answered me; teach me Thy statutes. *Make me understand the way of Thy precepts, so I will meditate on Thy wonders.*" The psalmist was not content simply to understand God's precepts, but he also wanted to know how to act on them. He was praying that God would help him to know both His moral and individual wills.

APPLICATION

1. When we pray this prayer, what are we really asking God to do?

2. How does Psalm 119:18–27 illustrate this?

Knowing God's Will for the What's, When's, Where's, and How's

I think at this point it would be good to address the frequently asked question, "How do I know what God's individual will for me is?" Many believers seem to think that we are at a disadvantage in this regard in modern times, because God no longer speaks in direct and dramatic ways to His people—none of us have ever encountered a burning bush or an angel of the Lord. And it's true that in Bible times God sometimes spoke directly to His people. He told them the exact what, when, where, and how of His will in certain situations.

That said, He did not often reveal His will in this way, and most of the time God's people had only His moral will by which to determine their actions. As we learned in the last chapter, God's moral will is clearly taught in Scripture and is quite sufficient for us in terms of teaching us how to live godly lives. Direct, specific revelation about God's individual will is actually a rare thing in Scripture. It is the exception rather than the rule.

Good and Bad Examples

Throughout the ages, God's people have had to discern His individual will by other means than from direct revelation. This may come as a surprise to some people, but it's true. For example, God occasionally gave Paul specific directions regarding his ministry, but there were many times when He did not. In Acts 16:6–10 we read:

> And they passed through the Phrygian and Galatian region, having been forbidden by the Holy Spirit to speak the word in Asia; and when they had come to Mysia, they were trying to go into Bithynia, and the Spirit of Jesus did not permit them; and passing by Mysia, they came down to Troas. And a vision appeared to Paul in the night: a certain man of Macedonia was standing and appealing to him, and saying, "Come over to Macedonia and help us." And when he had seen the vision, immediately we sought to

go into Macedonia, concluding that God had called us to preach
the gospel to them.

In this case, Paul and his companions were forbidden by the Holy
Spirit to preach in two different places, Asia and Mysia, but the text
does not indicate that the Holy Spirit communicated this directly
to them. God says simply that His Spirit did not allow them to enter
those areas. We have no reason to assume that they received any
kind of direct revelation regarding this. R. C. Sproul wisely said,
"Don't shout where God only whispers."

Since Paul had not received any direct revelation in terms of
what the vision meant, he had to interpret the meaning of his vision.
After all, for all he knew, Satan could have been behind his vision.
In the Old Testament, the witch of Endor conjured up a vision of
the prophet Samuel for King Saul to consult with. The counsel that
King Saul received was from Satan, not from the Lord. In this case,
Paul and his companions had to decide where to go next, and they
were aided, in part, by a vision.

I have often heard people say, when determining God's will
for some matter, "I got a holy nudge." Frankly, I wouldn't know
how to tell a holy nudge from an unholy nudge. Others say, "I just
had an impression." I wouldn't know whether my impression was
from God or from a bad night's sleep. Whatever we think that we
have heard or seen or felt, we still have to make a decision about
what it meant and from whom it came. Paul had a vision of a man,
and verse 10 says that they *concluded* that God had called them to
preach in Macedonia. The Greek word that is translated "conclude"
means to carefully assess and evaluate, that is, these men considered carefully this vision, measuring it against all the other things
that they knew about God's will. Their decision, in this case, was
that God had in fact indicated to them that they were to preach in
Macedonia.

From this event in Paul's life, we learn two things about determining God's individual will. One, sometimes we have no direct
revelation. Though the apostle Paul was occasionally given direct
revelation, he and his companions were simply prevented by the
Holy Spirit in their attempts to enter certain areas. How that hap-

pened we don't know, for the Bible doesn't specifically tell us. Two, if we believe that we have received some kind of direct revelation, we must carefully evaluate it before acting on it. (Incidentally, we really have no reason to expect that this will happen because the time of direct revelation is past. We now have a completed Scripture, which Paul and others in his day did not have.) Though Paul had a vision, he and the others with him still had to think through the meaning and validity of what he had seen.[1]

Consider another example where the matter is even clearer. Acts 15:1 says, "And some men came down from Judea and began teaching the brethren, 'Unless you are circumcised according to the custom of Moses, you cannot be saved.' " Paul and Barnabas disagreed with this teaching, so the early church had an important question to settle. "And the apostles and the elders came together to look into this matter" (15:6). Since there was no direct revelation from God about it, they carefully considered the matter together. After making a decision, they shared it with the rest of the church. "It seemed good to us, having become of one mind, to select men to send to you with our beloved Barnabas and Paul. . . . For it seemed good to the Holy Spirit and to us to lay upon you no greater burden than these essentials" (15:25, 28).

How did the apostles and elders know that it "seemed good to the Holy Spirit"? They knew because they had discussed it, prayed about it, and studied the Scriptures for insight into the matter. From all of that, these godly men had determined what the Holy Spirit wanted. There was no direct revelation involved. How do we come to know the individual will of God? In the same way, we search the Scriptures for insight and we go to God in prayer. We also look to godly people for help—elders and pastors whose job it is to give us guidance in understanding the will of God.

There is another example in this same chapter: "And after they had spent time there, they were sent away from the brethren in peace to those who had sent them out. (But it seemed good to Silas to remain there)" (Acts 15:33–34). Silas had to make a decision to go with the others or stay where he was. How did he decide to stay? Paul was Silas's mentor and companion at that time. It is clear in Scripture that Paul gave direction to his disciples, and so it is logical to conclude that Silas consulted with Paul about what to do. Silas then made his decision about what he deemed was good—most spiritually beneficial—for him to do.[2]

APPLICATION

1. What did R. C. Sproul mean when he said, "Don't shout where God only whispers"?

2. What did this section indicate about how to determine God's individual will for our lives?

3. In chapter 8 you were asked to write down some specific issues about which you needed to discern the godly thing to do. Review what you wrote at that time and reflect on the teaching in the section you've just read in chapter 9. Then think through how you will put this teaching into practice in discerning God's will for you on these specific issues.

Knowing God's Will Is Important

Understanding what the Lord's individual will is for each of us is very important. In fact, the Bible commands it: "So then do not be foolish, but *understand what the will of the Lord is*" (Eph. 5:17). Years ago, a man came to me for counseling who had failed in every job he had tried. At that point, he believed that God wanted him to be in the ministry. I asked him to spend a week studying 1 Timothy 3:1–7, which lays out the qualifications for the eldership. I asked him to determine the meaning of each qualification and then evaluate his own life in terms of those qualifications. I also asked him to have his wife and his pastor evaluate him with the same criteria. I did this because becoming a pastor is not a matter of what someone feels like doing. There are clear criteria in Scripture for the personal life of a man in the ministry.

When Paul asked Timothy to go with him on his second missionary journey, he did not have direct revelation from God about the decision. In Acts 16 we are told that when Paul was forming his missionary team, he made inquiries of other believers about Timothy's life. On the basis of what he learned, he decided to take Timothy with him. We need to act in a similar manner when faced with decisions about God's individual will for our lives. The decision-making process should always involve the counsel of other believers who are well informed about the situation and about what the Bible has to say on the matter.

For example, I think it's foolish for anyone to even think about getting married without consulting their pastor and other believing friends and family. There would be far fewer divorces and marital problems in the church if they would. In fact, the Scripture teaches us to seek such counsel. Proverbs 15:22 says, "Without consultation, plans are frustrated, *but with many counselors they succeed.*" Proverbs 12:15 instructs us, "The way of a fool is right in his own eyes, but *a wise man is he who listens to counsel.*" And Proverbs 18:1 teaches, *"He who separates himself seeks his own desire, he quarrels against all sound wisdom."* A person who refuses to get advice from other people is one who "separates himself." In doing so, Scripture says that this person is arguing against sound judgment.

I have often said that I would not be in the counseling ministry if godly people had not encouraged me to do it. The evaluation and judgment of others has kept me, sometimes, from giving up when the work was difficult or discouraging. When we pray "Thy will *be done,*" we are praying for God's help in knowing His will and in using the resources that He has given us: His inspired Word, prayer, and godly people who are able to give biblical, objective counsel. If we want to know and do His will, we must be humble and willing to make use of each resource.

More about the Meaning of Praying "Thy Will Be Done"

In addition to being satisfied with His sovereign will and searching out His individual will, when we pray "Thy will *be done,*" we are also asking that God would give us a desire to do His will. It's not enough that we know what God's will is; we must also have a desire in our hearts to do it. Scripture is full of illustrations of people who knew God's will and didn't do it. Jesus told a parable of two sons in Matthew 21:28–32. In the parable, a father sent his two sons to work in his vineyard. The first son said yes, but never went. The second said no, but later regretted it and went as he was asked. Both sons knew what the father wanted, but only one had the desire to actually do it. When we pray "Thy will *be done,*" we are praying that God would work in our hearts so that we would want to obey His will.

In Luke 12:42–47 Jesus told a parable about servants who knew their master's will. In the story, Jesus asked "Who then is the faithful and sensible steward, whom his master will put in charge of his servants, to give them their rations at the proper time? Blessed is that slave whom his master finds so doing when he comes" (12:42–43). This slave knew his master's wishes and was carrying them out, but another slave did not. Regarding that slave Jesus said, "The master of that slave will come on a day when he does not expect him . . . and assign him a place with the unbelievers. And that slave who knew his master's will and did not get ready or act in accord with his will, shall receive many lashes" (12:46–47). Jesus was teaching here that it is a very serious thing to know what God's will is and not do it.

In Romans 1:32 Paul said, "Although they know the ordinance of God, that those who practice such things are worthy of death, they . . . do the same." It is not enough to know God's will; we must pray for a desire to live in obedience to it. Adam and Eve knew that the will of God for them was to not eat of the tree of knowledge because God said, "For in the day that you eat from it you shall surely die" (Gen. 2:17). As we know, their knowledge did not translate into a desire to obey.

Philippians 2:13 says, "For it is God *who is at work in you,* both *to will and to work for His good pleasure.*" It is God who gives us the desire to do His will. The constant prayer of our hearts should be Psalm 119:36: *"Incline my heart to Thy testimonies,* and not to dishonest gain." The great hymn "Come, Thou Fount of Every Blessing" says, *"Tune my heart* to sing Thy praise." Unless God tunes our hearts, we would rather sing our own praises than the praises of God. The hymn continues, *"Prone to wander,* Lord, I feel it, prone to leave the God I love; here's my heart, O take and seal it; seal it for Thy courts above." If we know anything about our own hearts, we know that they are prone to wander and get out of tune. We need to pray "Thy will be done," asking God to incline our hearts to do His will.

I knew a man whose wife was a dear Christian, but he was not. Nevertheless, this man came to church with her every Sunday. For the nine years that I was the pastor of that church, that man attended Sunday services with his wife. He could have told anyone that asked him how to become a Christian. He knew that he needed to repent and turn his life over to Jesus, but he didn't want to. There are many people like that, people who know what God says, but do not wish to obey. When we pray "Thy will *be done,*" we are praying that God would give us a desire to repent of our sins and obey His Word. Fortunately, in the case of this man, he did repent and believe on Christ shortly before he died. Unfortunately, this is not the case with many others.

APPLICATION

1. In addition to praying that God would help us to know His will, what does this section indicate should rightly be included in our prayers as we pray this petition?

2. How does Romans 1:32 indicate the need for praying this kind of prayer?

3. What can we learn from Adam and Eve about the need for praying this petition?

4. In what areas of your life do you find it most difficult to actually do what you know God wants you to do?

5. Are there areas in your life where you not only find it difficult to do what God wants you to do, but more than that you just don't do it?

6. What are you going to do about these areas?

What We Need If We're Going to Do God's Will

Finally, when we pray "Thy will *be done,*" we are praying for God to give us the power to do His will. I have often heard people say,

"I know what God wants me to do and I want to do it, but I don't seem to *be able* to do it." If we are trying to obey God's will in our own power, that will be true of us as well. Everything that we do for God must be empowered by Him.

Consider Paul's words in Romans 8:5–8: "For those who are according to the flesh set their minds on the things of the flesh, but those who are according to the Spirit, the things of the Spirit. For the mind set on the flesh is death, but the mind set on the Spirit is life and peace, because the mind set on the flesh is hostile toward God; for it does not subject itself to the law of God, *for it is not even able to do so;* and those who are in the flesh cannot please God." Paul said that without God's Spirit, we cannot please God even if we know how to and want to. God's Spirit must enable us to do what pleases God.

Ephesians 2:1–3 says: "And you were dead in your trespasses and sins, in which you formerly walked according to the course of this world, according to the prince of the power of the air, of the spirit that is now working in the sons of disobedience. Among them we too all formerly lived in the lusts of our flesh, indulging the desires of the flesh and of the mind, and were by nature children of wrath, even as the rest." Until God works in our hearts, we will not have a desire to do His will or the power to do it. When we pray "Thy will *be done,*"we are praying, "Lord, give me the power to do Your will."

This, of course, requires that God puts a new spirit in us. In Ezekiel 36:26–27 God says, "Moreover, I will give you a new heart and put a new spirit within you; and I will remove the heart of stone from your flesh and give you a heart of flesh. And *I will put My Spirit within you and cause you to walk in My statutes,* and you will be careful to observe My ordinances." God says that we must have the power of His Spirit within us in order to obey Him. We cannot do God's will on our own; He must cause us to do it.

Paul said that we are to "consider [ourselves] to be dead to sin, but alive to God in Christ Jesus" (Rom. 6:11), and to "walk in newness of life" (Rom. 6:4). We cannot do that, even as believers, on our own. It is only by the power of God's Spirit that we can live the new life to which we have been called. Paul continued, "Do not go on presenting the members of your body to sin as instruments of unrighteousness; but present . . . your members as instruments of righteousness to God" (6:13). When we pray "Thy will *be done,*" we are praying that God would give us the power to be dead to sin and alive to Him, and that God would empower our bodies to be useful for His work—instruments of righteousness.

In Ephesians 1:18–19 Paul said, "I pray that the eyes of your heart may be enlightened, so that you may *know . . . what is the surpassing greatness of His power* toward us who believe." Later, in Ephesians 3:14–19, Paul said that his prayer for the Ephesian believers was this:

> For this reason, I bow my knees before the Father, from whom every family in heaven and on earth derives its name, that *He would grant you, according to the riches of His glory, to be strengthened with power through His Spirit in the inner man;* so that Christ may dwell in your hearts through faith; and that you, being rooted and grounded in love, may be able to comprehend with all the saints what is the breadth and length and height and depth, and to know the love of Christ which surpasses knowledge, that you may be filled up to all the fulness of God.

Paul wanted those believers to be filled up with the knowledge of God's love, and so he prayed for God's power to strengthen them through His Spirit. When we pray "Thy will *be done,*" we are praying for God to give us the power to love Him and to know to the fullest extent the greatness and richness of His love for us. We cannot love God or know His love on our own; it is only by God's power that we are able.

All these things are bound up in the words "be done" in this third petition of the Lord's Prayer. We are praying that God would help us to be satisfied and submissive to His will. We are praying that we might be able to do His will and that we might know God's individual will for us. We are also praying that God would give us the desire and power to do it. To pray in this way is to pray effectively, and it is to pray in the way that Jesus taught us.

APPLICATION

1. Summarize in your own words the most important truths presented in this chapter.

2. Write out and work on memorizing one or two verses found in this chapter.

3. In what ways were you encouraged, challenged, or convicted by the material in this chapter? In keeping with the material presented in this chapter, how should your prayer life be changed?

EXAMPLES OF PRAYING
FOR GOD'S WILL

I hope that the scope and depth of Scripture and its ability to address every area of our lives are becoming more and more apparent through this study. Psalm 119:96 says, "Thy commandment is exceedingly broad." In other words, there are innumerable truths contained in God's Word. We are looking at just a small portion of these things that God has to teach us in this passage in Matthew 6 known as the Lord's Prayer.

What It Means to Pray "Thy Will Be Done"

In the last chapter, we studied what Jesus was teaching us about God's will with the words "be done." We learned that Jesus was teaching us to pray for a number of things: for help in being satisfied with and submitted to His sovereign will, for help in being able to obey His will, and for help in finding out what His moral and individual wills are. Further, He was teaching us to ask God for a desire to do His will and the power to do His will. We turn now to one other important word in this phrase that we have not yet examined and that is the word "Thy." What was Jesus teaching us about effective prayer when He said *"Thy* will be done"?

First, Jesus was teaching us that we should pray that *His will,* rather than the will of other men, would be done. In 1 Peter 4:3 Peter said, "For the time already past is sufficient for you to have carried out *the desire of the Gentiles,* having pursued a course of sensuality, lusts, drunkenness, carousals, drinking parties and abominable idolatries." Peter was saying that as unbelievers we had long enough to live according to the will of other people. He went on to remind us that as believers we are now to live according to God's will.

A Dangerous Propensity: Some Examples

In John 12:42 Jesus prayed aloud for the benefit of some people who did not believe in Him. These people did not believe because they were afraid of what others would think. They preferred to do what other people wanted them to do rather than what God wanted them to do. Jesus taught us to pray *"Thy* will be done" because He knew that we are prone to live according to the will of other people rather than according to God's will.

The apostle Peter fell into this sin at one time. In Galatians 2:11–14 Paul reports:

> But when Cephas came to Antioch, I opposed him to his face, because he stood condemned. For prior to the coming of certain men from James, he used to eat with the Gentiles; but when they came, he began to withdraw and hold himself aloof, fearing the party of the circumcision. And the rest of the Jews joined him in hypocrisy, with the result that even Barnabas was carried away by their hypocrisy. But when I saw that they were not straightforward about the truth of the gospel, I said to Cephas in the presence of all, "If you, being a Jew, live like the Gentiles and not like the Jews, how is it that you compel the Gentiles to live like Jews?"

Paul had to rebuke Peter for succumbing to what other people wanted him to do rather than what God wanted. Peter's sin caused even Barnabas to go astray. These were godly men, but they were intimidated by what other people thought. It is a very real danger for any believer to become too concerned about doing the will of men rather than the will of God.

Aaron, the brother of Moses, struggled with this as well. God appointed Aaron to help Moses bring the Israelites out of Egypt. In

Exodus 32 Moses had gone up to receive the commandments from God. While he was on the mountain with God, Aaron remained in the camp in charge of the people. When Moses came down, he found that the people, and Aaron with them, had fallen into idolatry.

> And it came about, as soon as Moses came near the camp, that he saw the calf and the dancing; and Moses' anger burned, and he threw the tablets from his hands and shattered them at the foot of the mountain. And he took the calf which they had made and burned it with fire, and ground it to powder, and scattered it over the surface of the water, and made the sons of Israel drink it. Then Moses said to Aaron, "What did this people do to you, that you have brought such great sin upon them?" And Aaron said, "Do not let the anger of my lord burn; you know the people yourself, that they are prone to evil. For they said to me, 'Make a god for us who will go before us; for this Moses, the man who brought us up from the land of Egypt, we do not know what has become of him.' " (Ex. 32:19–23)

Aaron, whom God had made a leader of the Israelites, had become more concerned about the will of the Israelites than he was about the will of God. We are all tempted to such sin, and so we need to constantly pray *"Thy* will be done."

Proverbs 29:25 says, *"The fear of man brings a snare,* but he who trusts in the LORD will be exalted." Jeremiah 17:5 says, "Thus says the LORD, *'Cursed is the man who trusts in mankind* and makes flesh his strength, and whose heart turns away from the LORD." When we trust in people for our satisfaction and security, we have turned ourselves away from depending on God and seeking to please Him. If godly men like Peter and Aaron could experience this problem, then we certainly can too. None of us can honestly say that we have never struggled with being influenced to sin by other people. We all know what it is to be tempted by the will of men.

Areas in Which We Often Fail

Sadly, there are people who refuse Christ just because they are afraid of what other people might think or say about them. There are husbands who hesitate to be leaders in their homes because they are afraid that their wife won't like it. They are more concerned about their wife's will than they are about God's will. There are parents who do not discipline their children as God commands because they are more concerned about what other people think is right than they are about what God says is right.

There are believers who know what the Bible says about putting aside all bitterness and anger and slander (Eph. 4:31), and yet they enjoy putting others down and slandering. They are more concerned about the will of people than they are about the will of God. There are children who know the fifth commandment, "Honor your father and your mother" (Ex. 20:12), but they refuse to do it because other kids don't. It is more important to them to be like their friends than it is to obey God.

Some of us face tension between the will of men and the will of God in the area of ministry. For example, we may know that God wants us to go and preach the gospel—"And you shall be My witnesses . . . even to the remotest part of the earth" (Acts 1:8), but we would rather stay home and keep quiet because we are intimidated by people. In fact, God has called us to be witnesses wherever we are, but we don't even do that. We are more concerned about what our neighbors and friends think of us than what God thinks of our disobedience.

APPLICATION

1. Summarize what Jesus is teaching us by the word "Thy" in "Thy will be done."

2. What does Peter's experience in Galatians 2:11–14 illustrate in reference to the importance of praying this petition?

3. In what areas are you most prone to succumb to doing what others want rather than what God wants?

Examples of People Who Take This Petition Seriously

These are just a few illustrations of how we are tempted to do the will of men rather than the will of God. My mother-in-law, however, is a great example of someone who resisted this temptation in an area of her life. Her brother, who was not a believer, would make a point of visiting her on Sunday afternoons, even though he knew that she attended evening services at church. Because of this, my mother-in-law had to make a choice. She had to decide whether to stay home and visit with her brother, as he wanted, or join the believers in worship, as God wanted. "Not forsaking our own assembling together, as is the habit of some, but encouraging one another; and all the more, as you see the day drawing near" (Heb. 10:25). She chose the latter, telling her brother, "You know what I do on Sunday evening. I love God, and hearing the Word of God is of utmost importance to me. I wish you would go with me, but if you choose to stay, I'll visit with you when I get back." Her relationship with God was most important to her, and she was not afraid to tell her brother what she believed.

As a teenager, a friend of mine was offered a job that required him to be at work early in the morning. This new schedule conflicted with his family's regular practice of having devotions together before school. When he asked his dad what he should do, his father said, "Take the job, and we'll all just get up a half hour earlier for devotions." My friend never forgot the example his father was to him. His father considered the family devotion time to be important enough to change everyone's schedule to preserve it. When we pray *"Thy* will be done," we are praying that God would help us to be more concerned about doing His will than about doing the will of other people. We are praying that we will not make decisions on the basis of what other people might think or say or approve of, but that we will base all our decisions on what God's will is for us to do.

APPLICATION

Write Psalm 40:8 and John 4:34 and reflect on their connection to "Thy will be done."

More about What Praying This Petition Really Means

Second, when we pray *"Thy* will be done," we are praying that God would help us to do His will rather than *our own will.* In Mark 10:45 Jesus said, *"For even the Son of Man did not come to be served, but to serve,* and to give His life a ransom for many." For some people, the desire to please themselves is the entire focus of their lives. They are completely ruled by their passions. Instead of serving others with their time and resources, they think only about being served and pursuing whatever it is that they want, regardless of God's will.

There are people so consumed with sports that their team's record determines their emotional state. If the team wins, they are on top of the world; if the team loses, they are depressed and angry. They don't care about doing God's will. All they care about is satisfying their lust for sports. For some, God's command to "remember the sabbath day, to keep it holy" (Ex. 20:8) means nothing. Sunday is no longer a day dedicated to the Lord, it is a day of recreation. They pursue their own interests on Sunday—playing golf or sleeping in, rather than joining with others in worship.

Some people would rather feel sorry for themselves than think about what God says about being filled with self-pity. They would rather be bitter than deal with their anger as God commands. They would rather slander others than edify with their words. They would rather think evil of others than love their enemies. They would rather be proud before men than humble before God. They would rather do things that the world praises than the things that God praises. In all things, they would rather satisfy the lusts of their flesh than be filled with a desire for God.

Many times in his letters, Paul addressed this issue of living for our own interests rather than God's interests. In Romans 8:6–8 he said, "For the mind set on the flesh is death . . . because *the mind set on the flesh is hostile toward God; for it does not subject itself to the law of God, for it is not even able to do so;* and those who are in the flesh cannot please God." And in Ephesians 2:3, "Among them we too all formerly *lived in the lusts of our flesh, indulging the desires of the flesh and of the mind,* and were by nature children of wrath, even as the rest." Again, in Titus 3:3 Paul said, "For we also once were foolish ourselves, disobedient, deceived, *enslaved to various lusts and pleasures,* spending our life in malice and envy, hateful, hating one another." When we pray *"Thy* will be done," we are praying that God would help us to be more concerned about His will than the natural, sinful desires of our flesh.

Scripture contains many instructions regarding how we are to live according to God's will. In Philippians 2:14 we are told, *"Do all things without grumbling or disputing."* We ought to pray that God would help us to never complain because what He wants is more important than what we want. In Romans 12:10 Paul says, "Be devoted to one another in brotherly love; *give preference to one another in honor."* We ought to pray that God would help us not to honor ourselves, as we like to do, but to honor others according to His will. In Luke 9:23 Jesus said, "If anyone wishes to come after Me, *let him deny himself,* and take up his cross daily, and follow Me." Our natural desire is to puff ourselves up and push ourselves forward, not to deny ourselves or submit to God. We ought to pray that God would help us to take up our cross daily and follow Him. That is praying *"Thy* will be done."

Ephesians 4:29 teaches, *"Let no unwholesome word proceed from your mouth,* but only such a word as is good for edification according to the need of the moment, that it may give grace to those who hear." Though we are tempted at times to deceive or abuse others with our mouths, we ought to pray that God would help us to build others up with our words. Romans 14:23 says, "But he who doubts is condemned if he eats, because his eating is not from faith; and *whatever is not from faith is sin."* If we desire to do something that we are not sure God would approve of, but we do it anyway, we are asserting our own will over God's will. The Bible says that whatever we do without a conviction of God's approval is sin. When we pray *"Thy* will be done," we are praying that God would help us to live a life of faith according to His will.

Regarding humility, 1 Peter 5:6 says, *"Humble yourselves,* therefore, under the mighty hand of God, that He may exalt you at the proper time," and James 4:6 says, "But He gives a greater grace. Therefore it says, *'God is opposed to the proud, but gives grace to the humble.'* "A proud person focuses on himself and runs ahead with what he wants. When we pray *"Thy* will be done," we are praying that God would help us to be humble and teachable people who are eager to do His will, not our own.

The Bible declares that we are to submit ourselves to the church leadership. Hebrews 13:17 says, *"Obey your leaders, and submit to them;* for they keep watch over your souls, as those who will give an account. Let them do this with joy and not with grief, for this would be unprofitable for you." We ought to pray that God would help us to follow the counsel of godly leaders in our church. According to Proverbs 12:15, "The way of a fool is right in his own eyes, but a wise man is he who listens to counsel." According to God's Word, it is foolish to live apart from the wisdom and instruction of other believers. Not only is it pride, but it is disobedience to God's will. When we pray *"Thy* will be done," we are praying that God would help us to seek out and listen to godly counsel.

"Thy will be done" is a prayer for all of these things. Jesus was teaching us to pray to God that He would help us to do His will rather than the will of other people. He was also teaching us to pray to God for help in doing His will rather than our own will. We ought to examine both our prayers and our lives to determine if we are living according to *His will.*

APPLICATION

1. As you examine your past and present life, identify times and instances when you have been more concerned about and/or have actually done your will instead of God's will.

2. What have you done about past instances when this occurred?

3. What will you do about present instances where this is occurring?

4. To whom can you go for godly, biblical counsel?

God's Will on Earth

The next two words that we need to look at in this petition are "on earth." What was Jesus teaching us to pray for when He said,

"Thy will be done, *on earth* as it is in heaven"? The words "on earth" tell us what Jesus expected the scope of our prayers to be. He didn't say "in Galilee" or "in Judea." The Lord taught us to pray that God's will would be done throughout the whole earth. All too often, our prayers are focused around ourselves, our families, our churches, and a few missionaries that we happen to know.

Instead, Jesus was teaching us that we ought to have big prayers. We ought to be praying that God's will would be done throughout the world, every continent and every country. Our prayers should be like the psalmist's in Psalm 67:

> God be gracious to us and bless us,
> And cause His face to shine upon us—
> *That Thy way may be known on the earth,*
> *Thy salvation among all nations.*
> Let the peoples praise Thee, O God;
> Let all the peoples praise Thee.
> *Let the nations be glad and sing for joy;*
> For Thou wilt judge the peoples with uprightness,
> And guide the nations on the earth.
> Let the peoples praise Thee, O God;
> Let all the peoples praise Thee.
> The earth has yielded its produce;
> God, our God, blesses us,
> God blesses us,
> That *all the ends of the earth may fear Him.*

Like Jesus, the psalmist was praying, "Thy will be done, *on earth* as it is in heaven."

The apostle Paul prayed in the same way. In Colossians 1:3–4, he made a significant statement to the Colossian believers: "We give thanks to God, the Father of our Lord Jesus Christ, praying always for you, since *we heard of your faith* in Christ Jesus and the love which you have for all the saints." The apostle Paul had not visited Colossae on any of his missionary journeys, and therefore he had probably not met any of the believers in that city personally. Some people from Ephesus and other places had preached the gospel in Colossae, and Paul had only heard of the Colossians' faith. This epistle to the Colossians shows us that Paul was not only concerned for the people that he had met and to whom he had ministered personally, but his concern went far beyond that. When he wrote this letter of instruction and encouragement to them, he said that he had heard about their faith and love and that he was praying for them.

Paul exhorted all believers to do the same. In Ephesians 6:18 Paul instructed them, "With all prayer and petition pray at all times in the Spirit, and with this in view, be on the alert with all perseverance and *petition for all the saints.*" Paul wanted these believers to pray for not just others in their area, but all believers—those in Colossae, in Thyatira, in Laodicea, and in all the world. Paul desired that God's will would be known and would be done *on earth.* In 1 Timothy 2:1 Paul said, "First of all, then, I urge that entreaties and prayers, petitions and thanksgivings, *be made on behalf of all men.*" Paul did not distinguish between people that he knew and those whom he had never met. He instructed all believers to pray for every person *on earth.* When Jesus taught us to pray "on earth," He was teaching us to pray big prayers.

APPLICATION

1. In what ways are your prayers like or unlike those recorded in Psalm 67?

2. What missionaries and other Christian workers are you regularly praying for?

3. What changes should you and will you make in your prayer life to be more in accordance with this petition?

Praying for Those Who Are Still on the Earth

It is important to realize here that while Jesus was instructing us to pray for those who are on earth, He was teaching us to pray for those who *are still* on the earth. In other words, we do not need to pray for those who have died. If they are in heaven, they are doing God's will continually. If they are in hell, then it is too late for them. In Luke 16:19–31 Jesus told the story of the rich man and Lazarus. When the rich man died he went to hell. From hell, he looked up and begged Abraham to send someone to talk to his family, but Abraham refused. Not only was the rich man praying to the wrong person (he should have been praying to God), but he was also praying too late. While on earth, we are to pray for those who are also on earth.

There are some people who believe that it is right to pray for the dead. The Mormons pray for people who have died because they believe that the living can be a proxy for the dead. The Roman Catholic and Greek Orthodox churches do the same. They believe that they can speed the dead through purgatory with their prayers. In all of Paul's prayers, however, we never find a single hint or suggestion that he prayed for people who had died. Nowhere does the Scripture ever instruct us to pray for the dead.

The Bible does clearly teach us to pray for the living, and Jesus taught us to pray for all the world. We need to carefully examine our prayers, measuring them against His standard. Are we praying for missionaries in other parts of the world? Are we taking time to find out what is happening in the lives of the missionaries that our church supports? Do we know what their specific ministry and personal needs are, and are we praying for those needs? Are we praying for unsaved people in other parts of the world? Are we praying for missionaries to go to those people and share the gospel with them? Are we praying for believers who are experiencing persecution?

A pastor in Wales named Geof Thomas wrote this letter to me. Consider his words:

> Please pray and ask God to protect Christians and their families from being attacked and their properties from being destroyed in Pakistan. Ask God to stop the hand of the oppressor and exalt His own body in Pakistan. . . . Who will speak out for the many Christians falsely charged under the nation's blasphemy law, languishing in jails year after year without trial? . . . Who will speak out for them? Who will decry the injustice to the mother who is denied food and forced to watch her baby die of salvation? Christian women are often taken away and sold into slavery for pocket

change, their families paralyzed with no voice to protest. Our Christian sisters have only to curse their Lord and Savior Jesus and they would be promptly restored to all privileges and honor. Yet like Moses, they reject that option, choosing rather to share ill treatment with the people of God than to enjoy the fleeting pleasures of sin. Who will be the voice of Christian children beaten and forcibly trained into Islam? Rachel is weeping for her children and refusing to be comforted because her children are no more (Jeremiah 31:15). Will you join Rachel in her weeping? Will you join Christ as His body is mercilessly ravaged in Pakistan?

Not all of the persecution that the Pakistani church faces is blatant. Christians are not permitted to vote for Muslim candidates for the National Assembly. This robs the Christian of their lobbying power, since Muslim candidates do not need their votes. . . . Fair and equal voting rights would allow the Christians voice in the election of legislators . . . and the enactment of bills as laws. . . . The Messiah's own body is suffering in Pakistan, and the Bible says that when one member suffers, we all suffer.

The Christmas season is when Christians in Pakistan seem to be persecuted the most. These are the days when the least number of Christians are praying for them, since many Christians who would ordinarily intercede for the unreached and for the persecuted church are preoccupied during the Christians' Christmas season with festivities and merriment. The prayer shield over Pakistani Christians is very weak during this time. . . . Please take a stand for the persecuted church in Pakistan, and let your voice be heard before man and before God on their behalf. Please pray that God would promote fasting, prayer, and missionary outreach to Pakistan.

Pakistani Christians have no voice. Please, can you be their voice? Please write to your . . . congressman [or] senator . . . and ask them to use their influence on the Pakistani government to enact laws for the protection of the non-Muslim minorities. Please write . . . to newspapers and news media, asking them to report more stories on the abuse of Christians in Pakistan. . . . And please pray that the heads of states . . . and news media would champion the cause of Pakistani Christians. Our Lord is the Father to the fatherless, a Defender of widows, and a high tower for those without refuge. Please, can you adopt the Pakistani Christians into your hearts and prayers?

"Thy will be done, *on earth* as it is in heaven." Jesus instructed us to pray that God's will would be done, not our own or any other person's will. And He taught us to pray that His will would be done throughout the world. Praying for the people like the ones Pastor Geof Thomas mentions in this prayer letter is an example of praying the way Jesus taught us to pray in this petition. To pray this way is to pray Jesus' style, and to pray Jesus' style is to pray effectively. How could it be otherwise? May our prayers continue to be enriched and informed by Jesus' great teaching on the subject of true and effective prayer.

 **APPLICATION**

1. Summarize in your own words the most important truths presented in this chapter.

2. Write out and work on memorizing one or two verses found in this chapter.

3. In what ways were you challenged or convicted by the material in this chapter? In keeping with the material presented in this chapter, how should your prayer life be changed?

GOD'S WILL IN
HEAVEN

Throughout the ages, great leaders of the Christian faith have always regarded prayer as of utmost importance. In his sermon "True Prayer! True Power!" Charles Spurgeon indicated how important he believed prayer to be in life as well as in the ministry of the church:

Would it not be a vile crime if a man had an eye given him, which he would not open? Or a hand that he would not lift up, or a foot that grew stiff because he would not use it? And what must we say of ourselves when God has given us power and prayer, and yet that power lies still? Oh, if the universe was as still as we are, where would we be? Oh God, Thou hast given us light by the sun, and the sun shines with it. Thou hast given light even to the stars and they twinkle. To the winds, Thou hast given force and they blow. And to the air, Thou givest life and it moves, and men breathe thereof. But to Thy people, Thou hast given a gift that is better than force and life and light, and yet they permit it to lie still, forgetful almost that they wield the power, seldom exercising it though it would be blessed to countless myriads. Weep, Christian man. Constantine, the emperor of Rome, saw that on the coins of the other emperors, their images were in an erect posture triumphing. Instead thereof, he ordered that his image should be struck kneeling for he said that's the way in which I have triumphed. We shall never triumph till our image is struck kneeling. The reason why we have been defeated and why our banners trail in the dust is because we have not prayer. Go, go back to your God with sorrow, confess before Him that you were armed and carried bows but turned your backs on the day of battle. Go to your God and tell Him that if souls are not saved it is not because He has not power to save, but because you have never travailed as it were in birth, for perishing sinners. Wake up, wake up! Be astonished, ye careless ones! You who have neglected prayer, you sinners who have been at ease. Wake up, wake up yourselves! Wrestle and strive with your God, and then the blessing shall come. The early and the latter rain of His mercy and the earth shall bring forth plenteously, and all the nations shall call Him blessed. Look up then and weep![1]

Spurgeon truly believed the words of Scripture recorded in James 5:16, "The effective prayer of a righteous man can accomplish much."

In the past three chapters, we have been studying our Lord's teaching in the phrase "Thy will be done, on earth as it is in heaven." We have looked carefully at the words "Thy," "will," "be done," and "on earth." In the last chapter, we learned that the words "on earth" teach us about the proper scope and focus of our prayers. Jesus wanted us to pray for everyone, everywhere, who is still on this earth. We come now to the last phrase of this petition, "as it is in heaven."

What did Jesus mean when He taught us to pray, "Thy will be done, on earth *as it is in heaven*"? First, consider the meaning of the small but important word "as." It means "in the same manner" or "in the same way" or "to the same degree." We are praying, "Lord, I want Your will to be done on earth in the same way that it is done in heaven." That brings us to the focus of our study. How is God's will done in heaven, and what does that mean for us on earth?

APPLICATION

What does the word "as" mean in this petition?

Doing God's Will Universally

God's will is done in heaven *universally*. This means that in heaven, every creature does the will of God. There are no exceptions. There was a time when a high angel, who is now called Satan, and some other angels, now demons, rebelled against God in heaven. This event is recorded in Isaiah 14 and Ezekiel 28. We read in Isaiah 14:12–15:

> How you have fallen from heaven, O star of the morning, son of the dawn! You have been cut down to the earth, you who have weakened the nations! But you said in your heart, "I will ascend to heaven; I will raise my throne above the stars of God, and I will sit on the mount of assembly in the recesses of the north. I will ascend above the heights of the clouds; I will make myself like the Most High." Nevertheless you will be thrust down to Sheol, to the recesses of the pit.

According to these verses, Satan was one of the most glorious of all the angels. Why was he cast out of heaven? Satan wanted to do his will rather than the will of God. Five times Satan declared, "I will." Because of their rebellion, Satan and the unclean angels were cast out of heaven. For everyone in heaven, whether angels or men, does the will of God.

When we pray, "Thy will be done, on earth *as it is in heaven,*" we are praying first that we personally would do God's will here on earth as it is done in heaven. We are then also praying the same for our family, our church, our community, and our world. In 1 Timothy 2:1 Paul said, "First of all, then, *I urge that entreaties and prayers, petitions and thanksgivings, be made on behalf of all men.*" Our prayer concern should be that God's will would be known and obeyed universally, as David described it being done in heaven. "Bless the LORD, you His angels, mighty in strength, *who perform His word, obeying the voice of His word!*" (Ps. 103:20).

Doing God's Will Cheerfully

Second, when we pray, "Thy will be done, on earth *as it is in heaven,*" we are praying that God would help us to do His will *cheerfully.* In 1 Kings 10 the Queen of Sheba, who had heard of the wisdom and wealth of Solomon, came to Israel to see it for herself. When Solomon showed her his great kingdom and all his wealth, the queen responded, "Nevertheless I did not believe the reports, until I came and my eyes had seen it. And behold, the half was not told me. You exceed in wisdom and prosperity the report which I heard" (10:7). In fact, she was impressed with more than Solomon's wisdom and wealth; she was impressed by how happy his servants were. "How blessed are these your servants who stand before you continually and hear your wisdom" (10:8). Solomon's men served him with joy and delight.

The servants of God in heaven serve Him with joy as well. No one in heaven serves grudgingly, or because they are forced to, or out of fear of punishment. Psalm 16:11 promises, "In Thy presence is *fulness of joy;* in Thy right hand there are *pleasures forever.*" In the book of Revelation it is recorded many times how the angels in heaven constantly sing and give praise to God. Psalm 100:2 says, "Serve the LORD with gladness; come before Him with joyful singing."

In fact, that is the only kind of service that God accepts. God wants us to serve Him gladly, not because it is our duty. In Acts 5:41 the Bible tells us that the early believers accepted persecution, *"rejoicing* that they had been considered worthy to suffer shame for His name." God is not pleased with service that is done merely for duty's sake. Jonah gave God his grudging service when he preached to Nineveh after spending three days in the belly of a great fish. He went to Nineveh because he had to, and when God blessed his ministry, Jonah became angry. He did not serve joyfully, and God had to rebuke him for his disobedience. All too often, our service is as grudging as Jonah's was. When we pray, "Thy will be done, on earth *as it is in heaven,*" we are praying that God would make us cheerful servants of Jesus Christ. Remember 2 Corinthians 9:7 in this regard, "Let each one do just as he has purposed in his heart; not grudgingly or under compulsion; *for God loves a cheerful giver.*"

If we give to God of our money or our service in any other way, then our service is not pleasing to Him.

APPLICATION

1. Summarize the two things we have learned thus far about how God's will is done in heaven.

2. Reflect on Psalm 100:2 and think about what this kind of service would look like in actual experience. Be specific.

3. Reflect on Psalm 100:2 and think about what service that is not done with gladness looks like. Be specific.

4. How often do you serve the Lord with gladness: always? sometimes? seldom? never?

5. Give illustrations of times you have and times you haven't served the Lord with gladness.

Doing God's Will Constantly

Third, we are praying that God's will would be done *constantly*. In Revelation 7:9–15 John described the scene in heaven:

> After these things I looked, and behold, a great multitude, which no one could count, from every nation and all tribes and peoples and tongues, standing before the throne and before the Lamb . . . and they cry out with a loud voice, saying, "Salvation to our God who sits on the throne, and to the Lamb." And all the angels were standing around the throne and around the elders and the four living creatures; and they fell on their faces before the throne and worshiped God, saying, "Amen, blessing and glory and wisdom and thanksgiving and honor and power and might, be to our God forever and ever. Amen." . . . And he said to me, "These are the ones who come out of the great tribulation, and they have washed their robes and made them white in the blood of the Lamb. For this reason, they are before the throne of God; *and they serve Him day and night in His temple;* and He who sits on the throne shall spread His tabernacle over them."

All the creatures, angels, and people in heaven are giving God the glory and serving Him constantly. When my family and I lived in California, there was a river near our house called the Santa Clara River. Most of the time, when we would go by that river, it would be dry. The only time there was water in it was when it rained or when the mountain snow melted in the spring. That river ran in fits and starts, not constantly, and it is a good example of the wrong way to do God's will.

In Genesis 49:4 Jacob said of his son Reuben that he was "uncontrolled as water." In other words, he could not be trusted or relied on. All too often, that is true of us as well. We serve the Lord in fits and starts. At times, we get excited and devote ourselves to God's will. We read the Word, pray, witness, come to church, and seek after God, but then we lose our enthusiasm and our dedication falters. This does not happen in heaven, of course. In heaven, God is served and worshiped day and night. When we pray, "Thy will be done, on earth *as it is in heaven*," we are praying that God would help us to serve Him constantly, every hour and every day of our lives.

Charles Spurgeon, in a sermon on the perseverance of the saints, remarked that most new believers are excited about hearing the Word. They are excited about praying, about being part of the fellowship of God's people, about reaching out and talking to others about their faith. Spurgeon noted, however, that all believers tend to run out of steam. He gave the example of Noah, who sinned in drunkenness in his old age, and many others. In truth, there are many of us like the Galatians, of whom Paul said, "I am amazed that you are so quickly deserting Him who called you by the grace of Christ" (1:6), and "You were running well; who hindered you from obeying the truth?" (5:7). We need to pray, "Lord, help me to be constant in doing Your will."

Doing God's Will Completely

Fourth, when we pray, "Thy will be done, on earth *as it is in heaven*," we are praying that God would help us to do His will *com-

pletely. Again, consider David's words in Psalm 103:20, "Bless the LORD, you His angels, mighty in strength, who perform His word, obeying the voice of His word!" The angels listen to God's word and they do whatever He commands. If He sends them with a message of joy, then they proclaim that message of joy. If He sends them with a message of doom, they proclaim the message of doom. If He sends them to save, they save. If He commands them to destroy, they destroy. Whatever God says to do, they do. The angels of the Lord never refuse to obey His will.

It is interesting to study in the Scripture the things that angels were sent by God to do. In the book of Genesis, God used angels to accomplish His purposes a number of times. In Genesis 3 God banished Adam and Eve from the Garden of Eden: "So He drove the man out; and at the east of the garden of Eden *He stationed the cherubim, and the flaming sword which turned every direction, to guard the way to the tree of life*" (v. 24). In Genesis 16 Sarai was mistreating her servant Hagar out of jealousy. Abram, faithful and godly man though he was, sinfully yielded to his wife at that point and allowed her to abuse Hagar. Hagar then fled from the mistreatment that she experienced at Sarai's hand. "Now the angel of the LORD found her by a spring of water in the wilderness. . . . And he said, 'Hagar, Sarai's maid, where have you come from and where are you going?' And she said, 'I am fleeing from the presence of my mistress Sarai'" (vv. 7–8). God sent an angel to minister to Hagar in her time of great distress.

There are many more instances in Genesis where God sent an angel to do His will. In Genesis 19 angels were sent to tell Lot that Sodom and Gomorrah were going to be destroyed. In Genesis 21 the angel of God again ministered to Hagar when she was out in the wilderness, telling her where to find water for herself and her child. In Genesis 22 an angel stopped Abraham from sacrificing his son on Mount Moriah. In Genesis 24 Abraham assured his servant Eliezar that an angel of the Lord would help him in his task of finding a wife for Isaac. In Genesis 28 angels ministered to Jacob through a vision that he had while on the run from his brother Esau. On and on through Scripture, we read about how God used angels to do His will. An angel of the Lord struck dead the first-born in Egypt, and an angel of the Lord proclaimed Christ's birth to the shepherds. Though their tasks are both unpleasant and glorious, they always do God's will completely.

Earlier, we looked at Revelation 7 and saw that not only the angels, but also people who are in heaven are doing God's will completely. Before the throne of God, they are recognizing Him as King. They are constantly bowing in worship and adoration before God's throne. Likewise, we are to do God's will completely on this earth. In Matthew 23:23 Jesus condemned the Pharisees, "Woe to you, scribes and Pharisees, hypocrites! For you tithe mint and dill and cummin, and have neglected the weightier provisions of the law: justice and mercy and faithfulness; but these are the things you should have done without neglecting the others." The Pharisees served God in formal ways, scrupulously tithing their incomes, but they neglected to serve God with their hearts, showing love and mercy to others. They served Him in part, not completely.

In 1 Samuel 13 Saul went out to battle the Philistines. He waited for Samuel the priest to come as he had promised and offer a sacrifice to the Lord. Saul and the people with him waited seven days, but when Samuel still had not come, Saul took it upon himself to offer the sacrifice. When Samuel finally came, he rebuked Saul for his sin: "You have acted foolishly; you have not kept the commandment of the LORD your God, which He commanded you, for now the LORD would have established your kingdom over Israel forever. But now your kingdom shall not endure . . . because you have not kept what the LORD commanded you" (1 Sam. 13:13–14). When we pray, "Thy will be done, on earth *as it is in heaven,*" we are praying that we would not be like Saul, who refused to obey the will of God completely.

APPLICATION

1. Summarize the two things we have learned in the last two sections about how God's will is done in heaven.

2. Reflect on Psalm 103:20 and think about what the kind of service the angels render would look like in actual experience. Be specific.

3. Reflect on Psalm 103:20 and think about what service that is not done in the way the angels serve would look like. Be specific.

4. Evaluate your service: does it resemble the way the angels serve, or are you more like the Galatians or like Reuben or even the Pharisees?

5. In what ways and areas does your obedience need to be improved?

Doing God's Will Evangelically

Fifth, we are praying that God would help us to do His will *evangelically*. What does it mean to do the will of God evangelically? It means that we are not doing His will in an attempt to win His favor. Those in heaven already have the favor of God, so we know that they never do anything for that purpose. As inhabitants of heaven, they are assured of God's favor. They serve Him joyfully and willingly in response to His love for them. That is how we should serve God on earth.

Again, consider what the elder said to John in Revelation 7:14–15: "These are the ones who come out of the great tribulation, and they have washed their robes and made them white in the blood of the Lamb. *For this reason,* they are before the throne of God; and they serve Him day and night in His temple; and He who sits on the throne shall spread His tabernacle over them." The people who came out of the tribulation were serving God because they had experienced His grace. They served out of gratitude. Romans 12:1 says, "I urge you therefore, brethren, *by the mercies of God, to present your bodies a living and holy sacrifice,* acceptable to God, *which is your spiritual service of worship."* Paul said that because of God's mercy to us, we should present our bodies—our entire lives—to God for service. We are not to serve God so that He will give us favor; we are to serve God because He has already given us His favor. If we are motivated in our service by anything less than gratitude for God's mercies to us, our service will not be acceptable to God.

Paul explained what motivated him in his service for Christ in 2 Corinthians 4 and 5. Some people had accused Paul of being out of his mind, but Paul said that if he was out of his mind, it was for God's sake (5:13). He was zealous for serving God and willing to be persecuted because of God's great mercy and love for him. "For the love of Christ controls us" (5:14). When we pray, "Thy will be done, on earth *as it is in heaven,*" we are praying that God would help us to be motivated by His love for the purpose of doing His will. We ought to serve the Lord because we love Him and because He first loved us, not because we are trying to win His favor. If we are serving God in order to win His favor, that is works for righteousness. The Bible clearly teaches that we are saved by grace, that we live by grace, and that we will get home by grace. Our service is not for obtaining grace; it is gratitude for grace already received.

APPLICATION

1. What does it mean to serve the Lord evangelically?

2. Reflect on Romans 12:1 and think about what this text indicates about how we should serve the Lord.

3. What would it look like, what would be our attitude if we were motivated to serve the Lord because of His mercy?

4. Evaluate your service in terms of whether your motivation is grace or law. Do you serve primarily out of love and devotion or out of obligation?

Doing God's Will Eagerly

Sixth, when we pray, "Thy will be done, on earth *as it is in heaven,*" we are praying that the Lord would help us to do His will *eagerly.* In Isaiah 6 the prophet Isaiah had a vision of the Lord on a throne, high and lifted up. In this vision, he also saw the seraphim with their six wings. Two wings covered their faces, two covered their feet, and with two they flew constantly. Their wings were in constant motion because they were ready and eager to do the will of God at His command. Like hummingbirds, they hovered around God, waiting to fly off at a moment's notice. So also should we be eager and ready to serve God when He calls.

In Daniel 9:21 we read, "Yes, while I was speaking in prayer, the man Gabriel . . . *being caused to fly swiftly,* reached me about the time of the evening offering" (NKJV). The angel Gabriel flew swiftly at God's command. Our obedience should be like this angel's obedience to God's will. Consider the example of Philip in Acts 8:26–27, who was on his way back to Jerusalem from Samaria. "But an angel of the Lord spoke to Philip saying, 'Arise and go south to the road that descends from Jerusalem to Gaza.' (This is a desert road.) *And he arose and went;* and behold, there was an Ethiopian eunuch." The angel sent him to a desolate and dry part of the country, but Philip did not protest his new assignment. Though he had just been part of a tremendous ministry in Samaria and was headed back to a growing church in Jerusalem, Philip did not question the command to go into the desert. He simply arose and went.

Is that our response to the Word of God? If we don't fully understand God's purposes, do we eagerly and immediately obey anyway? Let us not be like Jonah, whom God had to send into the belly of a great fish in order to get obedience from him. Though Jonah eventually got to Nineveh, it was with great reluctance and a bitter heart. Let us not be like Moses, who told God that he couldn't speak when the Lord sent him to talk to Pharaoh. Moses made many excuses in an attempt to avoid doing God's will. How often do we do the same!

Instead, our obedience should be like that of Abraham in Genesis 22. Abraham had waited a long time for the fulfillment of God's promise to give him a son. Twenty-five years went by after God made that promise, and Sarah was past child-bearing age when she finally conceived. Little Isaac was surely a joy to Abraham when he finally arrived, but then God came to Abraham and asked him to sacrifice Isaac on Mount Moriah. What was Abraham's response? He could have argued with God about His promise to make a great nation out of Abraham's descendants. He could have asked for more time with his son. Instead, Abraham "rose early in the morning and saddled his donkey" (22:3). He didn't make excuses or try to get out of the task before him. He did the will of God eagerly, and that is the way that we should respond to God as well.

Doing God's Will Earnestly

Finally, when we pray, "Thy will be done, on earth *as it is in heaven,*" we are praying that God would help us to do His will *earnestly.* Romans 12:11 says that we are to be "not lagging behind in diligence, *fervent in spirit,* serving the Lord." Colossians 3:23 says, "Whatever you do, *do your work heartily,* as for the Lord rather than for men." In Galatians 4:18 Paul said, "But it is *good to be zealous in a good thing always"* (NKJV). And in Matthew 15:8–9 the Lord Jesus gave a strong warning to those who honored God with their lips, but whose hearts were far from Him. That should never be true of us.

John the Baptist was an example of a man who did God's will earnestly. In John 5:35 Jesus said that John was the "lamp that was *burning* and was shining." John the Baptist was not lukewarm about his faith or his message; he was on fire for the Lord. We too should be on fire for God, earnestly doing His will. More often, we serve the Lord with such little enthusiasm that we couldn't convince a flea that we were serious about spiritual things. We simply go through the motions. We're like a fake fireplace—we look good from a distance, but at close range there's no heat. Ecclesiastes 9:10 says, "Whatever your hand finds to do, verily, *do it with all your might;* for there is no activity or planning or wisdom in Sheol where you are going." Can we honestly say that whatever we do, we are doing it earnestly for the Lord? Are we lamps that are burning and shining?

Some time ago, I worked with a young lady who was experiencing depression. I asked her to make up some small cards. On one side, she was to write a Bible verse that spoke directly to her depression, like Philippians 4:6, and on the other side, she was to write the word "STOP." I told her to pull out a card whenever she found herself being ruled by her feelings, look at the word "STOP," and then meditate on the verse on the other side of the card. I asked her to practice saying "STOP" while she was with me in the office, and so she repeated the word very quietly. I told her, "That wouldn't stop a flea," and then I demonstrated what I meant by saying "Stop." I yelled, "STOP!" with everything I had in me (and probably almost gave her a heart attack).

The point that I was trying to make to her was that we are able to make ourselves do what we ought to do if we are really serious about it. And when we make ourselves do what we ought to do, we often end up feeling like it as well. However, until we take control and make ourselves obey, we will never experience the Lord's revival and restoration of our feelings. We need to pray that God would help us to serve Him earnestly.

There are times when I start praying because I know I ought to pray, not because I really want to, but as I do, the Lord gives me the desire to continue praying and honoring Him. There are times when I am very tired or have a headache and don't feel like preaching, but I do it because I know that the Lord wants me to preach. As I preach, I ask the Lord for help and He helps me to become excited about what I am saying. I find then that I am not only ministering to others, but I am ministering to myself as well. In fact, I am always the most blessed by my preaching because each time I preach, I believe a little bit more. I pack down more truth into my heart; I stir myself up more to love and good deeds. Some people never learn how to take control of themselves and do what God wills, trusting that God will bring the feeling and desire in time. We need to pray that God would make us earnest in doing His will.

APPLICATION

1. What examples were given about what it means to serve the Lord eagerly?

2. What examples were given about what it means to serve the Lord with earnestness or a lack of earnestness?

3. Can you think of other biblical examples of either of these practices?

4. If people who know you well were to describe your service, would they be able to say that you serve the Lord eagerly? Would they be able to say that you serve the Lord with earnestness?

When we pray, "Thy will be done, on earth *as it is in heaven,*" we are praying that God would help us to do His will in all these ways: universally, cheerfully, constantly, completely, evangelically, eagerly, and earnestly. Most important, though, what Jesus was teaching us in this passage in Matthew 6 is that we need *to pray*. Unless we practice what we are learning about prayer, it is of no value to us. If we do practice, however, we are going to experience the kind of power that Charles Spurgeon spoke about:

Look up, dear Christian brethren, and amend your prayers from this time forth. Look on prayer no longer as a romantic fiction, or as an arduous duty; look at it as a real power, as a real pleasure. When the philosopher discovers some latent power, they seem to have a delight to put it into action. I believe there have been many great engineers who have designed and constructed some of the most wonderful human works, not because they would be remunerated for it, but simply from a love of showing their own power to accomplish wonders, to show the world what skill could do and what man could accomplish. They have attempted companies into speculations that could never remunerate, apparently, so far as I could see, in order to see that they might have an opportunity of displaying their genius. Oh Christian men, and shall our great engineer attempt great works and display his power, and will you who have a mightier power than ever was wielded by any man apart from his God, will you let that be still? Nay, think of some great object; strain the sinews of your supplications forth. Let every vein of your heart be full to the brim with the rich blood of desire and struggle and wrestle and tug and strive with God for it, using the promises and pleading the attributes, and see if God does not give you your heart's desire. I challenge you this day to exceed in prayer my Master's bounty. I throw down the gauntlet to you; believe Him to be more than He is. Go to Him now for more faith and the promise warrants. Venture it. Risk it. Out-do the Eternal if it be possible. Attempt it. Or, I would rather put it thus, take your petitions and wants and see if He does not honor you. Try whether if you believe Him, He has not fulfilled the promise and richly blessed you with the anointing awe of His spirit by which you will be strong in power.[2]

We will be strong in power only as we put into practice our Lord Jesus Christ's marvelous teaching on effective prayer. Spurgeon was right, "True prayer, true power." Again, I say let's devote ourselves to praying this way because to pray this way is to pray effectively and it is to pray Jesus' style. How could it be otherwise since it was Jesus Christ, the Son of God in whom are hid all the treasures of wisdom and knowledge (Col. 2:3), who taught us to pray this way?

APPLICATION

1. Summarize in your own words the most important truths presented in this chapter.

2. Write out and work on memorizing one or two verses found in this chapter.

3. In what ways were you encouraged, challenged, or convicted by the material in this chapter? In keeping with the material presented in this chapter, how should your prayer life be changed?

PRAYING ABOUT YOUR
PHYSICAL NEEDS

*I*magine that you really wanted to do a certain thing, and along came someone who knew everything there is to know about what you wanted to do and could do it perfectly. Imagine that this person was willing to teach you everything he knew about what you wanted to do so that you also could do it successfully. I suspect that if you really wanted to learn how to do this thing, you would be excited about the opportunity to learn from this great expert. In fact, you would jump at the chance.

As we study Matthew 6:5–13, we are being taught by the One who knows everything about prayer, the One whose prayers were perfect prayers, the One whose prayers were always heard (John 11:42). Here we have Jesus, history's greatest expert on prayer, teaching us the secrets of effective prayer. If you really want to know how to pray effectively, you ought to be excited about this incredible opportunity to learn from "the expert" on the subject of prayer. You ought to be jumping at the chance!

In this chapter, we come to what Jesus taught about effective prayer in verse 11, where He said we should pray, "Give us this day our daily bread." As we casually look at this phrase, it may seem short and simple; but, as we study each word carefully, we will discover that this phrase contains great depth of meaning. We will discover that each of the seven words is important.

175

The Meaning of "Bread"

In seeking to get our arms around what Jesus was teaching about effective prayer, let's first consider what Jesus meant when he instructed us to pray for *bread*. Genesis 47:11–13 is a passage that helps to explain what *bread* represents. At this time, Joseph was the prime minister of Egypt, in control of all of the nation's resources. His whole family had moved to Egypt, as we read, "So Joseph settled his father and his brothers, and gave them a possession in the land of Egypt, in the best of the land, in the land of Rameses, as Pharaoh had ordered. And Joseph provided his father and his brothers and all his father's household with food, according to their little ones." The key word in this passage is "food," and the Hebrew word "food" that is used here can also be translated "bread." Does that mean that they ate only the substance we call "bread" (flour, water, and yeast)? No, bread is symbolic of all of their physical needs. The passage continues, "Now there was no food [or no bread] in all the land, because the famine was very severe, so that the land of Egypt and the land of Canaan languished because of the famine." So the word "bread" in Scripture often represents not merely what we call bread, but rather all of man's physical needs.

This word "bread" is used in the same way in 2 Samuel 9:6–7, where David speaks to the lame man Mephibosheth shortly after David becomes king of Israel. "And Mephibosheth, the son of Jonathan the son of Saul, came to David and fell on his face and prostrated himself. . . . And David said to him, 'Do not fear, for I will surely show kindness to you for the sake of your father Jonathan, and will restore to you all the land of your grandfather Saul; *and you shall eat at my table regularly.*' "Another translation of that last phrase is, "and you shall eat *bread* at my table regularly." Obviously, David is not saying that they will eat only bread. Bread is representative of all foods which, by interpretation, means all physical needs.

Since God is vitally concerned about everything in our lives, Jesus was teaching that we should pray for all our physical provisions. There is nothing "unspiritual" about praying for legitimate physical needs and blessings. Certainly, the main emphasis of our prayers ought to be for spiritual things. In prayer, as well as in life, we should make the truths found in Matthew 6:9–10 our primary concerns. We should be mainly concerned about hallowing God's name, seeing His kingdom come, and having his will be done. In keeping with what Jesus taught in Matthew 6:33, our main concern should be to "seek *first* the kingdom of God and His righteousness; and all these things shall be added to you." In Colossians 3:1–2 the Bible says we ought to set our minds on things above, not things on earth. Our primary concern in life as well as in prayer should be spiritual matters as outlined by Christ in the first three petitions. But this does not mean that it is wrong for Christians to ask God for physical things.

APPLICATION

1. Asking for our daily bread is really asking God to provide what?

2. Write out Matthew 6:25–26.

Wrong Ideas about Praying for Physical Needs

Indeed, there are some who believe that Christians should not bother God with requests about physical things. They think that Jesus is speaking here purely in spiritual terms. They support this idea with passages like John 6:35, where Jesus said, "I am the bread of life." They interpret this petition as a spiritual allegory, saying that we should be praying for God to minister Jesus to us. "Give me this day my daily bread" means "Give me my portion of Jesus; feed me more of Jesus today. Help me to come to know more of His sufficiency, to depend on Him more, to know Him better." Certainly we should pray in this way, but I do not believe that is what our Lord had in mind when He taught us to pray "Give us this day our daily bread."

There are others who seldom, if ever, pray this prayer because they have a good job; they know that if they work hard and do their job well their daily bread will be supplied. They have skills and job security, so why pray for daily bread? Instead of praying for daily bread, they would say, "Get out there and work for your daily bread. If you do, you will have what you need." Perhaps they think the petition for bread would be a good prayer for the very poor people in the time of Jesus or even for the many poor people in our world today. Certainly, it would be a good prayer for those who are out of work or severely handicapped and therefore cannot work for their daily bread. People with this perspective do not get very excited about praying this prayer because they already know where their daily bread is coming from. Others aren't excited about praying this petition because the government has already committed itself to providing their daily bread, or because they know that their funds in the bank, or their investments, or their affluent parents can adequately provide for them. Their attitude is, "Why pray when the refrigerator is full? There is no real need for us to pray 'Give us our bread.' "

APPLICATION

1. On the basis of what you have read in this chapter thus far, how would you respond to someone who told you, "I don't need to pray for my daily bread. I have a great job that provides all I need."

2. Have there been times in your life when you haven't wanted to bother God about physical needs or times when you didn't think you needed to pray about these things? When? Why?

Why These Ideas Are Unbiblical

In reference to these negative attitudes about praying this petition, I see no evidence in this passage (or elsewhere in Scripture) to think that Jesus meant for us to spiritualize it or to be excused from praying for food because we already have it in the pantry or already have resources to pay for it for the rest of our lives. I think the Lord teaches us to pray for these things, even though we might already have some of them, because God is interested in every aspect of our lives. He is interested not only in the big things—the spiritual aspects—but every aspect of our life. In Matthew 10:29

Jesus said, "Are not two sparrows sold for a cent? And yet not one of them will fall to the ground apart from your Father." God is so interested in this world and what is happening in it, that He knows every single sparrow (of the millions in the world) and knows when any one of them dies. Not only that, but God is the one who ordains that the sparrow should fall. He is interested in the little things as well as the big things—that is the point of Jesus' words in Matthew 10, which He goes on to clarify in verse 30 when He says that "the very hairs of your head are all numbered." God counts the hairs on our head, and He knows when we have one less than the day before. He is so omniscient, all-wise, and concerned that even these details do not escape His attention. Does God have bigger things to do? Of course, but God's concern for our details should be an enormous comfort to us. "Therefore do not fear; you are of more value than many sparrows" (v. 31). We can, and should, pray about the small things in life—the physical things—not just about the big, spiritual things.

APPLICATION

1. Why does God want us to pray for our daily bread?

2. How does God's concern for the little things in life comfort you?

3. What are some of the "small things" in life that you tend to forget to pray about?

Biblical Exhortations and Examples

Scripture is full of exhortations to this kind of prayer. Proverbs 3:6 instructs us to acknowledge God in *all* our ways—every detail of life. Philippians 4:6 says, *"In everything* by prayer and supplication . . . let your requests be made known to God." Colossians 4:2 and Romans 12:12 indicate that we should be *devoted* to prayer, which means we should be consistently and constantly doing it, talking to God about everything. God is never bothered by our requests. Earthly parents may be, earthly spouses may be, but God is always ready to hear us. In Genesis 32:11 Jacob came to God and prayed, "Deliver me, I pray, from the hand of my brother, from the hand of Esau; for I fear him, lest he come and attack me." He was praying for physical protection from his brother. In Numbers 12:13 we find Moses, who the Bible says was one of the two greatest men in the Old Testament, crying out to the Lord: "O God, heal her, I pray!" His sister Miriam had leprosy, so Moses prayed for her physical restoration. Essentially, he was praying for her daily bread. Praying that God would help Miriam physically was another way of saying, "Lord, give us this day our daily bread."

The prayer of a newly crowned Solomon in 1 Kings 3 is an example of another way of praying this petition. In verse 5 God said to him, "Ask what you wish Me to give you." Verses 6–8 continue: "Then Solomon said, "Thou hast shown great lovingkindness to Thy servant David my father, according as he walked before Thee in truth . . . Thou hast given him a son to sit on his throne, as it is this day. And now, O LORD my God, Thou hast made Thy servant king . . . yet I am but a little child; I do not know how to go out or come in. And Thy servant is in the midst of Thy people . . . a great people who cannot be numbered or counted for multitude.' " He began his prayer by praising and thanking God for His goodness to his father and then he made his request in verse 9. "So give Thy servant an understanding heart to judge Thy people to discern between good and evil. For who is able to judge this great people of Thine?" Solomon requested wisdom and the ability to rule over Israel. He, in effect, was praying that the Lord would give him his daily bread.

In Nehemiah 4:7–9 Nehemiah and the Israelites prayed to the Lord about their physical needs, or daily bread. Nehemiah was overseeing the rebuilding of the walls of Jerusalem, but the enemies of Israel were opposing their efforts. "Now it came about when Sanballat, Tobiah, the Arabs, the Ammonites, and the Ashdodites heard that the repair of the walls of Jerusalem went on, and that the breaches began to be closed, they were very angry. And all of them conspired together to come and fight against Jerusalem and to cause a disturbance in it. But we prayed to our God, and because of them we set up a guard against them day and night." Nehemiah and the

Israelites went to prayer and asked the Lord to protect them from their enemies. That is praying "Give us this day our daily bread."

In Acts 12:5 the whole church went to prayer for Peter who was in prison. Just prior to this, James, one of Jesus' disciples, had been imprisoned and then decapitated because of his faith in Jesus Christ. What did the church pray? They undoubtedly asked the Lord to protect and even deliver Peter, as that is exactly what happened. That is an application of what it means to pray "Give us this day our daily bread." Or in 2 Corinthians 12:7–8 Paul wrote about a thorn in the flesh that the Lord had given him and his prayers for it to be removed. Verse 10 gives a description of what this thorn may have been: weaknesses, insults, distresses, persecutions, and difficulties that Paul was facing in his ministry. His prayer for help in the midst of his difficulties was modeled after what Jesus taught His followers to pray. "Give us this day our daily bread." Paul's example teaches that we should pray about all our physical needs.

APPLICATION

1. What examples are found in the Bible that teach us the importance of praying about the "small things"?

2. Write out Philippians 4:6.

The Meaning of "Daily" Bread

The word "daily" in this petition is a second important word that we need to study if we are going to understand the teaching of Jesus on effective prayer. Jesus not only taught us to pray "Give us bread," but He also taught us to pray "Give us this day our *daily* bread." The Greek word translated "daily" is a very unusual word. It is used only two times in the Bible: here and in Luke's version of the Lord's Prayer (Luke 11). Most scholars are agreed that Jesus is teaching us to pray for physical or temporal things that we really *need*. The word "daily" means "that which I need today." In Job 23:12 Job said that he had esteemed God's precepts to be more important than his *necessary* food. By this he acknowledged that there are some things that, as far as our life in this world is concerned, are necessary. Therefore, when Jesus says, "Pray . . . give us this day our daily bread," He is teaching that we should pray for what we really need—that which is absolutely necessary. The prayer of Proverbs 30:8 refers to this concept of "daily": "Keep deception and lies far from me, give me neither poverty nor riches; *feed me with the food that is my portion.*" That is a prayer that says, "Give us this day our *daily* bread."

APPLICATION

1. What important truth is Jesus teaching us by using the word "daily"?

2. Make a list of the things in your life that would fit into the category Jesus is referring to in the word "daily."

What Praying for "Daily Bread" Doesn't Mean

The prayer for daily bread of course does not mean that God will never give us more than we need. Obviously, there are times when God does that very thing. When the prodigal returned to the father, the father gave him much more than he needed. He threw a party, put a ring on his finger, hugged and kissed him, and gave him new sandals. When we return to the Father, God often gives us more than we need as well. God's blessings to Solomon are a good example of this. Earlier, we looked at the passage where God told Solomon to ask for what he wished, and Solomon asked for understanding and wisdom (1 Kings 3:5–9). But in verse 13 God answers his prayer with much more than that. He tells Solomon, "And I have also given you what you have not asked, both riches and honor, so that there will not be any among the kings like you all your days."

God often gives us more than we ask for; praise God that He treats us that way! Back in Genesis 28:20, Jacob asked God for food and clothing, but God gave him much more. Later, in Genesis 32:5, Jacob recounted these added blessings from God, saying, "I have oxen and donkeys and flocks and male and female servants." Also, when Abraham asked God, in Genesis 15, for one child, God said, "Now look toward the heavens, and count the stars, if you are able to count them. . . . So shall your descendants be" (v. 5). God gave to Abraham much more than he asked.

APPLICATION

1. Have there been times and are there instances right now in which God has given you more than you need? Describe in what areas and ways God has done this.

2. What has been and is your response to God when He does this?

3. Why do you think God has done this for you?

4. What should we do when God gives us a surplus?

What Praying for "Daily Bread" Does Mean

At the same time, Jesus taught us in this prayer that we should not ask God for a surplus. If God wants to give a surplus, that is His prerogative, but we should not ask for it. We should ask Him only for what we need lest we manifest a covetous spirit. At this point, then, it is necessary for us to define the word "necessary." Some believers use the word in a very narrow way, thinking that anything that brings pleasure is unnecessary. For example, it is possible, even today, to get along without a car. In fact, we could even get along without a house, or without three or four suits in the closet, or more than one pair of shoes. These people believe it is wrong to have any more than is absolutely necessary, such as a full refrigerator or a well-stocked pantry. This is a very narrow interpretation of the word "daily" or "necessary." Still other believers go to the opposite extreme and interpret it in a very broad way. They say "necessary" refers to anything *they* think to be necessary for them. If they think three Cadillacs are necessary, then they pray for three Cadillacs. If they think thirty suits are necessary, then they pray for thirty suits.

I believe, however, that both of these views are wrong and that neither is what Jesus meant in Matthew 6:11. The first view, which interprets this word narrowly, is wrong because the Bible indicates in John 2 that Jesus went to a wedding feast. There would have been an abundance of food and wine at such a feast, but Jesus never condemned such feasts. He often went to dinner parties (recorded throughout the gospels) and was, in fact, criticized for it. In Mark 2:16–19 we read:

> And when the scribes of the Pharisees saw that He was eating with the sinners and tax-gatherers, they began saying to His disciples, "Why is He eating and drinking with tax-gatherers and sinners?" And hearing this, Jesus said to them, "It is not those who are healthy who need a physician, but those who are sick; I did not come to call the righteous, but sinners." And John's disciples and the Pharisees were fasting; and they came and said to Him, "Why do John's disciples and the disciples of the Pharisees fast, but Your disciples do not fast?" And Jesus said to them, "While the bridegroom is with them, the attendants of the bridegroom do not fast, do they? So long as they have the bridegroom with them, they cannot fast."

Jesus and His disciples were criticized for enjoying some of the good things in life, but He made no apologies.

In Matthew 11:19 He was criticized again: "The Son of Man came eating and drinking, and they say, 'Behold, a gluttonous man and a drunkard, a friend of tax-gatherers and sinners.' " Jesus replied, "Yet wisdom is vindicated by her deeds." Jesus was not a glutton or a drunkard, of course, but He was not against eating good food or having a good time, and He even associated with others who were not godly. But those who thought narrowly about these things believed that anything that was fun, or pleasant, or enjoyable was wrong. In Mark 6:31 Jesus took His disciples on a vacation. He said, "Come away by yourselves to a lonely place and rest a while." In Mark 7:24 he went into the country of Tyre and Sidon and stayed in a house. He could have slept out on the desert ground, but chose the comfort of a house instead.

In 1 Timothy 4:3–4 the apostle Paul spoke out against narrow interpretations of "necessary" things when he condemned those who said that it was unspiritual for believers to enjoy the pleasures of marriage or partake of certain foods. Paul argued, "[These things] God has created to be gratefully shared in by those who believe and know the truth. For everything created by God is good, and nothing is to be rejected, if it is received with gratitude." In 1 Timothy 6:17 Paul said, "God . . . richly supplies us with *all things* to enjoy." Enjoyment and pleasure are not wrong for a Christian, and do not contradict praying that God would give us our necessary food, or "daily bread." Again, if God gives us more than what is absolutely needful, that is His prerogative. We should realize that it is God who has given it, give Him praise and thanks, use it for His honor and glory, and not become so dependent on it that it becomes our source of meaning or direction in life.

So the first view, which interprets the word "daily" in a very restrictive way, is wrong, but the second is wrong as well. It is wrong to say that anything we desire is "necessary" because Jesus taught in Luke 9:23, "If anyone wishes to come after Me, let him deny himself, and take up his cross daily, and follow Me." In 1 Corinthians 9:27 the apostle Paul said, "I buffet my body and make it my slave, lest possibly, after I have preached to others, I myself should be disqualified." He denied himself; he exercised self-control. He was not ruled by his own desires or wants but was ruled by the desires of God. First Timothy 3:3 warns us to not be greedy for money. And in 1 Timothy 6:8 the Bible says that "if we have food and covering, with these we shall be content."

APPLICATION

1. What wrong views about material things do professing Christians sometime have?

2. When God gives us a surplus, what should we be on our guard against?

A Balanced Approach

The Scriptures, therefore, teach a balanced approach. On the one hand, it is not wrong to have pleasure. On the other hand, we must be satisfied with whatever God gives us, even if it is just food and clothing for today. Hebrews 13:5 says that our life is to be free from the love of money and we are to be content with what we have. In Philippians 4:12 Paul said, "I know how to get along with humble means, and I also know how to live in prosperity." In 2 Timothy 2:4, we are warned not to be entangled in the things of this world. Jesus said, in Matthew 6:19–20, "Do not lay up for yourselves treasures upon earth, where moth and rust destroy, and where thieves break in and steal." Rather, He said, "Lay up for yourselves treasures in heaven." He also said in Luke 12:15, "For not even when one has an abundance does his life consist of his possessions." Finally, in Galatians 5:24 the apostle Paul said, "Now those who belong to Christ Jesus have crucified the flesh with its passions and desires." We do not live to fulfill our own desires and passions. When we pray "Give us this day our daily bread," we are saying, "Lord, you know what is needful, and I'm praying that you would give me what is necessary."

APPLICATION

1. If you find yourself becoming discontented with God's provisions for you, how can the truths in this chapter be of help to you?

2. What Scripture verses will you focus on?

Two Things to Keep in Mind

In reference to what constitutes "necessary" bread, two things must be kept in mind. First, ultimately, only God really knows our needs. In 2 Corinthians 12 Paul thought he needed to have the thorn in his flesh removed. He asked the Lord to remove it, but God said no because He knew Paul's needs better than Paul did. Instead, God gave him something that was far better than the removal of the thorn: an abundant portion of His all-sufficient grace. Paul responded with thanks, saying, "Therefore I am well content with weaknesses, with insults, with distresses, with persecutions, with difficulties, for Christ's sake; for when I am weak, then I am strong." We need to remember, when we ask God for something that we believe is necessary, that God alone knows what we truly need.

For example, it is not wrong for single people who would like to be married to ask God for a godly mate. But if God does not give one, they should seek to use their free time and money to serve God in ways that otherwise they could not. If someone has a car that needs to be replaced, it is not wrong for that person to pray, "Lord, You know my problems with this car. I need to get to work, and to church, and to use it in ministry for You. Lord, please give me whatever's necessary to buy a better car." It is not wrong to ask that; but if God says no, our response must be, "Lord, Your grace is sufficient." It is not wrong to pray, "Lord, I would like to have a better job where I get paid more, so I can give more to the church, and not have as much pressure in terms of paying my bills." It is wrong, however, to get upset if God does not grant it because God promises to give us what we need, knowing far better than we do what that is.

Secondly, to properly understand what Jesus meant by "necessary" bread, we must recognize that necessary bread for one person may not be necessary bread for another. This is true because of our created differences. Some of us are weaker, physically, than others and have needs in the physical realm that stronger people do not. Husbands need to understand that in reference to their wives. I have had counseling situations where the husband cannot understand why his wife needs more sleep than he does. They are different and have different sleep needs. Some people have a faster metabolism than others and need more food. Some people need more encouragement or affirmation than others do.

Necessary bread may vary also because of our differences in occupation or other responsibilities. The physical needs of a person who leads are different from a person who does not. For example, those of us in ministry need books in a way that others may not. Books are expensive; therefore, asking, "Lord, give me the money to buy books," may be necessary. Those who have the gift of hospitality, who are using their home to entertain others, may have different needs than someone else who does not entertain often. Someone with an office job needs different things from what my father needed as a farmer. The needs of a person who has no children are different from the needs of parents, and the needs of parents are different from those without children. The needs of a single man will be different from the needs of a married man. God made each of us different, and we must recognize those differences when we pray for ourselves and for others, "Give us this day our *necessary* bread."

APPLICATION

1. What two things described in this section should we keep in mind about the matter of "daily bread"?

2. This section gives some illustrations of the two thoughts to be kept in mind. Can you give other illustrations?

3. How can keeping these two things in mind help us in our daily lives and prayers?

The Dangers of Covetousness

Jesus was including all of this when He taught us to pray for our daily, or necessary, food. Thus far we have looked at two words in this model prayer: "bread" and "daily." This wonderful pattern, or outline, says so much with so little. But there is one more thing that we need to learn from the words "daily bread," and that is what Jesus is teaching us about avoiding covetousness. This petition condemns covetousness; it condemns the man who has as his goal the accumulation of things. There are many warnings about this in God's Word because we are so prone to fall into the temptation of thinking that life consists in the abundance of things that we possess. In 1 Timothy 6:6–11 Paul warned against this tremendous danger:

> But godliness actually is a means of great gain, when accompanied by contentment. For we have brought nothing into the world, so we cannot take anything out of it either. And if we have food and covering, *with these we shall be content.* But those who want

to get rich fall into temptation and a snare and many foolish and harmful desires which plunge men into ruin and destruction. For the love of money is a root of all sorts of evil, and some by longing for it have wandered away from the faith, and pierced themselves with many a pang. *But flee from these things, you man of God; and pursue righteousness, godliness, faith, love, perseverance and gentleness.*

Again, in verses 17–18, Paul wrote, "Instruct those who are rich in this present world not to be conceited." It is so easy for us to be puffed up and to fix our hope on the uncertainty of riches rather than on God who richly supplies us with all things to enjoy. Instead, Paul continued, "Instruct them to do good, to be rich in good works, to be generous and ready to share."

APPLICATION

1. What is God forbidding in these verses?
2. In what areas are you tempted to be covetous?

No better conclusion and challenge could be given to us as we consider and apply the concepts presented in this chapter than the words of Thomas Watson.

> God, who gives us our allowance, knows what quantity of outward things is fittest for us. A smaller provision may be fitter for some; bread may be better than dainties. Everyone cannot bear a high condition. . . . Has anyone a larger proportion of worldly things? God sees he can better manage such a condition; he can order his affairs with discretion, which perhaps another cannot. As he has a large estate, so he has a large heart to do good which perhaps another has not. This should make us content with a shorter bill of fare. God's wisdom is what we must acquiesce in; he sees what is best for everyone. That which is good for one may be bad for another.
>
> If you have but daily bread enough to suffice nature, be content. Consider it is not having abundance that always makes life comfortable; it is not a great cage that will make the bird

sing. . . . A staff may help the traveler, but a bundle of staves will be a burden to him. A great estate may be like a long trailing garment, more burdensome than useful. Many that have great incomes and revenues have not so much comfort in their lives as some that go to hard labor.[1]

Praying as Jesus taught means that we will be praying for our necessary food. Let us, therefore, remember the prayer of King Agur in Proverbs 30:8 and pray in similar fashion, "Give me neither poverty nor riches; *feed me with the food that is my portion.*" We should be content with whatever God gives to us. If God gives much—whether wisdom, education, money, possessions—He has given it to be used for His honor and glory. If God gives little, He knows best what our needs truly are. Jesus taught us to pray for our *bread*—all our physical needs—and our *daily* (necessary) bread— that which God knows we really need.

Again, I remind you that to pray effectively means that we will pray as Jesus taught us to pray; this is the kind of prayer that pleases God; this is the kind of prayer that God loves to answer. How could it be otherwise since it was Jesus Christ, the Son of God, in whom are hid all the treasures of wisdom and knowledge (Col. 2:3), who taught us to pray this way?

APPLICATION

1. Summarize in your own words the most important truths presented in this chapter.

2. Write out and work on memorizing one or two verses found in this chapter.

3. In what ways were you encouraged, challenged or convicted by the material in this chapter? In keeping with the material presented in this chapter, how should your prayer life be changed?

PRAYING FOR THIS DAY

In chapter 3 of this book, we mentioned that Augustine, Martin Luther, and many other saints have said that there is nothing more wonderful in the entire Bible than the Lord's Prayer. By this time, as we've studied the words of this prayer, I think you will agree with me that the way in which Jesus summarized everything about prayer and reduced it all to a few sentences and words is remarkable. Never was so much meaning packed into so few words. Every word and sentence in the prayer is like a diamond whose every facet must be looked at carefully and individually in order to fully grasp its beauty and richness.

In the last chapter we began to study the petition "Give us this day our daily bread" (Matt. 6:11). We carefully examined the meaning of two words: "bread" and "daily." However, there is so much more for us to learn about effective prayer from the other words in this little petition that we will devote two more chapters to examine it.

The Meaning of "This Day"

In this petition Jesus taught us to ask God for bread for "this day." Why didn't Jesus teach us to ask God for enough bread to last the rest of our lives? Why didn't He encourage us to be like the prodigal son who wanted all of his inheritance at once (Luke

15:12)? Why did He want us to be like Jehoiachin, who received from the king of Babylon a regular portion, "a portion for each day, all the days of his life" (2 Kings 25:30)? Why did He want us to be like the Israelites, to whom God gave enough manna for each day? Why didn't He give them enough for a week, a month, or even for the rest of their lives?

God, being the wise and loving Father He is, wants us to come to Him asking for necessary provisions for *this day* for some very good reasons.[1] For one thing, God knows that if He gave us everything we needed for a lifetime at once, many of us would probably behave like the prodigal son. Scripture says that when he received his entire inheritance, he "gathered everything together and went on a journey into a distant country, and there he squandered his estate"(Luke 15:13). Unfortunately, when many people come into an inheritance or get a sizable increase in salary, they see it as an opportunity to increase their standard of living. They see it as an opportunity to purchase new things and to take longer vacations instead of seeing it as an opportunity to invest in God's work.

All too often, the abundance of physical privileges becomes a detriment to people's spiritual lives. Their increased resources become a snare for them, they give in to "many foolish and harmful desires," they yield to temptation and become more conformed to this world, and they become conceited (1 Tim. 6:9–10, 17; Rom. 12:2). Failing to recognize that they are stewards, they begin to think and act like owners—proprietors of what they have. These are not guaranteed outcomes, of course, but all too often these things happen. The words "this day" remind us to think of ourselves as stewards of whatever we have.

APPLICATION

1. What is the difference between being a steward and a proprietor?

2. How would the attitude of a steward differ from that of a proprietor?

3. How do you respond when God gives you a surplus?

4. What can help you to avoid making a mistake when this happens?

Promotion of Dependence

Praying for *this day's* bread teaches us the importance of depending every day on the Lord. It emphasizes the importance of walking by faith and not by sight (2 Cor. 5:7). God knows that we have a tremendous tendency to think that we don't need to depend on Him when we seemingly have everything wrapped up for the rest of our lives—when we are financially secure by the world's standards. Thomas Watson said that in this petition our Savior wanted us to pray this way so that we would remember that all "the good things of life are the gifts of God; He is the donor of all our blessings. 'Give us.' Not faith only, but food is the gift of God; not daily grace only is from God, but daily bread; every good thing comes from God. . . . All comes from God; He makes the corn to grow, and the herbs to flourish."[2]

God wants us to walk by faith. That's the way He worked with Hudson Taylor, the founder of China Inland Mission. Taylor started such a tremendous movement for God in China that hundreds of missionaries went there and thousands of Chinese people were converted. How did he support all of those people? He did it by faith. Hudson Taylor was one of those people who did not believe in asking people for money. I am not saying that this is the only way to live, but it was the way Taylor lived. He believed in praying "Give us *this day* our daily bread." He never got an enormous amount at once, but the money was always sufficient for the needs.

The same was true of George Mueller, who started an orphanage in Bristol, England. Thousands of orphans were cared for in that orphanage, but Mueller started many days not knowing how they were going to eat. There are some remarkable stories of how God provided for them. One morning, they began the day with no food and no money. Just in time for breakfast, there was a knock at the door and a milkman said, "My milk wagon broke down out here, and the milk is going to spoil. Could you use this milk?" So the Lord supplied their needs that day. Though never a great amount at once, He continued to supply their needs on a regular basis. That's the way God usually does it so that He can teach us to walk by faith and depend on Him.

APPLICATION

1. How does this petition illustrate what it means to "walk by faith"?

2. Write out 2 Corinthians 5:7.

3. How do the lives and ministries of George Mueller and Hudson Taylor illustrate walking by faith?

4. How does your life illustrate that you are or aren't walking by faith?

Promotion of Humility

Praying "give us *this day* our daily bread" is a means of making us humble. In 1 Timothy 6:17 Paul warned that those who are rich have a tendency to be conceited. They have a tendency to be arrogant, to think that they are in a class by themselves, and to think that they ought to be treated in a way that other people shouldn't be treated.

There was a time when a very wealthy man was supporting our ministry in a particular area. Before we came to work there, we talked very carefully about how we thought that the ministry should function, with a board of directors providing guidance and direction. At that time this wealthy man said, "That's fine with me. I don't want any special position or authority. I'll support the ministry, but the money I give really isn't my money. It's the Lord's money. I only want what God wants." So we formed a board in which all members were to be equal. Sadly, it soon became apparent that this man wanted to be just a little more equal because, after all, he was the one actually underwriting the entire expense of the ministry. In reality, because of his money, he treated people as though they were his servants rather than as his equals.

For this reason, the Lord often gives us bread for *this day* and continues to do it that way because He wants to keep us humble. He knows that there are dangers in getting things too easily and too abundantly. This is certainly the warning of Deuteronomy 8. In this chapter God was about to bring His people out of the wilderness and into the promised land, and He told them what the land would be like, "a land of wheat and barley, of vines and fig trees and pomegranates, a land of olive and honey; a land where you shall eat food without scarcity, in which you shall not lack anything; a land whose stones are iron, and out of whose hills you can dig copper. When you have eaten and are satisfied, you shall bless the LORD your God for the good land which He has given you" (vv. 8–10). In that last sentence, God warned His people not to forget that He had given them all these good things. He then exhorted them, "Beware lest you forget the LORD your God . . . lest, when you have eaten and are satisfied, and have built good houses and lived in them, and when your herds and your flocks multiply, and your silver and gold multiply, and all that you have multiplies, then your heart becomes proud, and you forget the LORD your God who brought you out from the land of Egypt, out of the house of slavery. . . . Otherwise, you may say in your heart, 'My power and the strength of my hand made me this wealth' " (vv. 11–14, 17). God knows that the propensity of people when "the good times roll" is to become proud and to trust in themselves rather than in God. So He carefully instructed His people about what they should and shouldn't do in their time of abundance.

In similar fashion, the apostle Paul indicated that when people have an abundance, there is a temptation for them to become conceited and dependent on their resources rather than on the Lord (1 Tim. 6:17). They are tempted to think that they have acquired what they have by their own might and power and forget that "it is the blessing of the LORD that makes rich" (Prov. 10:22). They take credit for what they have rather than giving the glory to God. Our Savior knows this propensity and teaches us to pray for *this day's* bread so that, through our praying, we would be reminded on a daily basis of our dependency on God. We have no reason to boast because there is nothing that we have not received from God (1 Cor. 4:7).

In his characteristic way, Thomas Watson warned about the danger that often attends prosperity:

> Pride, idleness, wantonness are three worms that usually breed of plenty. Prosperity often deafens the ear against God. . . . Soft pleasures often harden the heart. In the body, the more fat, the less blood in the veins, and the less spirits; so the more outward plenty, often the less piety. Prosperity has its honey, and also its sting. . . . The pastures of prosperity are rank and surfeiting. Anxious care is . . . the evil spirit that haunts the rich man, and will not let him be quiet. When his chests are full of money, his heart is full of care, either how to manage or how to increase, or how to secure what he has gotten. Sunshine is pleasant, but sometimes it scorches. . . . The spreading of a full table may be the spreading of a snare. . . . The world's golden sands are quicksands, which should make us take our daily bread, though it be but coarse, contentedly.[3]

Another comment by Watson is very appropriate as we consider the benefit of a proper understanding and use of this petition. Watson stated that this petition should cause us to

> see our own poverty and indigence. We all live upon alms and upon free gifts—"Give us this day." All we have is from the hand of God's royal bounty; we have nothing but what He gives us out of His storehouse; we cannot have one bit of bread but from God. The devil persuaded our first parents, that by disobeying God, they should "be as gods;" but we may now see what goodly gods we are, that we have not a bit of bread to put in our mouths unless God give it to us (Gen. 3:5). This is a humbling consideration.[4]

APPLICATION

1. What is one of the character qualities that God is trying to form in us by teaching us to pray for this day's bread?

2. Summarize the warning of Deuteronomy 8:10–17.

A Means of Confession

Praying this petition is a way of confessing to God and others that we're not serving Him for material reasons. That was the charge against Job that Satan brought to God. According to Job 1, there was a time when Satan approached God and asked, "Is there anybody who is really serving you?" (I have paraphrased this event, which is recorded in Job 1:6–12.) God answered, "Yes, just look at my servant Job." Satan replied, "Of course Job is serving you. He doesn't fear you for nothing. Look at all you've given to him: all his herds and his lands and all of his employees, the servants and slaves. He's serving you because of what he's getting out of it. Just take that away from him and you'll see whether or not he fears you and serves you."

What Satan said about Job's motives for serving God wasn't true, but unfortunately, it is true of some people. William Carey experienced this problem as a missionary in India. He went to India to proclaim the gospel and make disciples for Christ. In order to do that, he had to translate the Scriptures into the Indian dialects. After learning the various languages, he made plans to print the Scriptures so that the Indians could read and study the Scriptures for themselves. He purchased printing presses and set up a scriptorium (a building for printing Bibles). In addition to the machines and the building, however, Carey needed workers to run the presses. So he began to hire some national workers.

The India to which William Carey had come was very poor, and the possibility of making money by working for Carey was very appealing to the people. In fact, it was so appealing that some of them made professions of faith just to be hired. Carey faced the danger of producing what are called "rice Christians," people who profess faith in Christ because they expect to be rewarded materially for it. Missionaries often face this problem when ministering to poverty-stricken people. People make professions of faith for the wrong reasons, not because they have been convicted of their sins and want God's forgiveness, but because they think it will be to their economic advantage to claim Christ.

The Prosperity Gospel and This Petition

This tendency to think that becoming a Christian will elimi-
nate the need to pray "Give us *this day* our daily bread" is prevalent
in some "Christian" circles today. It comes to us in the form of what
has been called the "Prosperity Gospel." People are being told to
trust Jesus, give generously to a certain organization (this giving is
sometimes called "seed faith"), claim what they want, and God will
open the windows of heaven and pour out material and physical
blessings on them. This kind of teaching can be heard in many
churches today and almost every day of the week on radio and television programs.

Sometimes this Prosperity Gospel comes in very obvious forms,
but sometimes it comes in more subtle forms. I've heard a subtle
form of this gospel at some Christian men's organization luncheons. Often at these events, the men have invited non-Christian
friends to hear the guest speaker give his testimony in the hopes
that they will hear the Word and be saved. The speaker is usually a
businessman who is very successful financially. The testimonies
have a common theme: after becoming Christian, the business took
off. The impression given is that faith in Christ not only guaran-
tees heaven later, but it means all kinds of material blessings right
now.

While the motives behind these luncheons may be admirable,
the message is suspect. And though I'm sure that not all Christian
men's luncheons are like this, I honestly cannot remember ever
hearing a speaker get up and say, "I became a Christian and I went
bankrupt." The impression given by the speakers that I have heard
is that becoming a Christian means that the need to pray for *this
day's* bread is all but taken care of.

Promotion of Contentment

By teaching us to pray for bread on a daily basis, Jesus is encouraging us to be content with whatever we have, even if it comes in
small amounts. In a sense, our prayer becomes a testimony to God
and others that we are serving Him because He is worthy of being
served, not because we expect God to give to us an abundance of

things. Asking for *this day's* bread becomes a testimony to the fact that we are not serving Him for material gain and that we are content to have God mete out our provisions in small increments as He sees fit. Thomas Watson explained why believers should be content with *this day's* bread:

> The pearl of price, the Lord Jesus, He is the quintessence of all good things. To give us Christ is more than if God had given us the entire world. He can make more worlds, but He has no more Christs to bestow; He is such a golden mine, that the angels cannot dig to the bottom. . . . The sea of God's mercy in giving us Christ, says Luther, should swallow up all our wants. . . . If God has adorned the inner man of the heart with these sacred jewels, it may well make us content, though we have but short commons [i.e., only enough physical bread for today], and that coarse too [i.e., not very tasty].
>
> You that have but a small competence [i.e., limited resources in outward things] may be content to consider how much you look for hereafter. . . . A son is content though his father gives him but now and then a little money. The world is but a . . . great inn. If God gives you sufficient to pay for your charges in the inn, you may be content.[5]

APPLICATION

1. In what ways is praying this petition a confession?

2. In what ways does praying this prayer promote humility?

3. What is the Prosperity Gospel?

4. How does this petition demonstrate the error of this gospel?

5. Give other reasons why the Prosperity Gospel is unbiblical.

6. Have you ever fallen into the error of the Prosperity Gospel? Describe how we may subtly do this. How can we know if we have fallen into this error?

7. How can praying this petition help us to deal with discontentment?

Promotion of Gratitude

Praying some form of this petition on a daily basis is also beneficial in that it helps us to develop and sustain an attitude of gratitude. Scripture makes it clear that God wants us to be constantly thankful—not just now and then, but constantly. He wants gratitude to be our way of life. First Thessalonians 5:18 says, "In *everything* give thanks." If we are giving thanks in everything, then we are giving thanks all the time. Ephesians 5:20 says, *"Always giving thanks for all things* in the name of our Lord Jesus Christ." When we pray "Give us *this day* our daily bread" and the bread comes, we are being regularly reminded of its Source, and that recognition promotes gratitude.

Promotion of Sympathy

Praying this petition on a daily basis will also help us to be sympathetic with those who lack the provisions we have. There are many people in the world today who are desperately poor. Some of us may think we are poor, but there are people in this world whose poverty is far greater. I have seen the cardboard and scrap-metal huts of shanty-towns in South Africa. I have seen flies crawling in the eyes of children in Egypt, and I have heard those children begging for money. I can still see them holding up their small hands and crying out, "Baksheesh, baksheesh, baksheesh."

We Americans say, "Why are you asking me for money? I'm not wealthy." But these children think that everyone in America is wealthy, and in comparison to them, they are generally right. Because of our relative wealth, we have a tendency to be unsympathetic to people who are really poor. By traveling abroad, we can be reminded of two important things: one, how greatly blessed we are in the United States; and two, how great our sympathy should be to those who have so much less. Learning to pray for *this day's* bread is a helpful stimulant to remembering these things as well.

One summer our grandchildren went on a mission trip to the mountains of West Virginia. Because their father is a lawyer and makes a good salary, our grandchildren live very comfortably. This mission trip to a poor area of West Virginia was a blessing to them.

They were involved in spiritual ministry through a Vacation Bible School and personal contacts with people in the area. They were also challenged to be more grateful for what they had and more compassionate toward those with much less. It's one thing to hear about people who live in poverty, but it's quite another to meet and interact with them. Hopefully, the lessons of this trip will have a lasting impact on their spiritual lives. Regularly praying "Give us *this day* our daily bread" can have the same effect on us, reminding us of the fact that there are many that really live a day-to-day existence.

A Reminder

Praying daily for *this day's* bread is a benefit also in that it reminds us that God desires our constant fellowship. Proverbs 15:8b says, "The prayer of the upright is His delight." God loves to have us pray to Him. In Revelation 3:20 Jesus said, "Behold, I stand at the door and knock; if anyone hears My voice and opens the door, I will come in to him." Jesus delights to fellowship with us, and when we have a sense of need, we are more prone to desire that fellowship with Him. First John 1:3 says, "And indeed our fellowship is with the Father, and with His Son Jesus Christ." God sometimes doesn't give us everything at once because our need often drives us to think more about God and thus helps us to maintain our fellowship with Him.

APPLICATION

1. What connection is there between praying this prayer and developing an attitude of gratitude?

2. How does praying this petition help us to be sympathetic with others who lack the physical provisions we have.

3. Write out Ephesians 5:20.

A Word of Caution

At this point a word of caution is due lest we misunderstand and misapply the concept being taught by the words "this day." Saying that we ought to pray that God would give us *this day* our daily bread does not mean that it is wrong to make provisions for the future. Some people think that we should not at all be concerned about our financial future, and if we are, it reveals a lack of faith. They are opposed to Christians making investments, or being interested in a pension or retirement plan, or taking out life insurance. "Just focus on today and let God take care of tomorrow" is their attitude. They believe that seeking to provide for the future is violating this petition for *this day's* needs. They would suggest that it is also a violation of Matthew 6:25–34, where Jesus said that we should not worry about tomorrow, but rather focus on today.

I am convinced that this view is a misunderstanding and misapplication of both passages cited above. To rightly interpret Scripture, we must take into account everything the Bible has to say about a particular subject. We must compare Scripture with Scripture and let the Bible interpret itself. When studying a particular issue, we dare not simply look at isolated passages while ignoring others. On this and other issues, the Bible presents a balanced perspective. In Proverbs 6:6–8 the Bible says, "Go to the ant, O sluggard, observe her ways and be wise, which, having no chief, officer or ruler, prepares her food in the summer, and gathers her provision in the harvest." In other words, "Learn from the ants. They prepare for the future and so should you." There is nothing wrong with preparing for the future when it is kept in moderation.

Proverbs 19:14 says, "House and wealth are an inheritance from fathers." This verse indicates that it is appropriate and right for parents to leave an inheritance to their children. In reference to inheritances, Proverbs 20:21 states, "An inheritance gained hurriedly at the beginning, will not be blessed in the end." To think that in this verse God is condemning the giving of an inheritance, or even the wanting of an inheritance, is to misunderstand the point that is being made. This verse is condemning the wrong kind of giving an inheritance and the wrong way of attaining that inheritance. It is forbidding being in a hurry to get an inheritance, like the prodigal son who wouldn't wait until his father had died. He wanted what he wanted, and he wanted it right then. There are many ways in which people might attempt to get an inheritance hurriedly, but God says that they are all wrong and will not be blessed.

"A good man leaves an inheritance to his children's children" (Prov. 13:22). It's clear from Scripture that there is nothing wrong with saving for the future, unless that becomes the focus of our lives and we become overly concerned with the future to the point that we are worrying about it. Some people are so worried about the future that they hardly give anything to the church or to the needy right now. They reason, "I have to save everything I can because who knows what might happen," or "I need to prepare for retirement."

That kind of preparing for the future is wrong because it violates many biblical commands about giving. It also reveals a very selfish approach to life, an inordinate concern about the future, and a failure to trust God for daily bread. Further, the hoarding of resources shows a misplaced confidence in material things. Proverbs 10:15 warns against thinking that having great material resources will protect us from problems: "The rich man's wealth is his fortress." God says that it is wrong for us to think that our security is in our wealth.

First Timothy 6:17 also warns against trusting in riches, and it does so for two reasons. One, riches don't satisfy apart from God's blessing (Prov. 10:22), and two, they fly away and they can be lost (Prov. 23:5). We need to realize that God wants us to live one day at a time. Praying every day "Give us *this day* our daily bread" with knowledge of the truth that is found in these words, will surely help us to live in a way that is pleasing to God.

APPLICATION

1. How do you know that it is not wrong to prepare for the future in a material way?

2. What wrong attitudes and practices must we avoid in our preparations for the future?

3. Can you honestly say that you have a Matthew 6:11 attitude about physical provisions for today? For the future?

4. Write out 1 Timothy 6:17.

The Meaning of "Our" Bread

Bread That Really Isn't "Our Bread"

The next word we come to in our study of the fourth petition is the word "our." What is Jesus teaching us to pray for when He says we should pray "Give us this day *our* daily bread"? The only kind of bread that we can rightly call "our" bread is bread that is acquired in the way God wants us to acquire it. First, we cannot claim physical provisions to be "our" bread if we are lazy. Proverbs 31:27 talks about the godly woman who "does not eat the bread of idleness." We cannot call bread that we receive while doing nothing "our" bread. Proverbs 21:25 says, "The desire of the sluggard [the lazy person] puts him to death, for his hands refuse to work." If we are able to work and do not, depending on someone else to provide for us, our provisions are not rightly ours. God does not usually provide for us in that way. Proverbs 20:4 warns, "The sluggard does not plow after the autumn, so he begs during the harvest and has nothing." If we pray "Give us this day *our* daily bread," we cannot expect others to provide for us while we do nothing.

Second Thessalonians 3:10–12 instructs us to earn "our" bread through honest labor. Verse 10 says, "If anyone will not work, neither let him eat." God's usual way of providing for our needs is through our work. In Exodus 20:9 we are commanded, "Six days you shall labor," but this is not just a command about the Sabbath. Yes, we ought to emphasize the importance of setting aside a day that is devoted to the Lord. However, we must not fail to realize that God also says in this command that *we are to labor*. We sin against God if we do not labor, just as we sin against God if we do not honor His day of rest. Ephesians 4:28 says that we are to "labor, performing with [our] own hands what is good." In Genesis 3:19 God told Adam that He would supply his needs by the sweat of his brow. We cannot expect God to provide what we are not willing to work for. When we work, God will provide the strength and the opportunity and will bless our efforts with "our" daily bread.

Another kind of bread that cannot be called "our" bread is described in Proverbs 9:17. The Bible says, "Stolen water is sweet;

and bread eaten in secret is pleasant." Stolen bread is not "our" bread. That includes stealing in any form: getting a paycheck without fulfilling our responsibilities, providing services or materials that are less than we contracted for, defrauding the government of social security or welfare funds, or actually taking money that does not belong to us. Similarly, we cannot claim as "our" bread that which is obtained through lies, or violence, or abuse of others, or other wickedness. Proverbs 20:17 says, "Bread obtained by falsehood is sweet to a man, but afterward his mouth will be filled with gravel." This is not "our" bread.

Nehemiah 5:1–7 gives a description of bread obtained by wickedness. At that time the leaders of the Israelites were taking advantage of the people by exacting usury from them (charging exorbitant interest). Nehemiah said, "Then I was very angry when I had heard their outcry and these words. And I consulted with myself and contended with the nobles and the rulers and said to them, 'You are exacting usury, each from his brother!' Therefore, I held a great assembly against them" (5:6–7). The leaders of the people were getting bread, but they were getting it by taking advantage of others. We cannot claim anything as "our" bread that we have received by cheating or deceiving others, being unjust to others, or oppressing others.

Malachi 3:8–9 describes another kind of bread that cannot be called "our" bread. It says, "Will a man rob God? Yet you are robbing Me! But you say, 'How have we robbed Thee?' In tithes and offerings. You are cursed with a curse, for you are robbing Me, the whole nation of you!" There are people who withhold from God that which they owe to Him. They do not give generously or sacrificially to God, and they make excuses about their own needs. God says that the withholding of tithes and offerings is robbery. Indeed, Proverbs 3:9 instructs us, "Honor the LORD from your wealth, and from the first of all your produce." We are commanded to honor God by giving to Him out of what He has given to us.

And then also, we cannot call "our" bread that which we get by withholding from others what the Bible says we should be giving to them. We are responsible not only to give to God, but also to people in need. In Proverbs 3:27–28 the Bible says, "Do not with-

hold good from those to whom it is due, when it is in your power
to do it. Do not say to your neighbor, 'Go, and come back, and
tomorrow I will give it,' when you have it with you." If our neighbor has a need and we can supply that need, but we do not, the
Bible says that we are sinning against God. Ephesians 4:28 says we
are to "labor . . . in order that [we] *may have something to share with
him who has need.*" We are to work not just to supply our own needs,
but to help meet the needs of others as well. Galatians 6:10 says,
"So then, while we have opportunity, let us do good to all men, and
especially to those who are of the household of the faith."

First John 3:18 echoes this command, "Let us not love with
word or with tongue, but in deed and truth." The previous verse
defines what it means to love in "deed and truth": "But whoever
has the world's goods, and beholds his brother in need and closes
his heart against him, how does the love of God abide in him?" In
other words, we may talk about the love of God, we may talk about
loving our neighbor, but if we do not give to our brother in need,
we are sinning and we cannot call what we are keeping "our" bread.
In 1 Timothy 6:17a the Bible says, "Instruct those who are rich in
this present world not to be conceited." That is a grave danger for
the rich; they begin to think that they are better than others are
and deserve more than others do. Thankfully, not all who are physically blessed succumb to this sin. This is a stern warning to us, however, against fixing our hope on the uncertainty of riches. In verse
18 Paul continues, "Instruct them to *do good,* to *be rich in good works,*
to *be generous and ready to share.*" If God has blessed us with material
wealth, he has blessed us in order that we might give to others.

Leviticus 19 is a wonderful passage teaching what it means to
love other people. I call it the 1 Corinthians 13 of the Old Testament. Verse 18 gives this command, "You shall love your neighbor
as yourself." Previously in this passage, some specific instructions
are given about how to live that out. In fact, there are numerous
examples of "loving your neighbor as yourself" in verses 9–18. The
first is found in verses 9–10, which says that when you reap the harvest of your land, you shall "not reap to the very corners of your
field, neither shall you gather the gleanings of your harvest. Nor
shall you glean your vineyard, nor shall you gather the fallen fruit

of your vineyard." The Lord explains why, "You shall leave them for the needy and for the stranger." Loving our neighbors as we love ourselves means doing for them what we would want done for us.

Further, "You shall not steal, nor deal falsely, nor lie to one another. And you shall not swear falsely by My name" (Lev. 19:11–12) if we love our neighbor as we love ourselves. "You shall not oppress your neighbor, nor rob him. The wages of a hired man are not to remain with you all night until morning" (v. 13). We are commanded not to "curse a deaf man, nor place a stumbling block before the blind" (19:14). We are to be concerned about others and their individual needs. "You shall do no injustice in judgment; you shall not be partial to the poor nor defer to the great, but you are to judge your neighbor fairly. You shall not go about as a slanderer among your people, and you are not to act against the life of your neighbor; I am the LORD. You shall not hate your fellow countryman in your heart; you may surely reprove your neighbor" (vv. 15–17). If we love our neighbor as we love ourselves, we must be willing out of our genuine love and concern to rebuke our neighbor who is in sin. Whatever sin he is doing is destroying him, hindering his relationship with God, and may even be causing others to sin. "You shall not take vengeance, nor bear any grudge against the sons of your people, *but you shall love your neighbor as yourself.*" Therefore, if we have bread that should be given to other people and withhold it, we cannot rightly call that "our" bread, and it is not part of that for which Jesus was teaching us to pray.

APPLICATION

1. What are the kinds of bread mentioned in this section that cannot be rightly called "our bread"?

2. As you look over this list, are there any ways in which you have tried to attain your bread that are contrary to God's will? Describe them.

Bread That Is "Our" Bread

We have studied what "our" bread is not. What, then, are we asking for when we pray "Give us this day *our* daily bread"? We are praying for bread that is right for *us,* individually, in contrast to what is right for someone else. If God gives us something that He does not give to someone else, then He gives it to us so that we might use it for Him and use it for others. If God does not give to others what He has given to us, He may have done this in order for us to learn how to share, or so that we recognize that "our" bread comes from Him. For example, in 1 Samuel 8 the Israelites asked God for a king in order that they would be like the surrounding nations. God had not given them a king because it was not His best for them, but the people demanded bread that was not theirs. Or sometimes we want what someone else has just because we are selfish. In Genesis 30:1 Rachel wanted a child because she was jealous of her sister who had a child, but that was not God's best for her at that time.

In Psalm 106:13–15 the psalmist recalled the time in the wilderness when the children of Israel continually harassed God in reference to their food. God poured numerous blessings on them, but "they quickly forgot His works; they did not wait for His counsel, but craved intensely in the wilderness, and tempted God in the desert." He gave them their request, but He sent a wasting disease among them as punishment for their discontent with His provisions for them at that time.

In 1 Samuel 2:7 the Bible says that it is God who makes some to be poor and others to be rich. Two people can work equally hard, but receive different provisions from the Lord for their labor. He brings some people low and He exalts others (Ps. 75:7). When we pray to God for "our" bread, we are asking for God's will in terms of bread for ourselves, not anyone else.

This is the mistake Peter made when the Lord told Peter what was going to happen to him in the future. Wondering what would happen to the apostle John, Peter asked Jesus, " 'Lord, and what about this man?' Jesus said to him, '. . . what is that to you?' " (John 21:21–22). Peter needed to know only about Peter. In 2 Corinthians 10:12–13 Paul talked about the danger of comparing ourselves with others. So often we struggle with that. God has been very good to my family and me, but I have some friends and even relatives whom God has blessed much more in the material realm. I must not compare myself to them, thinking about how—by God's grace—I may have worked just as hard or been just as smart, how I may have more education or be more organized. What they have received from God is their bread; what I have received is mine.

First Corinthians 4:7 asks, "For who regards you as superior? And what do you have that you did not receive? But if you did receive it, why do you boast as if you had not received it?" In summary, "our" bread means bread that has been acquired in the God-ordained way of our own faithful and diligent work. We have been responsible and honest in acquiring it, not withholding bread that belongs to God or to others. It is the bread that God has ordained as particularly suitable to us, and is not tainted by envy or discontent.

At the beginning of this chapter, I mentioned that Augustine, Martin Luther, and many other saints have said that there is nothing more wonderful in the entire Bible than the Lord's Prayer. I also said that what Jesus has done in this prayer is remarkable, packing so much meaning into so few words. I also indicated that every word or phrase of this prayer is like a diamond with many facets; it needs to be carefully examined so that we can learn how to pray more effectively.

"Give us this day our daily bread." This is a petition with seven simple yet profound words, words that are rich with meaning for our prayer lives. Will we allow ourselves to be challenged, enlightened, and motivated by the profound spiritual concepts found in them? Having carefully studied the meaning of these words, let us dedicate ourselves to be more diligent in praying and living in the manner described by Jesus, the Master Prayer Teacher, in these words.

Again I remind you that to pray effectively means that we will pray as Jesus taught us to pray; this is the kind of prayer that pleases God; this is the kind of prayer that God loves to answer. How could it be otherwise since it was Jesus Christ, the Son of God, who taught us to pray this way?

APPLICATION

1. Summarize in your own words what can rightly be called "our" bread.

2. Write out and work on memorizing one or two verses found in this chapter.

3. In what ways were you encouraged, challenged, or convicted by the material in this chapter? In keeping with the material presented in this chapter, how should your prayer life be changed?

PRAYING DEPENDENTLY AND THANKFULLY

aving carefully examined the words "Give us *this day our daily bread,*" we come now to the other two words in this fourth main petition of the Lord's Prayer. The first of these two important words is "give." Jesus said to pray, *"Give* us this day our daily bread." First Timothy 6:17 reminds us that it is "God, who richly supplies us with all things to enjoy." Why does one person prosper and another struggle? We may answer that it is due to their diligence at work, or their intelligence. That is sometimes true, but not always. There are some people who work much harder than others and yet seem less blessed in the physical realm. Why? Because God has chosen not to bless them physically as much as He has others. God determines His blessings to each of us. There are tremendous implications to that truth, and we will study those implications a little later in this chapter.

Every Good Thing Comes from Our Father

James 1:17 says, "Every good thing bestowed and every perfect gift is from above, coming down from the Father of lights, with whom there is no variation, or shifting shadow." Do we look on our possessions in that way—really? Sometimes we glibly say, "God has given me this home," or "God has given me this car." We can say these things easily, but we do not often live as if we believe them. If we do, it will affect the way we care for and use what we have.

It will also affect our attitudes. Jesus commanded, in Matthew 5:44, "Love your enemies." After He gave that command, He made a tremendous statement about what that looks like in reality. The verse (NKJV) goes on to give us three specific ways in which our love for other people, including our enemies, should be shown. First, loving our enemies involves blessing them when they curse us. Second, loving our enemies means praying for them. Third, loving our enemies requires that we do good to them, just as God does. The Scriptures remind us, "For He causes His sun to rise on the evil and the good, and sends rain on the righteous and the unrighteous" (v. 45). When we give to our enemies, we are following God's example because the unrighteous enjoy many of God's blessings every day—His sunshine, His rain, His good food— just as the righteous do. If God continues to bless them, then so must we.

Psalm 145:14–16 reminds us of the important truth that everything we have comes from God. "The LORD sustains all who fall, and raises up all who are bowed down. The eyes of all look to Thee, and *Thou dost give them their food in due time.* Thou dost open Thy hand, and dost satisfy the desire of every living thing." God provides for all of our physical needs. When we pray *"Give* us this day our daily bread," part of what we are praying for is that God would remind us that everything we have is from Him and should be used for His glory.

APPLICATION

1. If we really believe that everything we have comes from God, how will this affect the way we care for and handle our possessions?

2. How will it affect our attitudes toward our possessions?

3. According to this section, what are we really praying for when we pray for God to give us our daily bread?

Idolatry: A Common and Terrible Sin

One of the most terrible sins that we can commit is worshiping things rather than the Creator of all things. Romans 1:25 says that people "exchanged the truth of God for a lie, *and worshiped and served the creature rather than the Creator,* who is blessed forever." When we worship things, our boss or our bank account becomes our provider, rather than God. We become man-centered people rather than God-centered people. Romans 1:21a explains, "For even though they knew God, they did not honor him as God." The evidence for God's existence is all around us, but many people refuse to acknowledge it. In truth, they do not *want* to believe it, so they deny it, suppress it, and explain it away. If they acknowledged and honored God, they would have to give Him thanks. As a result of their disobedience, they are given over to their sin; "but they became futile in their speculations, and their foolish heart was darkened" (Rom. 1:21b).

Ingratitude: An Evidence of Pride

One of the ways that our sinfulness is manifested, therefore, is in the failure to give God thanks—to recognize that everything we have ultimately comes from God. This was the sin of Nebuchadnezzar. King Nebuchadnezzar was, at one time, the greatest king on earth. In Daniel 4:30 he boasted, "Is this not Babylon the great, which I myself have built . . . by the might of my power and for the glory of my majesty?" Nebuchadnezzar believed he was great by virtue of his own wisdom, his own efforts, and his own ability. God saw his arrogance and humbled him.

The king's servant Daniel, a godly man, declared to Nebuchadnezzar God's judgment on his pride by means of the interpretation of a dream the king had: "This is the interpretation, O king, and this is the decree of the Most High, which has come upon my lord the king: that you be driven away from mankind, and your dwelling place be with the beasts of the field, and you be given grass to eat like cattle and be drenched with the dew of heaven; and seven periods of time will pass over you, until you recognize that the Most High is ruler over the realm of mankind, and bestows it on whomever He wishes" (Dan. 4:24–25). God humbled Nebuchad-nezzar until he acknowledged the truth. We must learn that lesson as well.

In Acts 12 we find another example of sinful ingratitude. King Herod was known to be a great orator and when he spoke, people listened in awe. They praised him highly, and Herod gladly accepted their praise, denying that his ability was a gift from God. Because he took glory that belonged only to God, the Scripture says that God struck him with a horrible and fatal disease. God dealt with Herod because of his sinful ingratitude. In Deuteronomy 8 God told the Israelites He would bring them into a rich land and bless them. Before they entered, He warned them that when they became established in the land, they would forget that He had given it all to them. He said to them, "But you shall remember the LORD your God, *for it is He who is giving you power to make wealth,* that He may confirm His covenant which He swore to your fathers, as it is this day" (Deut. 8:18). Any ability, any possession, anything that we have that is good has been given to us by God.

Psalm 104 has thirty-five verses reminding us that every pro-vision of life has been given to us by God. In Romans 8:32 Paul reminds us that God freely gives us all things to enjoy. Proverbs 10:22 says, "It is the blessing of the LORD that makes rich." Wealth is a result of God's blessing, not our own intelligence or wisdom. In Psalm 75:5–7, God says, " 'Do not lift up your horn on high, do not speak with insolent pride.' For not from the east, nor from the west, nor from the desert comes exaltation. But God is the Judge; He puts down one, and exalts another." If we have a better posi-tion, or more prestige, or more of something than others do, we must not be proud. It is God who raises up one and puts down another. When we pray *"Give* us this day our daily bread," we are recognizing that truth.

The Implications of Being Dependent on God

Thomas Watson, in his book on the Lord's Prayer, wrote about the implications arising from this truth. First, if it is true that God gives us all things, we must give more praise to God than we give to the secondary agent who may be the channel through whom God gives it. We ought to thank the secondary agent, of course, but we must give more praise and thanks to God. Second, we must seek every mercy primarily from God and from God alone by prayer. Watson wrote that "the tree of mercy will not drop its fruit, unless shaken by the hand of prayer." God gives, usually, in connection with our prayers. Third, if all we have received is a gift, then it is not a debt that God must pay to us. God owes us nothing but hell.[1] That is a truth easier said than really believed. In truth, we deserve nothing but hell. God owes us nothing, and we can give nothing to Him that He has not first given us. We must never give ourselves, or anyone else, too much credit for what we have received, because all good things have been given by God.

Fourth, if all we receive is a gift of God, we must recognize the heinousness of sinning against Him, ignoring Him, and living as if He did not matter. That is pure foolishness and blatant sin. Fifth, we must seek to use whatever He has given us in a manner that would be pleasing to Him. We, after all, are just stewards. Whatever we have—our time, our homes, our bank accounts—is to be used for God's glory. Everything we have belongs to Him, not just our tithes and offerings. Sixth, if God is the One who gives us everything, we must learn to be content and satisfied with whatever He chooses to give us. We are often like children whose parents have expended great amounts of money, time, effort, and suffering on their behalf, and who yet are ungrateful. Instead of giving thanks, they are critical, demeaning, and unappreciative. It bothers us to see such ingratitude toward good parents, but in reality, we frequently do that to God. When we pray *"Give* us this day our daily bread," we need to remember all the implications that Jesus included with this word "give."

APPLICATION

1. Why is ingratitude a terrible sin?
2. According to Thomas Watson, what are the implications that arise from this petition?

3. Use these six criteria to evaluate your prayer life. Does your life, especially your prayer life, indicate that you really believe that everything we have comes from God?

4. Read Psalm 104 and summarize what it teaches about our dependence on God.

5. Write out Romans 8:32 and think of how this verse relates to the petition we're studying.

The Importance and Meaning of the Word "Us"

Another important word in this petition is the pronoun "us." Jesus taught us to pray "Give *us* this day our daily bread," not "Give *me* this day my daily bread." Scripture is full of commands to put the needs of others ahead of our own. In Matthew 22:39 He said we are to love our neighbor as we love ourselves. We have already looked at Matthew 5:44, which says we are to love our neighbors (and enemies), pray for them, bless them, and do good to them. Galatians 6:2 says that we are to "bear one another's burdens." Philippians 2:4 says we are to look not only to our own interests, but also to the interests of others. In Ephesians 6:18 Paul instructed us to pray for all the saints. In 2 Corinthians 1:11 Paul thanked the Corinthian church for joining with him in his ministry by their prayers. They had not just been praying for themselves, but they had been praying for Paul and for the people to whom Paul was ministering. First John 3:16 commands, "And we ought to lay down our lives for the brethren."

In 1 Corinthians 12 Paul said that if one member of the body suffers, every member should suffer with it, and if one member of the church is honored, every member of the body should be honored with it. In other words, though we join in the honor of a brother or sister, we should be just as concerned about them when they are in need as we are about ourselves. In 2 Corinthians 11:29 Paul said, "Who is weak without my being weak? Who is led into sin without my intense concern?" He was just as concerned about his fellow believers as he was about himself. First Timothy 6:18 instructs us to be generous and to share with others.

APPLICATION

1. What can we learn from the word "us" in this petition?

2. In what ways are you showing concern for your fellow believers?

3. List three things you can do this week to demonstrate practically that you are really concerned about other believers.

God's Concern for the Poor

Recently, I was studying the book of Proverbs again and I was struck by the number of references God makes to the poor. He refers to the poor thirty-seven times in the thirty-one chapters of Proverbs. The point that is made is that true believers will be concerned about people who are poorer than they are. Proverbs 14:21 says, "He who despises his neighbor sins." The verse defines this neighbor as it continues, "But happy is he who is gracious to the poor." If we despise our poor neighbor and are not gracious, we are going to be withheld happiness from the Lord. Proverbs 14:31 says, "He who oppresses the poor reproaches his Maker, but he who is gracious to the needy honors Him." All throughout the book of Proverbs, we are exhorted to show concern for others, especially the poor.

The Bible says that Jesus came so that we who are poor might become rich (2 Cor. 8:9). There are many different kinds of wealth—spiritual and physical. The Bible also says that some are spiritually rich in joy, some in contentment, some in peace, or in gentleness, or patience, or faith. Physically, some are rich in education, or in insights into the Word of God, or in hospitality and social relationships, or in discipline. They are rich in those physical ways, but there are people who are poorer in all those ways as well. Ultimately, we are to be concerned about people who are poorer than we are in any area of life, not just finances.

It is important to point out that it is not a sign of pride to acknowledge our differences in gifts. Yes, we may be poorer or richer in both spiritual and physical ways. Scripture makes it clear that it is not our place to pat ourselves on the back for these things. Instead, we should humbly thank God for whatever He has given, remembering He has given it to us in order that we might use it to help others, not to criticize, mock, or ridicule them. God has given to us so that we may give to others. His salvation makes us a part of a body, and every part of the body must contribute to the needs of the rest of the body. In my own body, my ears do not exist for the sake of my ears; they exist for the rest of my body. Nor does my nose exist for itself; it exists to help the rest of my body. The fact that we are a body means that each individual part of that body exists not for itself, but for everyone else.

In 2 Kings 6 and 7 we read about a period of time when a famine had come upon the land of Israel. 2 Kings 7:3–5 records an interesting event: "Now there were four leprous men at the entrance of the gate; and they said to one another, 'Why do we sit here until we die? . . . Now therefore come, and let us go over to the camp of the Arameans. If they spare us, we shall live; and if they kill us, we shall but die.' And they arose at twilight to go to the camp of the Arameans." As two lepers approached the camp, they discovered that it was empty because the Lord had caused the Arameans to hear the sounds of an approaching army. The Arameans had fled their camp, leaving everything behind. "When these lepers came to the outskirts of the camp, they entered one tent and ate and drank, and carried from there silver and gold and clothes, and went and hid them; and they returned and entered another tent and carried from there also, and went and hid them. Then they said to one another, 'We are not doing right. This day is a day of good news, but we are keeping silent.' " (2 Kings 7:8–9). They realized that they were wrong to keep all the spoils for themselves. " 'If we wait until morning light, punishment will overtake us. Now therefore come, let us go and tell the king's household.' So they came and called to the gatekeepers of the city. . . . And the gatekeepers called, and told it within the king's household" (2 Kings 7:9–11).

These lepers had come upon a great deal of wealth in a time of great need, and their initial response was typical of sinful men,

"Let's gorge ourselves and keep it all." Eventually, though, God worked in their hearts and they agreed, "We're not doing right." That is what it means to pray "give *us.*" "Lord, give me whatever you want me to have, so that I might be able to be your instrument in helping others to have their daily bread." This is what Christ came to do in us and for us. He came and died for all, says the Scripture, that "they who live should no longer live for themselves, but for Him who died" (2 Cor. 5:15). We must realize that everything we have has been given to us by God and is to be used for Him.

A woman was driving her son to a game when they came on an accident. She said to her son, "We'd better pray." What she meant was, "Let's pray for the people in that accident who may be hurt." But when she said, "Let's pray," her young son responded, "Oh God, please, please, don't allow this accident to keep us from getting to the game on time." The selfishness of his heart came out in his understanding of his mother's statement. He was concerned only about himself. Frequently, that is true of us as well in our prayers and in our lives. Jesus taught us to pray, *"Give us* this day our daily bread." May God then help us to pray as Jesus taught, acknowledging our dependence on God for everything and giving generously to others out of His blessings to us.

APPLICATION

1. Are there different kinds of wealth and poverty?

2. What are some of the different kinds of wealth and poverty that people may have?

3. In what ways are you rich and in what ways are you poor when compared to other people?

4. In terms of the areas in which you are rich, what are some ungodly ways of handling your riches?

5. Write out Ephesians 1:3.

6. Write out 2 Corinthians 8:9.

7. Write out James 2:5.

Again I remind you that to pray effectively means that we will pray as Jesus taught us to pray; this is the kind of prayer that pleases God; this is the kind of prayer that God loves to answer. How could it be otherwise since it was Jesus Christ, the Son of God, who taught us to pray this way?

APPLICATION

1. Summarize in your own words the most important truths presented in this chapter.

2. Write out and work on memorizing one or two verses found in this chapter.

3. In what ways were you encouraged, challenged, or convicted by the material in this chapter? In keeping with the material presented in this chapter, how should your prayer life be changed?

PRAYING ABOUT
YOUR DEBTS

*I*n his opening comments on the petition "forgive us our debts" Thomas Watson calls attention to the fact that in this prayer, there is but one petition for the body, which is "give us our daily bread," but two petitions for the soul: "Forgive us our trespasses," and, "lead us not into temptation, but deliver us from evil." Observe hence, that we are to be more careful for our souls than for our bodies, more careful for grace than for daily bread, and more desirous to have our souls saved than our bodies fed. In the law, the weight of the sanctuary was twice as big as the common-weight, to typify that spiritual things must be of far greater weight with us than earthly. The excellency of the soul may challenge our chief care about it.[1]

Watson then goes on to tell us why we should be more concerned about our soul than our body. He gives two reasons. First, he says, "The soul is an immaterial substance; it is a heavenly spark, lighted by the breath of God. It is the more refined and spiritual part of man. It is of an angelic nature. It has some faint resemblance to God. The body is the more humble part; it is the cabinet only, though curiously wrought, but the soul is the jewel. It is near akin to angels; it is capable of communion with God in glory." Secondly, he says our concern should chiefly be for our souls because "the soul is immortal; it never expires. The soul can act without the body, but the body cannot act without the soul. Though the body dissolves into dust, the soul lives. The essence of the soul is eternal; it has a beginning but no end. Surely then, if the soul be so ennobled and dignified, more care should be taken about it than the body. Hence, we make but one petition for the body, but two petitions for the soul."[2]

Then, having emphasized the supremacy of the needs of the soul over the needs of the body, he goes on to say that this petition reproves us for making the care of our bodies more important than the care of our souls:

> The body is but the animal part, yet many people take more care for it than they do for the soul. They take more care about dressing their bodies than their souls. They put on the best clothes; they are dressed in the richest garb, but they care not how naked or undressed their souls are. They do not get the jewels of grace to adorn the inner man; they are more concerned about feeding their bodies than their souls. They are caterers for the flesh, they make provision for the flesh, they have the best diet for the flesh, but they let their souls starve, as if one should feed his hawk, but let his child starve. The body must sit in the chair of state, but the soul—that princely thing—is made a lackey, or servant, to run on the devil's errands.[3]

The Right Focus in Our Personal Prayers

How true that we are often more concerned with putting nice clothes on our bodies than we are about, as Romans 13:14 says, "putting on the Lord Jesus Christ." We spend more time purchasing and taking care of our clothes—washing, ironing, folding, repairing—than we spend attending to our spiritual needs, as Paul admonished us in that verse. Paul listed the qualities that we are to dress ourselves with in Colossians 3:12–14. In this passage Paul said, "As those who have been chosen by God, holy and beloved, *put on* a heart of compassion, kindness, humility, gentleness, and patience; bearing with one another, and forgiving each other, whoever has a complaint against anyone; just as the Lord forgave you, so also should you. And beyond all these things, *put on* love, which is the perfect bond of unity."

We are usually more concerned about dressing our bodies than demonstrating love, compassion, kindness, humility, gentleness, patience, forbearance, or forgiveness. Peter emphasized one of these traits in 1 Peter 5:5–6. "*Clothe yourselves with humility* toward one another, for God is opposed to the proud, but gives grace to the humble. Humble yourselves, therefore, under the mighty hand of God." Humility is often of little concern to us, while hunger for physical food is of great concern. We have little desire for the righteousness that Jesus describes in Matthew 5:6: "Blessed are those who *hunger and thirst for righteousness.*" We are quick and eager to satisfy our constant physical hunger, but we rarely even feel a need for righteousness.

For example, there are people who would never think about missing a day of work. They get there on time, no matter how early, but given an opportunity to study the Word of God at an early service, they complain that it is too early. It is amazing how our priorities and values become so inverted. This applies also to parenting. Those of us who are parents should be far more concerned about feeding our children spiritually than we are about feeding them physically. That means reading God's Word with them and using every opportunity we have to present the Word of God and live it before them. It also means bringing them to the services of the church, where they will be taught the Word of God. In James 2 we are reminded that if we say that spiritual things are more important, we must prove it by our actions. If we do not, then we do not really believe it.

This petition for our soul in Matthew 6:12 reproves us for this great deficiency. As we look at this text we should notice that it contains a confession. When we pray, if we are praying rightly, we should be confessing to God that we are in His debt due to our sin. The Bible uses various words when referring to sin, each with a slightly different meaning. God uses these different words to help us understand how complex and serious sin is. For example, sin is referred to in the Bible by all of the following words: iniquity, transgression, disobedience, lawlessness, trespass, guilt, corruption, being depraved or evil, wickedness, rebellion, error, defiance, defilement, pollution, filthiness, and vileness. In Matthew 6:12 Jesus expands our understanding of sin by describing our sin as a "debt." He says that we are to pray "forgive us our *debts.*" The word "debt" is used to describe our sin because Jesus wants us to know that sin is a failure to pay God what we owe Him. When we pray, we should do so with the awareness that we have failed to give to God what He deserves and demands of us. Acceptable, God-approved prayer will always include an acknowledgment that we have not given, and are not giving God what we owe Him.

APPLICATION

1. In what ways do people indicate that they are more concerned about their bodies than they are about their souls?

2. In what ways do you sometimes evidence that you are more concerned about your body than your soul?

3. What are two reasons we should be more concerned about the soul than the body?

4. What do we confess in this petition?

The Debts We Owe to God

What is it that we owe to God and have not paid? Matthew 22:37 says that we owe God all of our love: "You shall love the Lord your God with all your heart, and with all your soul, and with all your mind." None of us has done that. We have not loved Him as He deserves to be loved, and so we are in debt to God for that deficiency in our love. Deuteronomy 10:12 asks, "What does the LORD require from you, but to fear the LORD your God . . . and love Him, and to serve the LORD your God with all your heart and with all your soul . . . ?" None of us has done that. We have not perfectly feared Him, loved Him, or served Him, and so we are in debt to God for that. Ecclesiastes 12:13 says, "Let us hear the conclusion of the whole matter: Fear God and keep His commandments, for this is man's all" (NKJV). None of us has perfectly feared God and kept His commands. We owe that to God and are in debt to Him for it.

Matthew 6:33 says, "Seek first the kingdom of God and His righteousness." None of us, any day in our lives, has perfectly sought first the kingdom of God and His righteousness. Colossians 1:18 says that we are to make Jesus Christ preeminent in all things. In every area of our lives—our thoughts, our speech, our behavior, our desires, our family life, our business life, our social life, our recreational life—Jesus Christ should be preeminent. He deserves that, we owe it to Him, and yet none of us has perfectly done that. First Corinthians 10:31 says, "Whether, then, you eat or drink or whatever you do, do all to the glory of God." Romans 3:23 defines sin in this way: "For all have sinned and fall short of the glory of God." We have not glorified God in the way that He deserves to be glorified. None of us has perfectly done everything to the glory of God. God deserves and demands it. We owe it, and so we are in debt.

Proverbs 3:5–6 says, "Trust in the LORD with all your heart, and do not lean on your own understanding. In all your ways acknowledge Him." Does any believer trust in the Lord with all his heart all the time? We are to lean upon the understanding of God in every situation and let God determine the truth. Yet none of us has perfectly trusted in God and perfectly acknowledged him in all our ways. Proverbs 3:9 says, "Honor the LORD from your wealth, and from the first of all your produce." In other words, we are to honor God in our stewardship—with what we give back to Him—and not only that, but it is to be our first thought in using our resources. More often, what we give to the Lord is our leftovers. We are in debt in our actions and in our intentions.

Ephesians 5:20 instructs us to be *"always giving thanks* for all things in the name of our Lord Jesus Christ to God, even the Father." Has any believer constantly bowed the knee, hour by hour, thanking God in prayer for everything? First Thessalonians 5:16 teaches us to *"rejoice always."* We owe God our constant praise and rejoicing. Paul continues, *"Pray without ceasing."* No man has done that. *"In everything give thanks;* for *this is God's will for you* in Christ Jesus." God wants this from us, He deserves it from us, but we have not paid our bill.

Second Corinthians 10:5 exhorts us to take "*every thought* captive to the obedience of Christ." Has our every thought this day, even this hour, been under our control and made obedient to Jesus Christ? We are in debt to God.

Luke 9:23 says, "If anyone wishes to come after Me, let him deny himself, and *take up his cross daily,* and follow Me." To die to self and to live for Jesus should be our daily determination. None of us has followed Jesus Christ in every area of our lives—our thoughts, our words, our actions, our behavior, our relationships with people, in the way we use our time, in the way that we use our money or even our opportunities. "Make the most of your time," Paul said in Ephesians 5:16. In other words, we are to use every situation that comes in our lives to glorify God. If we do not, we are in debt to God. First Timothy 4:7 says we are to exercise ourselves for the purpose of godliness. All our lives, we are to pursue that which will help us to become godly. "Orient your life toward godliness" is another way that 1 Timothy 4:7 could be translated. None of us does that perfectly and continuously. We are in debt.

In 1 Peter 4:10–11 Peter says that God has given us gifts, and as those who have received the various gifts, we are to "employ [them] in serving one another as good stewards of the manifold grace of God." We are to use everything we have in service to other people, as well as service to God. No one has done that. In fact, we have all too often served ourselves. The apostle Paul said in Philippians 2:20–21 that he had no one who was serving others perfectly or completely. "For they all seek after their own interests," he said, "not those of Christ Jesus." If Paul said that of the Christians in his day, he would say the same of us. Yet we owe God that kind of service as our Lord, our Master, our Creator, our Father, and our Redeemer. As such, He deserves our obedience in all of these things, but none of us has perfectly done His will. We are greatly in debt to God.

APPLICATION

1. What is Jesus referring to when He teaches us to pray for forgiveness of our debt? To whom are we indebted?

2. Why is sin described as a debt?

3. Make a list of the debts each of us owes to God but none of us has paid.

4. Why do we owe these things to God?

5. Write out Matthew 6:33.

Our Most Serious Indebtedness

Truly, there is never a day in the life of any one of us in which we give God all the obedience, praise, love, and worship that He deserves. There is never a day when we fully give to God what we owe Him. Watson says that this sin debt is serious. In fact, he says it is the worst debt any of us will ever have. Many of us have been overwhelmed by a debt we owe to the bank, but does it even bother us that we have not paid, *and cannot pay,* our debt to God? It ought to, because this sin debt is the most serious debt we will ever have.

Watson gives several reasons why this is true. First, he says that this sin debt is the worst debt we could ever have because it is a debt that *we can never fully pay.* In Matthew 18:21–35 Jesus tells the parable of a servant who owed his king a great debt. He begged the king, "Have patience with me and I will repay you all." That is a statement we can *never* make to God. We do not have the resources to pay the enormous debt we have run up, and continue to run up, to God.

Second, he says this is our most serious debt because of the *nature and the identity of the One to whom we owe this debt.* Our sin is against the God who made us: "Know that the LORD Himself is God; it is He who has made us, and not we ourselves" (Ps. 100:3). We owe this debt to a God who is omniscient, omnipresent, omnipotent, and who will bring us all into final judgment. He is holy, righteous, just, and unchangeable. This is not a debt owed to someone who is less than we are, or even to an equal. We owe this debt to the One who has given us everything and who deserves everything as well. This is a serious debt.

Third, this is the worst debt that we could have because our debt is not a single debt but a multiplied debt. Notice that in Matthew 6:12 Jesus teaches us to pray "forgive us"—not our *debt*—but "our *debts."* In Psalm 40:12 David acknowledged his multiplied debt to God when he wrote, "For evils beyond number have surrounded me; my iniquities have overtaken me, so that I am not able to see; they are more numerous than the hairs of my head; and my heart has failed me."

David continued on that same theme in Psalm 38:4: "My iniquities are gone over my head; as a heavy burden they weigh too much for me." David described himself as drowning in his sin because he understood how serious and enormous his sin debt to God was.

David dwelt on the enormity of his sin over and over in the psalms. In Psalm 65:3 he said, "Iniquities prevail against me; as for our transgressions, Thou dost forgive them." Psalm 19:12 says, "Who can discern his errors?" The Psalmist realized that no man is capable of fully understanding how sinful he is. Have we really been gripped by the fact that we are so sinful that we can never fully know just how sinful we are? Jeremiah 17:9 says it well: "The heart is more deceitful than all else and is desperately sick; who can understand it?" None of us knows how indebted we are to God, and so this is a most serious debt. In Genesis 6:5 our Creator saw that "every intent of the thoughts of [man's] heart was only evil continually." God counts not only our disobedient actions as sin, but He knows and counts our thoughts as well. He knows everything we have thought, every day of our lives. He knows every desire that we have had that has not been godly and every word that we have spoken that has not honored Him. Our sin is a multiplied debt.

Fourth, this is the worst debt we could have because we cannot hide from or escape from the One to whom we are indebted. In Psalm 139:7–12 the psalmist had this to say: "Where can I go from Thy Spirit? Or where can I flee from Thy presence? If I ascend to heaven, Thou art there; if I make my bed in Sheol, behold, Thou art there. If I take the wings of the dawn, if I dwell in the remotest part of the sea, even there Thy hand will lead me, and Thy right hand will lay hold of me. If I say, 'Surely the darkness will overwhelm me, and the light around me will be night,' even the darkness is not dark to Thee, and the night is as bright as the day. Darkness and light are alike to Thee." Every one of us will someday give an account of ourselves to God—every thought, intention, and action. We are all going to be judged by God.

Often we hear about people who have committed horrible crimes and somehow are able to escape man's judgment. On September 11, 2001, Osama Bin Laden and others executed one of the most horrible crimes ever committed. Thousands of people died, and thousands more are searching for Osama Bin Laden and his associates. They have not been found and brought to judgment before men—and may never be—but we all will face judgment before God. No one can hide from God, and that makes our sin debt the most serious debt we could ever incur.

Finally, sin is the worst debt we could ever incur because it carries men, in the case of nonpayment, to a worse prison than any prison on earth. It is a prison where there is "outer darkness." We have never seen darkness as it is in hell. It is a prison of torment, the likes of which no prisoner in this world has ever experienced. Some horrible things have been done to prisoners of war in this world, but there is no torment on this earth that will compare with what the Bible says people will experience in hell. There will be "weeping and gnashing of teeth" (Matt. 8:12). To be sure, people will begin to realize at that point how serious their sin debt really is.

APPLICATION

1. What are the five evidences given in the previous section that support the idea that sin is a very serious debt, the worst we could ever incur?

2. There are a number of things in this pattern prayer that indicate we should be praying about the issues mentioned on a daily basis. What is Jesus teaching us by the fact that praying for forgiveness of our sin debt should be something we do on a daily basis?

3. Do you view your sin in this way?

The Petition "Forgive Us Our Debts" and Effective Prayer

The Necessity of Confessing Sin

What does all this have to do with effective prayer? Jesus was teaching us that if we are going to pray effectively, we must take our sin seriously. Proverbs 14:9 says, "Fools mock at sin." They make jokes and laugh about it. The Bible indicates that sin is not a joking matter. To pray effectively, we must recognize that we have *grievously sinned against God.* Our sins are beyond counting. If we could go back to our birth and record every thought, desire, word, and action that has not been pleasing to God, we would run out of numbers with which to count our sins. We have grievously sinned against God.[4]

Jesus is also teaching us here that if we are going to pray effectively we must be willing to confess and acknowledge our sin to God. When Adam and Eve sinned against God and became aware of it, they tried to cover themselves. They used fig leaves to hide their nakedness, and men have been covering up ever since. Today we often attempt to run away from our sin by making excuses, rationalizing, justifying, blaming other people, blaming our circumstances, or blaming some innate character flaw. Our prayers to God are so often filled with requests for things, but so seldom filled with confessions of our sin. Jesus taught us to come to God in prayer, confessing and acknowledging our sin.

There are many examples in the Bible of sinners coming to God in this way. As they stood in the presence of a holy God, they realized their need to acknowledge their sins to Him. In Nehemiah 1:4–7 Nehemiah received news about the plight of his people and the city of Jerusalem. He wrote, "Now it came about when I heard these words, I sat down and wept and mourned for days." Nehemiah was greatly distressed by what he had heard. He then prayed, "I beseech Thee, O Lord God of heaven, the great and awesome God, who preserves the covenant and lovingkindness for those who love Him and keep His commandments, let Thine ear now be attentive and Thine eyes open to hear the prayer of Thy servant which I am praying before Thee now, day and night, on behalf of the sons of Israel Thy servants, confessing the sins of the sons of Israel which we have sinned against

Thee; I and my father's house have sinned. We have acted very corruptly against Thee and have not kept your commandments."

Nehemiah began his prayer acknowledging who God is and what God is. He then went on to confess his sins and the sins of the people before God. That theme is repeated again and again in Bible prayers. God's people came to Him, confessing and acknowledging their sins because they took sin seriously. In our day we are calling evil good and good evil, which means that our world does not take its sin seriously. Indeed, most churchgoers would rather be entertained by their pastor than convicted by the truth of the Word of God. They refuse to confront their sin, and they prefer instead to be told stories and jokes.

A number of years ago I was being interviewed for the pastorate at a particular church. I met with the men of that church, and they questioned me on many topics. At one point I was asked, "Do you tell jokes?" Apparently, this man wanted a pastor who would be entertaining. He did not ask me if I believed and exposited the Word of God, if I was a godly man, or if I loved my family. I almost replied, "You're a joke." Most people just do not want to deal with their sins today. They want to build up their egos and strengthen their self-esteem. In 2 Timothy 4:3 Paul said, "The time will come when they will not endure sound doctrine; but wanting to have their ears tickled, they will accumulate for themselves teachers in accordance to their own desires." They want to be told how wonderful, good, and talented they are. This goes on not just in liberal churches, but in churches said to be evangelical, which claim to believe and proclaim the Bible. Jesus clearly taught otherwise in this petition of the Lord's Prayer.

God Owes Us Nothing: We Owe Him Everything

Second, Jesus wanted us to know that if we are going to pray effectively, we must realize that God does not owe us anything—except eternal punishment in hell. Every one of us is so in debt to God that He has every right to cast us into hell. God is not indebted to us; we are indebted to Him. We cannot come to God as a person who has done a great amount of work for someone else, looking to collect what we are owed. Indeed, we often have the idea that God owes us something because, after all, we have done so much for Him. Have we not attended church regularly, read our Bibles faithfully, prayed, and given to the poor? I know of someone who once said, "I prayed that God would heal my dog. He didn't, so I'm not going to church anymore," as though God were his debtor. God does not owe us anything.

Instead, we are to come to God with the humility of a man who owes a great debt that he is completely unable to pay. This is the clear teaching of a parable Jesus told in Matthew 20:1–16. "The kingdom of heaven is like a landowner who went out early in the morning to hire laborers for his vineyard. And when he had agreed with the laborers for a denarius for the day, he sent them into his vineyard." The landowner repeated this four more times throughout the day, promising each group fair payment for their work.

> And when evening had come, the owner of the vineyard said to his foreman, "Call the laborers and pay them their wages, beginning with the last group to the first." And when those hired about the eleventh hour came, each one received a denarius. And when those hired first came, they thought that they would receive more; and they also received each one a denarius. And when they received it, they grumbled at the landowner, saying, "These last men have worked only one hour, and you have made them equal to us who have borne the burden and scorching heat of the day." But he answered and said to one of them, "Friend, I am doing you no wrong; did you not agree with me for a denarius? Take what is yours and go your way, but I wish to give to this last man the same as to you. Is it not lawful for me to do what I wish with what is my own? Or is your eye envious because I am generous?" Thus the last shall be first, and the first last.

Jesus was teaching us about the kingdom of heaven, and we must consider carefully the meaning of His words here. He was saying that God, as the landowner, does not owe us anything. Anything He gives to us is by His grace. We have not perfectly obeyed Him, served Him, or done His will. Thankfully, God does not deal with us on the basis of our works, because we are so hopelessly in debt to Him that even if we could live a perfect life from this day forward, it would not make up for all the debt we have already incurred. Sin is serious, and when we come rightly to God in prayer, we will come with full awareness of this enormous debt, and be humbled in His presence. We will not come swaggering or laughing, but we will come with a sense of great reverence and gratitude that this God to whom we owe so much would even be willing to hear us when we pray "Forgive us our debts." Let's devote ourselves to praying this way because to pray this way is to pray effectively and it is to pray Jesus' style. How could it be otherwise since it was Jesus Christ, the Son of God in whom are hid all the treasures of wisdom and knowledge (Col. 2:3), who taught us to pray this way?

APPLICATION

1. What does this petition teach us about the way we should come to God in prayer?

2. What can we learn from Matthew 20:1–16 about the attitude we should have as we approach God?

3. Summarize in your own words the most important truths presented in this chapter.

4. Write out and work on memorizing one or two verses found in this chapter.

5. In what ways were you encouraged, challenged, or convicted by the material in this chapter? In keeping with the material presented in this chapter, how should your prayer life be changed?

REMEMBERING
FORGIVENESS
AND FORGIVING

atthew 6:12 contains a confession, a petition, and a promise or commitment. In the previous chapter we studied the confession—the acknowledgment of *our debts*—and we turn now to the petition, which is *"Forgive us* our debts." Jesus wanted to teach us some truths about the forgiveness that we are asking of God, and we must understand these truths in order to pray this prayer properly.

The Bible uses a number of descriptive phrases—or metaphors—to describe God's forgiveness. In Job 7:21 the Bible indicates that when God forgives our sins, He takes them away: "Why then dost Thou not pardon my transgression and *take away my iniquity?"* Forgiveness involves removing our iniquity from us. Galatians 6:2 pictures sin as a burden. Verse 1 says, "Brethren, even if a man is caught in any trespass, you who are spiritual, restore such a one in a spirit of gentleness; each one looking to yourself, lest you too be tempted." The next verse, describing the sin in which people are caught, says, "Bear one another's burdens." For a child of God, sin is a burden.

Forgiveness: A Wonderful Blessing and a Great Need

John Bunyan picks up on that theme in *The Pilgrim's Progress.* In chapter 1, Christian has a burden on his back that is weighing him down, and it is not until he comes to the cross that his burden rolls off his back. When God forgives us, He lifts our burden of sin. In Psalm 38:4–6 David pictured his sin as a burden that was weighing him down: "My iniquities are . . . as a heavy burden[;] they weigh too much for me. . . . I am bent over and greatly bowed down; I go mourning all day long." When a person becomes aware of sin, it is a great burden that can be lifted only by God's forgiveness.

Psalm 85:2 describes a different aspect of what happens when we are forgiven: "Thou didst forgive the iniquity of Thy people; Thou didst *cover all their sin.*" Being forgiven means to have our sins covered. David used this metaphor in Psalm 32:1 when he said, "How blessed is he whose transgression is forgiven, whose sin is covered." When God sent the flood waters to judge the sins of mankind in Genesis 7:20, "the water prevailed . . . and the mountains were covered." When God forgives, He covers our sins so that, as far as He is concerned, they are out of His sight. In Isaiah 43:25 God said, "I, even I, am the one who wipes out your transgressions for My own sake; and I will not remember your sins."

Isaiah 44:22 says essentially the same thing about God's forgiveness: "*I have wiped out* your transgressions like a thick cloud, and your sins like a heavy mist." We have all seen the sun shining brightly all day in a cloudless sky. At other times, though the sun still shines, it is blotted out by thick clouds and cannot be seen. God is saying that just as thick clouds can blot out the sun completely, when He forgives, our sins are blotted out so that He no longer sees them. How wonderful it is that God chooses to hide our sin from His sight!

Micah 7:19 paints a telling picture of another aspect of God's forgiveness: "Thou wilt *cast* all their sins *into the depths of the sea.*" If we were to stand on the beach and throw something into the ocean, someone might find it. But if we were to throw it into the deepest part of the ocean—almost seven miles down—it could not be found. God says He buries our sin in the depths of the oceans, so that they cannot be recovered. What a wonderful picture!

In Jeremiah 31:34 God declared another facet of his forgiveness: "I will forgive their iniquity and their sin I will *remember no more.*" He said the same thing in Isaiah 43:25, and again in Hebrews

8:12. We must notice, however, that the Bible does not say He "forgets" our sins. Forgetting is passive; when we forget something, it is not because we decide to—it just happens. God, on the other hand, chooses not to remember our sins for the purpose of condemnation or punishment. Obviously, since God is omniscient, He cannot "forget" our sins. He could remember them if He wanted to, but He *chooses not to remember* them against us.

I know of a man who grievously sinned against his wife fifteen years ago. His wife claims to have forgiven him, and yet she constantly thinks about it, mentions it to others, and brings it up as an accusation against him. She is allowing it to hinder their relationship by punishing him for it. From a biblical perspective, her claim to forgiveness is invalid, because true forgiveness means choosing not to remember the sin any longer. That is the kind of forgiveness God offers to us in Christ Jesus: "There is therefore now *no condemnation* for those who are in Christ Jesus" (Rom. 8:1).

Psalm 103:12 tells us that when God forgives our sins, He removes them "as far as the east is from the west." Think about the meaning of this great metaphor that God uses to describe His forgiveness. If we traveled south from the North Pole, we would eventually get to the South Pole. If we continued to travel in the same direction, we would soon be going north again. But if we were to start east from somewhere in Pennsylvania, and continue to go east, would we ever go west? No, as long as we continued in that same direction, we would never go west. East and west can never meet, and when God forgives us our sins, they are gone forever.

Isaiah 38:17 has another description of God's wonderful forgiveness: "It is Thou who hast kept my soul from the pit of nothingness, for Thou hast *cast all my sins behind Thy back.*" When God forgives us, He puts our sins behind His back, which means they are out of His sight. Some time ago a dermatologist told me there were some marks on my back that I needed to check every six to twelve months. Obviously, I could not do that on my own. I could try twisting around in front of a mirror, but it would not be very effective. Instead, I have to ask my wife to check my back, because what is on my back is out of my sight. God uses this metaphor to help us understand that when He forgives us, our sin is put out of His sight.

In Acts 7:60 Stephen refers to God's forgiveness in this way: "Lord, do not *hold this sin against them!*" In other words, when God forgives us, He remits the guilt and penalty of our sin. They are not charged to us and will never be brought as an accusation against us. The word "remit" literally means "to put or send back." If something is "remitted," it is sent back. In monetary terms, it means to cancel a debt. When God remits our sins, He cancels out the debt that we have. Colossians 1:22 says that when God forgives us through Jesus Christ, he regards us as "holy and blameless and beyond reproach." We are free from accusation and now considered by God to be blameless.

In 1 Corinthians 6:9–11 the apostle Paul wrote of people who *used to be* homosexuals, adulterers, fornicators, idolaters, thieves, covetous, drunkards, revilers, and swindlers. Then he said, "But you *were washed.*" Sin had defiled these people—had made them dirty—but when God forgave them, they were washed. Ezekiel 36:25 conveys the same truth. God said, "Then I will sprinkle clean water on you, and you will be clean; I will cleanse you from all your filthiness." Imagine for a moment a very dirty person, who is so covered in mud and filth that no one will even approach him. God says that we are that person—and even more so than we can imagine—because of our sin. We are covered in filthiness, but God's forgiveness cleanses us.

Finally, in Colossians 2:13–14 Paul said, "When you were dead in your transgressions and the uncircumcision of your flesh, He made you alive together with Him, having forgiven us all our transgressions." What does that forgiveness entail? Paul continued, "having *canceled out* the certificate of debt consisting of decrees against us and which was hostile to us." Our debt is canceled—erased. Paid in full! How wonderful, that though we owed God a debt we could never pay, He has canceled that debt through the blood of Jesus Christ.

Remember how we learned that sin is so awful that God cannot describe it with just one word? In the same way, God cannot adequately describe His forgiveness with just one word. The fact that all of these different words are used to describe forgiveness teaches us two things: first, it indicates how serious sin is, and second, it indicates how wonderful forgiveness is. Man's greatest need is forgiveness, according to the Bible, not good self-esteem or material wealth, according to the wisdom of this world. And it is not only our greatest need, it is the most wonderful thing that we could ever experience, because sin is that serious.

APPLICATION

1. What figures of speech or word pictures does God use to describe what it means to be forgiven? List them.

2. What may we learn from the fact that God uses so many word pictures to describe what forgiveness involves?

3. Which of these word pictures is most meaningful to you?

4. Choose one of the passages that describe an aspect of God's forgiveness and write it out.

Important Aspects of God's Forgiveness

Forgiveness by Grace

Let us continue our study of this petition by looking at several other things the Bible teaches about our forgiveness. First, forgiveness is *by grace alone*. Ephesians 1:7 says: "In [Christ] we have redemption, through His blood, the forgiveness of our trespasses, according to the riches of His grace." Forgiveness is granted to us according to—or in keeping with—the riches of God's grace. It is not because of anything we do, but only because of God's grace that we are forgiven. Romans 4:4–5 says, "Now to the one who works, his wage is not reckoned as a favor, but as what is due. But to the one who does not work, but believes in Him who justifies the ungodly, his faith is reckoned as righteousness." Romans 11:5–6 also teaches, "There has also come to be at the present time a remnant according to God's gracious choice. But if it is by grace, it is no longer on the basis of works, otherwise grace is no longer grace." Forgiveness is all grace.

Suppose a beggar were to approach Bill Gates—reputed to be the world's wealthiest man—and ask for some money. If Gates were to write that beggar a check for four hundred dollars that would be nice, but Gates would not be giving *according to his riches*. It would be a small donation *out* of His riches—a pittance—that he gave to the beggar. Suppose, however, that Gates were to write out a check for a billion dollars instead. Gates would not then be giving *out* of His riches; he would be giving *according to* his riches. In the same way, God does not merely forgive us *out of* his riches; the Scripture says we are redeemed *according to* the riches of His grace.

Furthermore, 2 Corinthians 12:9 says this grace is "sufficient." Ephesians 2:7 goes beyond that and speaks of "the surpassing riches" of God's grace. First Timothy 1:14 refers to grace as "exceedingly abundant" (NKJV). In other words, God's grace goes beyond (exceeds) having more than enough (having an abundance). First Peter 4:10 speaks of the "manifold" grace of God, and Isaiah 43:25 says he forgives us for his "own sake." Therefore, God's forgiveness is always on the basis of grace—not because we deserve it—and He forgives us according to the riches of His grace, which is exceedingly abundant, or far more than we could ever imagine.

 **APPLICATION**

1. What does it mean to be forgiven by God's grace?
2. What does it mean to be forgiven "according to the riches of God's grace"?
3. What point was made about God's forgiveness in the Bill Gates illustration?
4. List some of the adjectives (modifying words) that Scripture uses to describe God's grace.
5. What is your response to this great fact about forgiveness?

The Death of Christ and Forgiveness

Ephesians 1:7 teaches: "In Him we have redemption through His blood." God always saves us *through the blood of Christ*. No one is ever forgiven apart from that, and that has been true not only since the time of Christ, but before He came as well. Old Testament people looked forward to the sacrifice that Christ was going to make.

We, in New Testament times, look back on the sacrifice that Christ has made. Romans 3:24–25 says that we are "justified [declared righteous] as a gift by His grace through the redemption which is in Christ Jesus, whom God displayed publicly as a propitiation in His blood through faith." Forgiveness is not granted because we go to church or read our Bibles, or even because we repent (though repentance is important and essential), but God forgives us and accepts our repentance because of the blood of Jesus Christ.

There are many opinions about the death of Christ. There is the example, or pattern, theory: that Jesus died to be an example of a man so committed to principle that He would willingly die for it. There is the ransom theory: that when Jesus died on the cross, He was paying a ransom to Satan to release us from his captivity. The Bible teaches, however, that Jesus did not die merely to pay a ransom to Satan or to provide us with an example. His death was a "propitiation," or atoning sacrifice: "whom God displayed publicly as a propitiation in His blood" (Rom. 3:25). When something is propitiated it is satisfied, and in this case, what was satisfied was the justice and wrath of God against sin. Jesus died on the cross as our *substitute:* He took what did not belong to Him, our sin, so that we might have what does not belong to us, His righteousness. We are forgiven because of Christ's sacrificial death. William Cowper said rightly:

> There is a fountain filled with blood drawn from Emmanuel's veins,
> And sinners plunged beneath that blood lose all their guilty
>   stains. . . .
> Dear dying Lamb, Thy precious blood shall never lose its power,
> Till all the ransomed church of God be saved to sin no more.

It is only by our trust in the Lord Jesus and the repentance of our sins that the forgiveness of God, through the blood of Jesus, becomes our portion.

APPLICATION

1. What does the death of Christ have to do with our forgiveness?

2. What is meant by the Bible truth that Christ's death on the cross was a propitiation for our sins?

3. Write out Ephesians 1:7.

Forgiveness for Every Sin

The Bible also teaches that God forgives *all* sin. First John 1:7 says, "But if we walk in the light as He Himself is in the light, we have fellowship with one another, and the blood of Jesus His Son cleanses us from *all* sin." First John 1:9 reiterates: "If we confess our sins, He is faithful and righteous to forgive us our sins and to cleanse us from *all* unrighteousness." In Jeremiah 33:8 God said, "I will cleanse them from *all* their iniquity by which they have sinned against Me, and I will pardon *all* their iniquities." It is a wonderful thing that God is willing to forgive all our sins.

I have heard people say they would be willing to forgive their spouse for most things, but there is often something they could never forgive. Thankfully, it is not so with God. David committed adultery and murder, and yet God forgave him. Zacchaeus robbed and stole from the poor, but God forgave him. Mary Magdalene was a prostitute, and the woman of Samaria was living in adultery; God forgave them both. Those who crucified Christ in Matthew 27 were forgiven in Acts 2. Saul blasphemed God and persecuted the church, but God forgave him. In 1 Corinthians 6:9–11 God forgave homosexuals, adulterers, swindlers, and revilers. God is willing to forgive *all* sin.

APPLICATION

1. Prove from the Scripture that God is willing to forgive every sin.

2. What biblical examples of God's willingness to forgive are most meaningful to you?

3. Are there any particular sins from your present or past that you find yourself being bothered by?

4. How can this great truth about God's willingness to forgive all sin be used in your life and in your attempts to help others?

A Caveat about Forgiveness

There is, however, a caveat here that must not be overlooked in terms of God's forgiveness. There is a sense in which, while His forgiveness extends to all sin, God's forgiveness is conditional. Our forgiveness is always by grace and through the blood of Christ, yes, but those who are forgiven must repent, according to Luke 24:46–47. In the Bible, God's forgiveness is always connected with repentance. In Acts 2 Peter preached the gospel, and people, under conviction of their sin, asked, "Brethren, what shall we do?" Peter responded, "Repent . . . for the forgiveness of your sins." Acts 3:19 says the same. The clear teaching of the Bible is that where there is no repentance, there is no forgiveness. If that were not true, everyone would be going to heaven, as there would be universal forgiveness and salvation. We know, however, that there will be many people spending eternity in hell. This is not because the cross is ineffective, but because they have never repented. God's forgiveness is always associated with repentance.

APPLICATION

1. What is meant by the statement that God's forgiveness is conditional?

2. Demonstrate the biblical validity of this statement.

3. What implications does this fact have for our own lives and for our ministries to others?

The Commitment God's Forgiveness Calls For

Finally, we come to the commitment, or promise, in Matthew 6:12, which is: "Forgive us our debts, *as we also have forgiven our debtors.*" With this statement we are promising the Lord that we will forgive others. Since we are constantly sinning, we need to constantly ask God for forgiveness and repent. And since others will constantly sin against us, we will have to constantly forgive them. We are committing to do that, just as God forgave us.

And if God's forgiveness is truly our pattern for forgiveness, then we must remember four important aspects of this promise we make to forgive others. First, we are promising never to bring up the sin to them again. Second, we are promising never to bring it up to ourselves again. If we have chosen not to remember a sin, when it pops back into our thoughts we will deliberately fill our mind with something else. Third, we are promising never to talk to someone else about it in a condemning way—including even spouses, other family members, and close friends. Fourth, we are promising to not allow the sin to affect the way we feel about or relate to that person. When God forgives us, He remembers our sins no more and restores us to fellowship with Himself. We must be willing to do the same.

Donald Grey Barnhouse told a story that illustrated this God-like attitude toward those who sin against us. It is about a wife speaking to her husband, when he told her about his past sinful lifestyle. The woman responded:

> John, I want you to understand something very plainly. I know my Bible well, and therefore I know the subtlety of sin and the devices of sin working in the human heart. I know you are a thoroughly converted man, John, but I know that you still have an old nature and that you are not yet as fully instructed in the ways of God as you soon will be. The devil will do all he can to wreck your Christian life, and he will see to it that temptations of every kind will be put in your way. The day might come—please, God, that it never shall—but the day might come when you will succumb to the temptation and fall into sin. Immediately, the devil will tell you that it is no use trying to resist—that you might as well continue on in the way of sin—and that, above all, you are not to tell me because it will hurt me. But John, I want you to know that here in my arms is your home. When I married you, I married all of you, and I want you to know that there is full pardon and forgiveness in advance for any evil that may ever come into your life.[1]

That woman had learned the truth of Matthew 6:12, and she made a commitment in terms of what she would do when she was sinned against. She committed herself to forgive, even as God had forgiven her. Because she had done this, she could rightly pray: "Father . . . forgive us our debts, as we also have forgiven our debtors." When Jesus taught us to pray these words, He meant that we should take our sin seriously. Confession is required: acknowledging our sins to God; recognizing that our only hope for forgiveness is by grace alone, through the blood of Christ; and coming to God with a repentant heart, desiring to renounce our sin and live a life pleasing to Him. A petition is also involved: asking God to do with our sin everything that the Bible says forgiveness entails—lifting the burden, throwing it into the depths of the sea, covering it, and remitting the penalty. And finally, true prayer involves a promise: to forgive others as God forgives us, never bringing it up again and always restoring fellowship with the offender. Let's devote ourselves to praying this way because to pray this way is to pray effectively and it is to pray Jesus' style. Again I ask, how could it be otherwise since it was Jesus Christ, the Son of God in whom are hid all the treasures of wisdom and knowledge (Col. 2:3), who taught us to pray this way?

APPLICATION

In applying this chapter it is important to ask yourself a few questions in addition to the ones we usually include at the end of each chapter.

1. Do your prayers frequently include confessions of your sin to God?

2. Are you really aware of how greatly you are in debt to God?

3. Do you think often about how you have failed to render to God what you owe to Him?

4. Still further, do your prayers frequently contain requests for His forgiveness, or do you just take His forgiveness for granted?

5. Do you understand what true forgiveness involves? How would you explain it to others?

6. Do you know how much you need the grace of God?

7. Do you really understand and appreciate the work that Christ did for us on the cross?

8. Is confession of sin and repentance from sin a regular practice with you?

9. Are you willing to forgive others in the way that God has forgiven you? Do you relate to others on the basis of their performance and their works—the way they treat you—or on the basis of grace?

10. Are you committed to a lifestyle of forgiveness, and do you practice it in your relationships with others?

11. Summarize in your own words the most important truths presented in this chapter.

12. Write out and work on memorizing one or two verses found in this chapter.

13. In what ways were you encouraged, challenged, or convicted by the material in this chapter? In keeping with the material presented in this chapter, how should your prayer life be changed?

HELP TO AVOID
GOING THROUGH
THE GATE

Certainly the primary purpose of our Lord's instructions in Matthew 6:9–13 was to teach us how to pray effectively. A secondary purpose could be to teach us a lot about the Christian life:

1. A Christian is a person who knows God as his heavenly Father, so he prays, "Our Father who art in heaven."
2. A Christian is a person who wants God's name to be hallowed, so he prays, "Hallowed be Thy name."
3. A Christian is a person who wants God's kingdom to come, so he prays, "Thy Kingdom come."
4. A Christian is a person who depends on God for all his needs, so he prays, "Give us this day our daily bread."
5. A Christian is a person who is concerned about his sin, so he prays, "Forgive us our sins."

In the next two chapters we will see that a Christian is also a person who wants to avoid sin, a person who hates sin and loves holiness, and so he prays, "And do not lead us into temptation, but deliver us from evil."

Evidence That Sin Is the Most Awful Thing in the Universe

An Abomination to God

There are countless reasons why Christians should regard sin as the most awful thing in the universe: first, because God sees it that way. In Psalm 53:1 God said, "The fool has said in his heart, 'There is no God.' They are corrupt, and have committed abominable injustice." Notice the adjective describing the word "injustice." God said that people have committed *abominable* injustice. Throughout Scripture the word "abominable" is frequently used by God to describe our sin, and when God says that our sin is an abomination, He is using the strongest possible word to describe how terrible it is. God does not merely dislike our sin; He is not merely displeased with it or offended by it. He says that it is an *abomination,* and He says it again and again in reference to our sin.

Proverbs is full of references to specific sins that God calls an abomination. For example, God hates the man who deviates from His commands: "The crooked man is an abomination to the Lord" (3:32). "A false balance is an abomination to the LORD" (11:1), that is, cheating and deceiving others in business. God hates those who deny Him: "The perverse in heart are an abomination to the LORD" (11:20). God abhors any kind of deceitfulness: "Lying lips are an abomination to the LORD" (12:22). "The sacrifice of the wicked is an abomination to the LORD" (15:8). "Evil plans are an abomination to the LORD" (15:26). God hates pride: "Everyone who is proud in heart is an abomination to the LORD" (16:5). In reference to those who make light of sin: "He who justifies the wicked, and he who condemns the righteous, both of them alike are an abomination to the LORD" (17:15). Then finally, "He who turns away his ear from listening to the law, even his prayer is an abomination to the LORD" (28:9). Sin, as far as God is concerned, is an abomination.

We find this word also in Jeremiah 44:2–4: "Thus says the LORD of hosts, the God of Israel, 'You yourselves have seen all the calamity that I have brought on Jerusalem and all the cities of Judah; and behold, this day they are in ruins . . . because of their wickedness which they committed so as to provoke Me to anger by continuing to burn sacrifices and to serve other gods. . . . Yet I sent you all my servants the prophets, again and again, saying, 'Oh, do not do this abominable thing which I hate.' " If the God who knows all hates sin, then we ought to hate sin as well.

APPLICATION

1. What do the words "abomination" and "abominable" suggest about God's perspective on sin? How would you define or describe what they are telling us about sin?

2. Can you honestly say that you view sin in this way?

3. If we do view sin in this way, what implications will that have for our praying and our lives?

What Christ Had to Do

Second, sin is serious because of what Christ had to do to remove it. In order for our sins to be forgiven, Jesus Christ had to be born a man, had to experience abuse and mistreatment throughout His life, and then had to die a cruel death on a cross. Ephesians 1:7 says that "in Him we have redemption through His blood, the forgiveness of our trespasses, according to the riches of His grace." First Peter 2:24 also tells us that Jesus Christ "bore our sins in His body on the cross, that we might die to sin and live to righteousness." Christ had to bear our sin burden and suffer agony on the cross for our forgiveness.

Isaiah 53:1–9 creates a strikingly detailed picture of what Jesus Christ had to do in order for us to be forgiven of our sins. Consider the words that are used in this passage: the Servant of God was despised, smitten, afflicted, pierced through, crushed, forsaken, chastened, scourged, slaughtered, oppressed, and cut off. He experienced great sorrow and grief. Of course, these words only begin to describe for us the horror and agony that Jesus went through on our behalf. Second Corinthians 5:21 describes his sacrifice this way: "He made him who knew no sin to be sin on our behalf, that we might become the righteousness of God in Him." Galatians 3:13

tells us that Jesus became a curse: "Christ redeemed us from the curse of the Law, having become a curse for us."

The Gospel of Matthew recounts the horrible way our Lord was treated while on earth: He was tested, lied about, accused of demon possession, and taken as a criminal before Pilate. A crown of thorns was pressed into His head, His back lacerated to a raw mess, spikes driven through His hands and feet, and a spear thrust into His side. Jesus Christ endured all of that for us to experience God's forgiveness. We cannot look at the cross, truly understanding what Christ went through, and think lightly about sin. And when we find our sinful hearts beginning to forget, we must remind ourselves of what Christ went through on our behalf.

APPLICATION

1. How does the death of Christ illustrate the seriousness of sin?

2. What is meant by the statement "We cannot look at the cross . . . and think lightly about sin"?

3. What is the practical value of such thinking for our prayers and Christian life?

Rebellion against God

Third, sin is serious because the Bible says it is rebellion against God. The seriousness of sin needs really to be evaluated in terms of *who* it is we sin against. In Nehemiah 9:26 we read: "They became disobedient and rebelled against Thee, and cast Thy law behind their backs." When we disobey the Law of God we are in rebellion. In Leviticus 26:40 God said: "They committed [sins] against Me, and act[ed] with hostility against Me." Our sin is an act of hostility toward the Almighty God, our Creator and Judge, and thus it is no small thing. Job 15:25 describes sin: the person who sins has "stretched out his hand against God, and He conducts himself arrogantly against the Almighty." Every sin we commit amounts to rebellion against God, and so sin is a serious matter.

APPLICATION

1. What is meant by the statement that "every sin we commit amounts to rebellion against God"?

2. What is the practical value of such thinking for our prayers and Christian life?

An Act of Ingratitude

Fourth, sin is also serious because it is an act of terrible ingratitude. God condemned the ingratitude of His people through the prophet Hosea: "She does not know that it was I who gave her the grain, the new wine, and the oil. And I lavished on her silver and gold, which they used for Baal" (Hos. 2:8). God had given them everything they had, and yet they used it against him. Acts 17:24–25 has this same perspective on sin: "The God who made the world and all things in it . . . does not dwell in temples made with hands; neither is He served by human hands, as though He needed anything, since He Himself gives to all life and breath and all things." Every breath that we take is a gift from God, and when we sin, we are expressing terrible ingratitude to our Creator. In Romans 1:21 the apostle Paul said of sinful men: "Even though they knew God, they did not honor Him as God, or give thanks." Instead of giving thanks and using their gifts for His glory, they used them for themselves and for disobedience. Ingratitude is a mark of a sinful heart. Luke 6:35 says, "But love your enemies . . . and you will be sons of the Most High; for He Himself is kind to ungrateful and evil men."

APPLICATION

1. What is meant by the statement that "when we sin, we are expressing terrible ingratitude to our Creator"?

2. What is the practical value of such thinking for our prayers and Christian life?

A Defilement and Pollution

Fifth, sin is serious because it defiles and pollutes us. In 2 Corinthians 7:1 the Bible says that sin makes us filthy in our body and in our soul. Titus 1:15 says sin defiles both the conscience and the mind: "To those who are defiled and unbelieving, nothing is pure, but both their mind and conscience are defiled." Sin is an awful thing, and we ought to see it the way God sees it.

An Enslavement

Sixth, sin is an abomination because it enslaves us. In 2 Timothy 2:26 the Bible says that we are taken captive by sin. Sin does not come into our lives and simply influence a little. When we yield to sin, we come under its control. Ephesians 2:3 says that sin causes us to live "in the lusts of our flesh, indulging the desires of the flesh . . . and [we are] by nature children of wrath." Sin makes us slaves to our own desires. Romans 6:14 and 8:2 say that sin masters us and rules over us. Romans 6:19 says that we "became slaves to impurity and to lawlessness." In other words, when sin takes over in our lives, everything we are and do is impure and lawless. In John 8:34–44 the Lord Jesus says that whoever commits sin is enslaved to it. People in this country may boast about their freedom, but the Bible says they are slaves to the cruel master of sin. Sin is awful because it is not content to be just a small influence; it becomes our master.

APPLICATION

1. What is meant by the statement that "sin makes us slaves"?

2. Prove the truth of this statement from Scripture. What verses teach this?

3. What is the practical value of such thinking for our prayers and Christian life?

Separation and Alienation

Seven, sin is awful because it separates us from the Almighty God; if we truly understood the implications of that, we would not take sin so lightly. In Isaiah 59:1–2, the Bible says: "The LORD's hand is not so short that it cannot save; neither is His ear so dull that it cannot hear. But your iniquities have made a separation between you and your God, and your sins have hidden His face from you." Anyone not redeemed by the blood of Jesus Christ is separated from God.

In fact, such people are more than separated. Colossians 1:21 says they are *alienated* from God by their sin. Separation is bad enough, but alienation is far worse. A few times in our marriage, my wife and I have been separated while I was away on ministry, but we were never alienated. Being alienated means that there is a problem—some source of hostility or antagonism—between us and somebody else. The Bible says our sin not only separates us, it alienates us from God, so that we become God's adversaries. Our relationship with God is broken because of sin. Ephesians 2:13 says that sinners are far off from God because of their sin.

Destruction

Eight, sin is awful because it is so destructive. Isaiah 57:20 says: "The wicked are like the tossing sea, for it cannot be quiet." Sin destroys our peace and our usefulness to God. Romans 6:21–23 says that our sin brings death and enslaves us. "For the wages of sin is death" (6:23a). Sin brings death in terms of our relationship with God, our usefulness to God, and our joy and peace in Him.

APPLICATION

1. What is meant by the statement that sin separates?

2. What is meant by the statement that sin destroys?

3. Prove the truth of these statements from Scripture. What verses teach these concepts?

4. What is the practical value of such thinking for our prayers and Christian life?

The Ultimate Cause of All Our Physical Problems

Nine, we ought to regard sin as an abomination because it is the cause of all of our physical problems. Every physical problem that anyone has ever had is the result of sin. In Romans 5:12 the Bible says, "Through one man sin entered into the world, and death through sin, and so death spread to all men." Death would not exist apart from sin. Nor would there be any disease, earthquakes, tornadoes, droughts, or difficulties in making a living. In Genesis 3:16–18 we are told that physical pain and thorns and weeds are the result of sin coming into the world through Adam.

In fact, many of our physical problems are the results of our own sin. God said to the Corinthians: "For this reason many among you are weak and sick, and a number sleep. For if we judged ourselves rightly we should not be judged" (1 Cor. 11:30–31). Because they had not dealt with their own sins, they were experiencing sickness and physical infirmity, and some had even died. First John 5:16 teaches that "there is a sin leading to death." Death and disease were brought into this world by sin and ought to remind us of its horrific nature.

APPLICATION

1. What is meant by the statement that sin is the ultimate cause of all our physical problems?

2. Prove the truth of this statement from Scripture. What verses teach this?

3. What is the practical value of such thinking for our prayers and Christian life?

The Ultimate Cause of All of Our Problems

Still further, sin is the cause of *all* the problems that we have. In James 4:1–3 we learn that sin is the cause of our problems with other people. James asked, "What is the source of quarrels and conflicts among you?" He answered his question by naming the sins that make it difficult for us to get along with others. Romans 1:29–31 has a long list of the problems caused by sin: greed, envy, murder, fighting, deceit, malice, gossip, slander, hating God, insolence, arrogance, inventions of new evils, and disobedience to parents. And yet sinners, "although they know the ordinance of God, that those who practice such things are worthy of death, . . . not only do the same, but also give hearty approval to those who practice them" (1:32). There are people who not only know God's commands and choose to disobey them, but they get a perverse satisfaction out of seeing others sin as well.

Romans 3:13–17 tells us that slander and cursing are the result of sin: "Their throat is an open grave, with their tongues they keep deceiving, the poison of asps is under their lips; whose mouth is full of cursing and bitterness; their feet are swift to shed blood, destruction and misery are in their paths, and the path of peace they have not known." We cannot read these verses and still think lightly of sin. People do these evils because they are under sin's control.

In Galatians 5:19–21 the Bible lists more outcomes of sin: immorality, impurity, sensuality, idolatry, contentiousness, enmity, jealousy, outbursts of anger, disputes, dissensions, drunkenness, and drug addiction. First Corinthians 6:9–11 says that, because of sin, people are homosexuals, adulterers, thieves, revilers, and swindlers. Whenever we see someone behaving brutally or thoughtlessly toward another person, we ought to remember that he is doing it because he is under the control of sin. Sin is serious.

According to 2 Timothy 3:2–5 sin makes us lovers of self, lovers of money, ungrateful, unholy, unloving, without self-control, brutal, haters of good, treacherous, reckless, conceited, and lovers of pleasure rather than lovers of God. Since sin is the cause of all these things, believers should see sin as the most abominable thing in the universe. Do we? Would we rather experience an awful disease or live in abject poverty than sin against God? The man who wrote these words in Psalm 119:163 saw sin rightly: "I hate and despise falsehood." In Proverbs 8:13 Solomon said: "The fear of the LORD is to hate evil; pride and arrogance and the evil way, and the perverted mouth, I hate." Do we really hate sin? If we understand how awful it is, we will not take it lightly; we will see it as God sees it.

Romans 12:9 instructs: "Abhor what is evil; cling to what is good." The word "abhor" is a very strong word, and it literally means "to shudder at." It can also be translated "be nauseated by." In other words, to abhor something is to consider it repulsive, disgusting, and odious. The Scripture is teaching that we ought to think about sin as we would about something that has the most disgusting, sickening smell imaginable. Sin is that awful. If we see it rightly, we will want to do what 2 Corinthians 7:1 says: "cleanse ourselves from all defilement of flesh and spirit." Do we like to touch or even be around things that are filthy? The Bible wants us to see sin like that.

APPLICATION

1. What is meant by the statement that sin is the ultimate cause of all our problems?

2. Prove the truth of this statement from Scripture. What verses teach this?

3. What are some of the specific problems we experience that are linked to sin by the Scripture?

4. What is the practical value of such thinking for our prayers and Christian life?

The Only Proper Response

Scripture teaches us what the proper response to a true understanding of sin is. Hebrews 12:14 says it should cause us to pursue holiness. First Peter 1:15 says the same: "like the Holy One who called you, be holy yourselves also in all your behavior." Colossians 3:5 says we should put sin to death. In Titus 2:12–13 we are instructed to deny ungodliness and worldly lusts and to "live sensibly, righteously and godly in the present age." If we see sin as the most awful thing in the universe, we will want to pray what Jesus taught us to pray in Matthew 6:13, "Do not lead us into temptation, but deliver us from evil." The heinousness of sin is our motivation to constantly pray that prayer.

The Gate of Temptation

Keeping all this in mind, let us focus our attention on the prayer petition in Matthew 6:13. Let's come to an understanding of the meaning of this prayer petition by examining some of the words that Jesus uses in this statement. The text begins: *"Do not lead us into* temptation." The Greek verb translated "lead us into" literally means "to bring in" or "to bring into something." The noun form of this verb is a word that means "gate," that is, something through which you go into someplace else. Jesus was essentially saying here: pray that God would prevent you from going through the gate of temptation and into sin.

This same word translated "do not lead us into" also means to be brought under the control of something. It is used in Luke 5:18–19, where we read: "And behold, some men were carrying on a bed a man who was paralyzed; and they were trying to *bring him in,* and to set him down in front of Him." That is what sin wants to do to us through temptation; it wants to bring us in and set us down in the midst of it so that we will yield. The word is also used in 1 Timothy 6:7, where it says: "We have *brought* nothing *into* the world." In Matthew 26:41 Jesus used the word when He said, "Keep watching and praying, that you may not *enter into* temptation." Jesus was teaching that when we pray "do not lead us into," we are praying that God would not allow us to be brought through the gate of temptation into the midst of sin. We are asking God to keep us from coming under the control of our temptation, so that we do disobey Him.

APPLICATION

1. Given what we have just noted about the awfulness of sin, why is praying "do not lead us into temptation" the only proper response?

2. To pray this petition as Jesus meant it, what are we really praying for? What does the idea of going through a gate suggest
about the meaning of this petition?

Prayer for Deliverance

A second Greek verb is found in the second part of this text,
where Jesus said we should pray *"Deliver* us from evil." The word
translated "deliver" is also found in Matthew 27:43. Those who were
mocking Jesus while He was on the cross said: "He saved others;
He cannot save himself. . . . He trusts in God; let Him *deliver* him
now, if He takes pleasure in Him." In Romans 7:24 this word is used
by the apostle Paul: "Wretched man that I am! Who shall *set me free*
from the body of this death?" He used it again in Romans 8:2 when
he wrote: "Christ Jesus has *set you free* from the law of sin and of
death."

When we pray *"Deliver* us from evil," we are asking the Lord to
rescue us, to set us free, and to preserve us from evil. The word is
used in 2 Thessalonians 3:2, when Paul asks the church to pray for
him that he would "be *delivered* from perverse and evil men." In
2 Timothy 4:18 Paul said, "The Lord will *deliver* me from every evil
deed, and will bring me safely to His heavenly kingdom." If God
the Holy Spirit brings an understanding of the seriousness of sin
to us with power and force, we will be praying constantly to be kept
from the control of temptation. We will want to be delivered and
preserved from its grasp, because we recognize that sin is the most
horrible thing we could ever experience. The only way that we will
be excited about praying this prayer is if we truly understand how
horrible our sin is. When that happens, we will not hesitate to pray
"Do not lead us into temptation."

It is no accident that this petition follows the prayer "Forgive
us our debts, as we also have forgiven our debtors." The point being
that, as we have come to God for forgiveness, we will not want to
fall back into the same sin. If we understand what sin is, we will
know our need for forgiveness, we will not take sin lightly, we will

ask for forgiveness, and we will then desire to be delivered from the temptation to fall into sin again.

This is just the beginning of the important teaching in this last phrase of the Lord's Prayer. In the next chapter, we will finish our study by looking at the terms: "temptation," "evil," and "us." All these words have tremendous meaning and should guide us as we pray in terms of our understanding of what we are asking to not be led into, what we are asking to be delivered from, and what the inclusiveness of "us" means in this context.

Again I ask, do you want to be effective in prayer? Well, then, part of your praying will involve asking God to not allow you to be brought under the control of temptation (to go through the gate into temptation). Praying this way must become a part of your daily prayer times. As you do this, you will be structuring your prayers according to the teachings of history's greatest teacher on the subject of prayer. And to pray this way must be effective because all the treasures of wisdom and knowledge about this and all other subjects are hidden in the Lord Jesus Christ.

APPLICATION

1. Summarize in your own words the most important truths presented in this chapter.

2. Write out and work on memorizing one or two verses found in this chapter.

3. In what ways were you encouraged, challenged, or convicted by the material in this chapter? In keeping with the material presented in this chapter, how should your prayer life be changed?

PRAYING FOR
DELIVERANCE

*I*n the last chapter, we wrote that it is no accident that the petition "Do not lead us into temptation, but deliver us from evil" (Matt. 6:13) should follow the petition "Forgive us our debts, as we also have forgiven our debtors" (Matt. 6:12). The point being that, as we have come to God for forgiveness, we will not want to fall back into the same sin. If we understand what sin is, we will know our need for forgiveness, we will not take sin lightly, we will ask for forgiveness, and we will then desire to be delivered from the temptation to fall into sin again.

Forgiven People Want to Be Delivered

Real believers have always seen the heinousness of sin and wanted to be delivered from its power. They have always known the importance of praying this sixth petition. Newman Hall expressed the real believer's conviction and concern:

> After God has forgiven us, there is nothing that we have so earnestly to pray for as that we fall not again into the same filth. Since therefore, as David said, there are in the great sea of this world things creeping innumerable, we have a need to pray from the inmost heart, "Oh Father, lead us not into temptation. We are surrounded with temptations, but be thou our help, that we

consent not unto them, and thus be taken and overcome by them." We cannot avoid temptations, but we can, by calling upon God for aid, take heed that they do not overcome us. This prayer is the natural heart utterance of every believer. We say, "Our Father, we mourn because of past sins committed against You. Oh, keep us from fresh grief and grieving You. We lament that we have often failed to hallow God's name and to do His will; help us in the future. We hate the sins that dishonor You and wound our own soul; enable us to conquer them. We distrust ourselves, for we have proved how inconstant are our best resolves, how weak are our strongest efforts, how numerous our evil inclinations, how slippery are the paths on which we walk, how many are the snares laid for our feet; uphold us. We lean on You. We follow You. But, oh, bring us not where temptation might be too strong for us."[1]

Many statements made by the psalmist in Psalm 119 indicate his understanding of the awfulness of sin and his intense desire to be delivered from the power of temptation and evil:

Do not let me wander from Thy commandments. (v. 10b)

Remove the false way from me, and graciously grant me Thy law. (v. 29)

Make me walk in the path of Thy commandments. (v. 35a)

Incline my heart to Thy testimonies, and not to dishonest gain. (v. 36)

Sustain me according to Thy word, that I may live; and do not let me be ashamed of my hope. (v. 116)

Uphold me that I may be safe. (v. 117a)

Establish my footsteps in Thy Word, and do not let any iniquity have dominion over me. (v. 133)

All of these quotes indicate that a Christian is a person who takes sin seriously. In our world there are many people who do not take sin seriously. In fact, it often seems as if the worst thing we could do would be to call someone a sinner. We hardly even use the word anymore, but Proverbs 14:9 says, "Fools mock at sin." Indeed, there are many fools around us, because many people laugh at sin.

Not so the Christian. The Christian sees sin as an abomination because that is how God sees it. We know how God regards sin because of how he describes it in his Word: rebellion, ingratitude, defilement, slavery, and destruction. We see the seriousness of sin in its results: alienation from God, physical death, disease, and all other problems known to man. Sin is so awful that it required the sacrifice of God's Son to take it away.

Temptation

One Kind of "Peirasmos"

Having studied the two verbs in this petition in the last chapter, we turn our attention now to the three nouns. The first is the Greek word *peirasmos* translated "temptation." This word is used in two ways in the Bible. First, it is used to describe the trials or difficulties that we sometimes face that are not a direct result of our sin. In James 1:2 the Bible says, "Consider it all joy, my brethren, when you encounter various *trials.*" This same word is found also in James 1:12, "Blessed is the man who endures *temptation* (NKJV)," meaning "trials." In Luke 8:13 Jesus used the word in the parable of the sower when he spoke about people who "believe for a while, and in time of *temptation* fall away." In Mark 4:17 we learn that this time of temptation is "affliction or persecution." Paul used the word in Acts 20:19 when he said that he served the Lord "with all humility and with tears and with *trials.*" He used it again in 1 Corinthians 10:13 when talking about difficulties we face as believers: "No *temptation has* overtaken you but such as is common to man."

These trials, when handled biblically, can be extremely beneficial. James said that God uses trials to make us "perfect and complete, lacking in nothing" (1:4). Later, he said, "Blessed is a man who perseveres under *trial;* for once he has been approved, he will receive the crown of life" (1:12). Job knew the benefits of trials and said, "But He knows the way I take; when He has *tried* me, I shall come forth as gold" (23:10). Paul knew the benefits as well. In 2 Corinthians 1:3–4 he spoke of "the Father of mercies and God of all comfort; who comforts us in all our *affliction* so that we may be able to comfort those who are in any affliction with the comfort with which we ourselves are comforted by God." Paul knew that God would use the trials in his life to help him minister to others.

Consider the example of Joseph. Joseph had all kinds of trials: mistreatment by his brothers, slavery in Egypt, false accusations of sexual perversion, jail time, and a broken promise from a friend. His trials went on for seventeen years, but at the end of it all he was able to say to his brothers, "You meant evil against me, but God meant it for good in order to bring about this present result, to preserve many people alive" (Gen. 50:20). Joseph knew that his trials had brought about God's good purposes.

We have already mentioned John Bunyan. He preached the Word of God and, as a result, spent twelve and a half years in prison. Yet Bunyan's trials did not make him bitter; they did not send him into depression and despair. Instead, he used his time for Bible study, for witnessing to other prisoners, and for writing some forty books, most notably *The Pilgrim's Progress.* Bunyan's trials and difficulties were beneficial both to himself and to all the people who have been taught and ministered to by his books. More than three hundred years later we are still benefiting from them.

APPLICATION

1. What is meant by the statement that "forgiven people take sin seriously"? Why is this so?

2. Demonstrate the truth of this statement from the quotes from the Bible and from Newman Hall.

3. What is the first way in which the Greek word "temptation" in Matthew 6:13 is used in Scripture?

4. What is the purpose of God in allowing us to be tested?

5. What examples of the value of testing were given? How were testings beneficial for these people?

The outcome of our trials depends on how they are responded to. When our response is godly, they are wonderful opportunities for spiritual growth and ministry. When our response is ungodly, these trials can be extremely destructive. Consider the testing by God of the Israelites in the wilderness. His people responded to their trials with immorality, grumbling, and tempting of God, according to 1 Corinthians 10. In Hebrews 3:7–10, we are given a warning against responding to difficulties in the same way: "Therefore, just as the Holy Spirit says, 'Today if you hear His voice, do not harden your hearts as when they provoked Me, as in the day of *trial* in the wilderness, where your fathers tried Me by testing Me, and saw My works for forty years. Therefore, I was angry with this generation.'" God was testing their hearts out in the wilderness, and they failed the test.

Abraham was put to the test in Genesis 12, and failed also. He came into the land of Canaan, and found that God had sent a severe famine. Without asking God for guidance, Abraham packed up his household and went to Egypt. Because he acted without God's counsel, he created problems for himself, for Pharaoh, and for all Egypt. When Pharaoh discovered what Abraham had done to him, he sent him out of his kingdom.

God allowed his servant Job to be tested by Satan. In the midst of his trial Job said: "Let the day perish on which I was born, and the night which said, 'A boy is conceived.' May that day be darkness; let not God above care for it, nor light shine on it. . . . Why did I not die at birth?" (Job 3:3–4, 11). For a period of time, Job struggled greatly with his difficulties. It is not until the end of the book of Job (chapters 38–42) that we see a lasting change in Job's attitude as he allowed himself to be humbled before God.

APPLICATION

1. Explain the statement "the outcome of our trials depends on how they are responded to."

2. What biblical illustrations were used to demonstrate the accuracy of this statement? How did these examples illustrate this fact?

Another Kind of "Peirasmos"

The word "temptation" (*peirasmos*), then, is sometimes used in Scripture as a synonym for trials or difficulties that we face in life. These trials may be of many kinds—financial, social, physical, or other. But there is another way in which this same Greek word, translated "temptation," is used in the Bible. The second use is always in reference to being tempted to sin. This is how the word is used in Matthew 4:1, where we read about Jesus being led by the Spirit into the wilderness to be tempted by the devil to sin. It is also used in reference to sin in Matthew 26:41, when Jesus told His disciples, "Keep watching and praying, that you may not enter into *temptation.*" In this instance, he was talking about a temptation to sin. It is found in 1 Corinthians 7:5, when Paul addressed married couples, instructing them to avoid temptation by not abstaining from sexual relations without agreement.

What kind of temptation did Jesus have in mind when He taught us to pray "Do not lead us into temptation"? Primarily he meant the second kind: temptation to sin. We know this from the fact that this statement follows the petition "Forgive us our debts." In our previous study, we learned that the word "debt" was one of the ways that God described sin in the New Testament. Jesus taught us to pray first for forgiveness from sin and then for deliverance from the temptation to sin. Jesus' intention in this petition is also indicated by the fact that He used the word "evil" in connection with "temptation."

Primarily, then, Jesus was saying that we ought to constantly pray that God would not allow the temptations in our lives to overcome us, not that we would be kept out of them entirely. In this world, that would be impossible. Paul said in 1 Corinthians 5:10 that to escape all temptation, we would "have to go out of the world." Occasions for temptation are everywhere around us, and inside of us as well. Thomas Watson said, "The meaning is that God would not suffer us to be overcome by temptation, that we may not be given up to the power of temptation and be drawn into sin."[2]

Martyn Lloyd-Jones has written:

We are asking that we should never be led into a situation where we are liable to be tempted by Satan. It does not mean that we are dictating to God what he shall or shall not do. God does test his children and we must never presume to tell God what he is or is not to do. He knows that we need much training in our preparation for glory. But, though it does not mean that we are to dictate to God, it does mean that we may request of him—if it be in accordance with his holy will—that he should not lead us into positions where we can be so easily tempted, and where we are liable to fall. . . . This is what our Lord meant when he said to his disciples at the end, "Watch and pray that you enter not into temptation."[3]

Newman Hall explains the meaning of this petition this way:

We should pray that God would so guide us that we may not be tempted beyond our strength. . . . Each has his special perils from inward tendencies or outward circumstances, and we reasonably pray to be protected in our most vulnerable part. . . . We ask God to guide us in such a way that outward circumstances may not so accord with inward tendencies that the resulting temptation might overpower us.

We pray not to be brought into temptation as to be overcome by it . . . we pray that no temptation will be beyond our strength, but that our escape may be in the way of endurance and victory.[4]

Indeed, if we understand the power of temptation both outside of us and in our own hearts, we will constantly pray to God for victory over sin and the power to not succumb to the temptations that will inevitably come our way.

APPLICATION

1. What examples of the second kind of "peirasmos" were given in this section?

2. How do we know that Jesus is referring to this second kind of testing or temptation in this prayer petition?

3. Summarize what Jesus was really teaching us to pray for in this petition. Reflect on the explanations of Martyn Lloyd-Jones and Newman Hall.

4. Given Jesus' indication that this is a prayer we should pray daily, what implications does this have for our prayer lives and life in general?

Evil

Situational Evil

The second noun we need to look at is the word "evil." Just as the word "temptation" has two meanings, the word "evil" has two meanings in Scripture as well, and we will not understand Jesus' intention unless we know which He meant. When we come to the word "evil" in Scripture, sometimes it is being used in reference to situational evil; in other words, that which is painful and unpleasant. In Psalm 112:7 the psalmist said that the man who fears God "will not fear *evil* tidings," meaning that he will not be constantly anxious that something terrible is going to happen. He will not live in fear because he knows God is in control and works all things together for good.

The word "evil" is also used to denote situational evil in Proverbs 1:33: "He who listens to me shall live securely and shall be at ease from the dread of *evil.*" In other words, he will not be afraid of the challenges and difficulties of life. Again, in Proverbs 27:12, "A prudent man sees *evil* and hides himself." He sees, for example, that if he overextends himself financially, the day will come when he will be held accountable by the law for his debts. Being prudent, he decides to avoid this trouble in the first place. He foresees this evil, or difficulty, and is careful to avoid it.

Isaiah 45 is a passage that has been often misunderstood. Verse 7 says, "[I am] the One forming light and creating darkness, causing well-being and creating *calamity* [evil]; I am the LORD who does all these." Is God saying that He is responsible for sin? No, this is another case of "evil" being used in reference to situational evil, not moral evil. We know that our God is in control of all things: "Our God is in the heavens; He does whatever He pleases" (Ps. 115:3). God creates situations that are difficult; Satan may be the instrument that God uses to bring these difficulties into our lives, but God is still in control. Satan can do only what God allows him to do, that which ultimately glorifies God and brings good to His people.

In Isaiah 47:11 "evil" is used in the same way: *"Evil* will come on you which you will not know how to charm away; and disaster will fall on you for which you cannot atone, and destruction about which you do not know will come on you suddenly." In Acts 16:28 the word often translated "evil" is translated "harm" instead. An earthquake destroyed the prison that Paul and Silas were in, and the head jailer was about to commit suicide, thinking his prisoners had all escaped, when Paul said to him, "Do yourself no *harm.*" In 2 Timothy 4:14 Paul said, "Alexander the coppersmith did me much harm." This man had been an instrument of difficulties— situational evil—in Paul's life and ministry.

Moral Evil

The second and more common use of this word "evil" is in connection with moral evil. In Matthew 5:37 Jesus told us to be careful about making false vows: "But let your 'Yes' be 'Yes,' and your 'No,' 'No.' For whatever is more than these is from the *evil* one" (NKJV). He was expositing the commandment "Thou shalt not bear false witness," and teaching that a false vow was sinful. In Mark 7:21 Jesus said: "For from within, out of the heart of men, proceed *evil* thoughts, adulteries, fornications, murders . . . ," and He goes on to list many more sins, all referring back to "evil." Romans 1:30 talks about people who are "inventors of *evil.*" In 2 Thessalonians 3:2 Paul prayed for deliverance "from perverse and *evil* men." The use of "perverse" with "evil" indicates moral evil.

The kind of evil that Jesus meant in Matthew 6:13 was, of course, primarily the second kind. God uses situational evil for His glory and for our good, and so Jesus was not instructing us to pray for deliverance from necessary trials. He was primarily teaching us to pray for deliverance from moral evil. Martyn Lloyd-Jones said, "Evil here includes not only Satan, but evil in every shape and form. It certainly includes Satan. We need to be delivered from him and his wiles, but there is evil also in our hearts. 'Lord, keep me from the evil that is in my heart!' . . . We need to be delivered from it all. It is a great request; a comprehensive petition."[5]

APPLICATION

1. What does this section teach us about the two ways in which the word "evil" is used in Scripture?

2. Which of these kinds of evil is Jesus primarily referring to in Matthew 6:13?

3. Why did you answer question 2 the way you did?

4. What practical implications will understanding what Jesus is really teaching us to pray for in this petition have for us in our daily prayers and lives?

Don't Limit the Seriousness or Meaning of Evil

We tend to limit not just the seriousness, but also the meaning of sin. In reference to moral evil (sin) J. C. Ryle wrote:

> Sin consists in doing, saying, thinking, or imagining anything that is not in perfect conformity with the mind and Law of God. Sin,

in short, as the Scripture says, is the transgression of the Law. The slightest outward or inward departure from the absolute mathematical parallelism with God's revealed will and character constitutes a sin and at once makes us guilty in God's sight. I need not tell anyone who reads his Bible with attention that a man may break God's Law in heart and thought when there is no overt and visible act of wickedness. Our Lord has settled that point beyond dispute in the Sermon on the Mount. Even a poet of our own has truly said, "A man may smile and smile and be a villain."

Again, I need not tell a careful student of the New Testament that there are sins of omission, that is, things that we should do which we do not do, as well as sins of commission. And that we sin by leaving undone the things which we ought to do, as really as by doing the things which we ought not to do. The solemn words of our Master in the gospel of St. Matthew placed this point also beyond dispute. It is there in the gospel of Matthew written, "Depart ye cursed into everlasting fire, for I was hungry and you gave me no meat. I was thirsty, and you gave me no drink." It was a deep and thoughtful saying of Pastor [Archbishop] Ussher, just before he died, "Lord, forgive me all my sins, and especially my sins of omission."

But I do think it is necessary in these times to remind my readers that a man may commit sin and yet remain ignorant of it, and fancy himself innocent when he is guilty. I fail to see warrant for the modern assertion that sin is not sin to us until we discern it and are conscious of it. On the contrary, in the fourth and fifth chapters of that unduly neglected book, Leviticus, and in the fifteenth of Numbers, I find Israel distinctly taught that there were sins of ignorance which render people unclean and for which they needed atonement. And I find our Lord expressly teaching that the servant who knew not his Master's will and did it not was not excused on account of his ignorance, but he was beaten and punished. We shall do well to remember that when we make our own miserably imperfect knowledge and consciousness the measure of our sinfulness, we are on very dangerous ground.[6]

God takes all sin seriously, both in gravity and in scope. Consequently, we ought to constantly pray "Do not lead us into temptation, but deliver us from evil."

APPLICATION

1. Carefully reflect on J. C. Ryle's description of sin and then write down all of the ideas about sin that you find in this statement.

2. Is this the way you view sin in your life?

A Third Noun in the Form of a Pronoun

Finally, we come to the pronoun "us" which is used twice in this petition: "Do not lead *us* into temptation, but deliver *us* from evil." As with all the petitions before, Jesus was teaching that in all of life, including our prayers, we should be concerned about others as well as ourselves. If we want to pray effectively, we need to pray unselfishly. We need to pray unselfishly about God's concerns, that His name might be hallowed, that His kingdom might come, that His will might be done. And we need to pray unselfishly about man's concerns, that God might give to others as well as ourselves our daily bread, that God might forgive the sins of others as well as our own sins, and that God might not allow others as well as ourselves to be brought under the power of temptation and into the actual practice of sin.

In Ephesians 6:18 Paul said that we are to pray "with all perseverance and petition for all the saints," and Paul himself was an example of this. In reference to this concept of "us" Newman Hall wrote:

> This prayer, like the rest, is unselfish. It embraces our brethren who are exposed to the same temptations, as on board a ship in danger, we cannot pray for our own preservation without including all the crew. For the whole church we pray, for struggling tempted souls altogether unknown to us in distant lands of other tongues. We realize the communion of the saints, the brother-

hood of all who are on their pilgrimage of trial. Oh, strange and mysterious privilege, that some bedridden woman in a lonely bedroom, who feels tempted to distrust the love and mercy of God, should wrestle with that doubt, saying the Lord's Prayer; and that she should be thus asking for help for those who are dwelling in palaces, yet in their own way are in a peril as great as hers; for the student haunted with questions which would seem to her monstrous and incredible, but which to him are agonizing; for the minister in his terrible assaults from cowardice, despondency, vanity, from the sense of his own heartlessness, from the shame of past neglect, from the appalling discovery of evils in himself which he has denounced in others; from vulgar temptations into which he had proudly fancied he could not fall. Of all this, the sufferer knows nothing, and yet for these she prays, and for the government leaders, and for her country, and for all other countries in their throes of anguish. For one and all she prays, "Lead us not into temptation." Their temptations and hers, different in form, are the same in substance. They, like her, are tempted to doubt that God is, and that he is the author of good and not of evil; and that he is mightier than the evil and that he can and will overthrow it, and deliver the universe out of it.[7]

APPLICATION

1. Carefully reflect on Newman Hall's statement; then write down all of the ideas about prayer that you find in this statement.

2. Is this the way you pray? Are your prayers filled with "us" or just me? Can you honestly say that your prayers are unselfish?

The Sin of Prayerlessness

Jesus has taught us in this prayer very clearly the fundamental principles of effective prayer. We should meditate upon them often and spend much time in prayer. We ought to desire that God's name would be hallowed, that His kingdom would come, and that His will be done. We ought to depend on Him for our daily bread and constantly ask for forgiveness from our sins. We ought to pray that God would give us victory and triumph over temptation in us and around us, and that God, by His grace, would deliver us and rescue us from evil, because sin is a horrible thing.

We fail in so many ways as Christians. Truly, we must say with the psalmist, "My sins have gone over my head." And yet, I believe that one of the greatest sins for which we should be seeking forgiveness from God is the sin of prayerlessness. The prophet Samuel said, "Far be it from me that I should sin against the LORD by ceasing to pray...." (1 Sam. 12:23). We need to confess our sin of prayerlessness, and then we need to take seriously what Jesus taught us here.

Sometime ago I read a story about some guests at a certain hotel who were being made uncomfortable by the repeated banging on a piano by a little girl who possessed no musical knowledge. They complained to the owner with the hope of having the annoyance stopped. "I am sorry you are annoyed," he said. "But the girl is the child of one of my very best guests. I can hardly ask her not to touch the piano. But her father, who is away for a day or so, will return tomorrow. You can approach him and have the matter settled." When the father returned, he found his daughter in the reception room thumping on the piano. He walked up behind the child, put his arms around her shoulders, took her hands in his, and produced some beautiful music.

I include that story as an illustration of what I hope will happen to all of us as a result of studying the teaching of Jesus on the subject of effective prayer. That little girl in the story represents all of us as we attempt to bang away at this matter of prayer. In and of ourselves, we don't know much about the kind of prayer that pleases God, the kind of prayer that is effective, the kind of prayer that God delights to answer. We stumble and fumble around doing the best we can. We hope we're praying according to the will of God because we know that God has promised to answer the prayers that are made in accordance with His will (1 John 5:14–15). But how can we know for sure what is His will?

Well, understanding this teaching of Jesus ought to forever remove our clumsy efforts at prayer; it ought to remove our uncertainty about knowing what to pray for that is in accordance with God's will. We don't have to bang away at prayer anymore. If we're willing to listen and learn from this wonderful passage in Matthew

6:5–13, we will have the privilege of having Jesus, history's greatest expert on how to pray effectively, come to us and provide the direction we need for knowing how to pray the kind of prayers that are in accordance with the will of God. If we follow His teaching on prayer in this passage, we will, in effect, be allowing Jesus to come up behind us, take our prayer hands in His, and then help us to pray in such a way that our prayers will be as beautiful music in the ears of God.

The instructions that Jesus gave about prayer in this section of Scripture are simple and yet they are profound. The depth and breadth of the teaching found here is incredible. Lloyd-Jones was absolutely right when he wrote of this prayer:

> The Lord's Prayer covers everything; and all we do is take these principles and employ and expand them and base our every petition on them. That is the way in which it should be approached. And as you look at it that way, I think you will agree with St. Augustine and Martin Luther and many other saints who have said that there is nothing more wonderful in the entire Bible than the Lord's Prayer. The economy, the way in which He summarizes it all, and has reduced everything to but a few sentences, is something that surely proclaims the fact that the speaker is none other than the very Son of God Himself.[8]

Will you allow yourself to be challenged, enlightened, and motivated by the profound prayer concept found in Matthew 6:5–13? Do you want to want to pray effectively? Do you want to know that God will hear and answer your prayers? Then listen to what Jesus said and follow the pattern He laid out for us in this marvelous section of Scripture. As we close this study, I encourage you to dedicate yourself to being more diligent in praying and living in the manner described by Jesus the Master Prayer Teacher in these words. Will you do this? I certainly hope so!

APPLICATION

1. Summarize in your own words the most important truths presented in this chapter.

2. Write out and work on memorizing one or two verses found in this chapter.

3. In what ways were you encouraged, challenged, or convicted by the material in this chapter? In keeping with the material presented in this chapter, how should your prayer life be changed?

Notes

Introduction

1. E. M. Bounds, *The Possibilities of Prayer* (New Kensington, Pa.: Whitaker House, 1997), 268–69.

Chapter 1: The Naturalness of Prayer

1. J. C. Ryle, *Practical Religion* (New York: Thomas Crowell, 1959), 48.
2. Ibid., 58–59.

Chapter 2: Getting the Big Picture

1. D. Martyn Lloyd-Jones, *The Christian Soldier* (Grand Rapids: Baker, 1978), 342.
2. John Piper, *A Godward Life* (Portland: Multnomah, 1997), 164–65.
3. E. M. Bounds, *E. M. Bounds on Prayer: Power through Prayer* (New Kensington: Whitaker House, 1997), 468.
4. Richard Newton, quoted in *E. M. Bounds on Prayer*, 483.
5. Ibid.

Chapter 3: Coming to Your Father

1. D. Martyn Lloyd-Jones, *Studies in the Sermon on the Mount* (Grand Rapids: Eerdmans, 1960), 2:45.
2. Ibid., 2:51–52.

Chapter 4: Coming to Your Heavenly Father

1. Daniel DeHann, "What Motivates God?" *Moody Monthly* 83.6 (Feb. 1983): 70–73.
2. D. Martyn Lloyd-Jones, *Studies in the Sermon on the Mount* (Grand Rapids: Eerdmans, 1960), 2:55–56.

Chapter 5: Putting God's Concerns First

1. D. Martyn Lloyd-Jones, *Studies in the Sermon on the Mount* (Grand Rapids: Eerdmans, 1960), 2:59.
2. Adapted from Thomas Watson, *The Ten Commandments* (London: Banner of Truth, 1965), 84–92.
3. Lloyd-Jones, *Sermons on the Mount,* 2:61.

Chapter 6: Kingdom Praying

1. Jay Adams, *Theology of Christian Counseling,* (Phillipsburg, N.J.: P&R, 1979), 67.

2. Ibid., 67–68.

Chapter 7: Praying for the Kingdom to Come

1. Arnold Dallimore, *Spurgeon* (Chicago: Moody, 1984), 48–49.

2. Thomas Watson, *The Lord's Prayer* (London: Banner of Truth, 1965), 76–78.

3. Al Mohler, commencement address at The Master's Seminary, Sun Valley, Calif., May of 2001.

4. Watson, *The Lord's Prayer,* 59–60.

Chapter 9: Praying for God's Will to Be Done

1. Just having a vision was not enough for Paul and his companions to determine God's individual will for them at this point. It's clear from the context that they had to use their minds to determine that this present vision was really from God. And more than that, they had to interpret the vision's meaning. Determining what it meant in terms of God's will required some serious thinking. The text tells us that after receiving the vision they concluded God was calling them to preach the gospel in Macedonia. In other words, the vision didn't come with a self-contained explanation. To determine its meaning they had to do some concluding. In the original, the word describing what they did after receiving the vision includes the concept of comparing, evaluating, or proving. "Comparing" involves looking at all the possibilities. "Proving" involves seeking validation for their conclusion, or looking at all the facts or possibilities before drawing a conclusion. Undoubtedly, there were some unique features about the way Paul and his team came to know the will of God in this instance. But it is wrong for us to assume that they were completely passive in the endeavor, or for us to think that knowing God's will for them at this time was a cut-and-dried matter requiring no serious biblical thinking.

2. How do we who live since the time of the apostles come to know the individual will of God? In the same way Christians in the early church did: we search the Scriptures for insight and we go to God in prayer. We gather all the information we can about whatever the situation may be and compare it with scriptural principles (Prov. 18:13, 15). We empty ourselves of self interest, and determine to seek only that which glorifies God (Prov. 3:5–6; Luke 9:23; John 7:17; Phil. 1:20; 1 Cor. 10:31; 2 Cor. 5:9). We look to godly people for help and counsel. We go to our elders and pastors, whose job it is to give us guidance in understanding the will of God (Prov. 11:14; 12:15; 15:22).

Chapter 11: God's Will in Heaven

1. Charles Spurgeon, "True Prayer! True Power!" 1860, The Spurgeon Archive, www.spurgeon.org/index/c06.htm.
2. Ibid., 335.

Chapter 12: Praying about Your Physical Needs

1. Thomas Watson, The Lord's Prayer (London: Banner of Truth, 1965), 205, 207.

Chapter 13: Praying for This Day

1. The following material is adapted from Thomas Watson, *The Lord's Prayer* (London: Banner of Truth, 1965), 94–208.
2. Ibid., 195.
3. Ibid., 206.
4. Ibid., 195.
5. Ibid., 206–7.

Chapter 14: Praying Dependently and Thankfully

1. Thomas Watson, *The Lord's Prayer* (London: Banner of Truth, 1965), 185–98.

Chapter 15: Praying about Your Debts

1. Thomas Watson, *The Lord's Prayer* (London: Banner of Truth, 1965), 209.
2. Ibid.
3. Ibid.
4. Ibid., 211–13.

Chapter 16: Remembering Forgiveness and Forgiving

1. Donald Grey Barnhouse, *God's Methods for Holy Living* (Grand Rapids: Eerdmans, 1951), 72–74.

Chapter 18: Praying for Deliverance

1. Newman Hall, *The Lord's Prayer* (Edinburgh: T&T Clark, 1889), 292–93.
2. Thomas Watson, The Lord's Prayer (London: Banner of Truth, 1965), 258.
3. D. Martyn Lloyd-Jones, *Studies in the Sermon on the Mount* (Grand Rapids: Eerdmans, 1960), 2:76.
4. Hall, *Lord's Prayer*, 290–91.
5. Lloyd-Jones, *Sermon on the Mount*, 2:77.
6. J. C. Ryle, *Holiness* (New York: Thomas Crowell, 1959), 2–3.
7. Hall, *Lord's Prayer*, 293–94.
8. Lloyd-Jones, *Sermon on the Mount*, 2:49.

INDEX OF SCRIPTURE

Wayne A. Mack (M.Div., Philadelphia Theological Seminary; D.Min., Westminster Theological Seminary) is adjunct professor of biblical counseling at The Master's College and director of Strengthening Ministries International. Mack is an executive board member of F.I.R.E. (Fellowship of Independent Reformed Evangelicals) and co-pastor of Grace Fellowship Church of the Lehigh Valley. He is a charter member of the National Association of Nouthetic Counselors, and he conducts seminars and conferences around the world.

Mack has authored a number of books including *Strengthening Your Marriage; Your Family, God's Way; A Homework Manual for Biblical Living, Vols 1 and 2, Family and Marital Problems;* with David Swavely, *Life in the Father's House;* and with John MacArthur, *An Introduction to Biblical Counseling.* He and his wife, Carol, have four children and twelve grandchildren.